Choral Music
Methods and Materials

Developing Successful Choral Programs (Grades 5 to 12)

BARBARA A. BRINSON

Southern Methodist University

SCHIRMER

THOMSON LEARNING

Australia • Canada • Mexico • Singapore • Spain • United Kingdom • United States

Wadsworth Group/Thomson Learning
10 Davis Drive
Belmont CA 94002-3098
USA

For information about our products, contact us:
Thomson Learning Academic Resource Center
1-800-423-0563
http://www.wadsworth.com

For permission to use material from this text, contact us by
Web: http://www.thomsonrights.com
Fax: 1-800-730-2215
Phone: 1-800-730-2214

Printed in the United States of America
10 9 8 7 6 5 4 3

Library of Congress Cataloging-in-Publication Data

Brinson, Barbara A.
    Choral music methods and materials : developing successful choral
programs, grades 5 to 12 / Barbara A. Brinson.
       p. cm.
    Includes bibliographical references (p.) and index.
    ISBN 0-02-870311-1 (alk. paper)
       1. Choral music—Juvenile—Instruction and study. 2. Choral
music—Instruction and study. 3. School music—Instruction and
study. I. Title.
MT930.B82 1996
782.5—dc20
                                              95-34459
                                                CIP
                                                MN

This paper meets the requirements of ANSI/NISO Z39.48–1992 (Permanence of
Paper).

Choral Music
Methods and Materials

Contents

Preface and Acknowledgments   ix

1   Philosophical Foundations   1

Formulating Your Philosophy of Music Education   5
Summary   13
Mini-Projects   14
References   15
Additional Reading   16

2   Recruitment and Retention of Singers   18

Motivation to Sing   18
Where Do You Find Students to Recruit?   23
Summary   26
Mini-Projects   27
Additional Reading   28

3   Auditions and Placement of Singers   29

Information to Be Gathered During an Audition   31
Audition Form   37
Implementing an Audition   37
Which Choirs Should You Offer?   40
Placement of Voices and Seating Arrangements   43
Summary   49

Mini-Projects   53
Reference   54
Additional Reading   54

**4   Development and Evaluation
      of a Choral Curriculum   55**

Developing a Choral Curriculum   55
Evaluation of Students   62
Summary   70
Mini-Projects   71
References   71
Additional Reading   72

5   Repertoire   73

Selection of Repertoire   73
When to Order Music   81
Where Do You Find Music?   83
Creating Music Files   87
Summary   87
Mini-Projects   89
Additional Reading   90

6   Programming Music   91

General Programming Tips   92
Several Programming Ideas   96
Sample Programs   97
Summary   103
Mini-Projects   104
Additional Reading   105

7   Musical Analysis and Score Preparation   106

Aural and Visual Study of the Music   107
Marking the Score   118
Connecting Your Study with Rehearsal Activities   125
Summary   125
Mini-Projects   126
Additional Reading   126

8   The Rehearsal   127

    I. *Planning the Rehearsal*   127

    Sample Rehearsal Plan   133
    Explanation of Rehearsal Plan   137
    Summary of the Rehearsal Plan   141

    II. *Rehearsing the Choir*   141

    Flowchart for Choral Rehearsals   142
    Summary   151
    Mini-Projects   152
    Reference   154
    Additional Reading   154

9   Behavior Management in Rehearsal   155

    Whom Are You Teaching?   156
    Discipline Takes Courage   160
    Preventive Discipline   162
    Summary   172
    Mini-Projects   173
    References   176
    Additional Reading   176

**10   Vocal Techniques
and Musicianship Skills**   177

    Vocal Techniques   177
    Musicianship Skills   197
    Summary   205
    Mini-Projects   206
    References   206
    Additional Reading   207

11   The Changing Voice   209

    Signs of a Change   210
    Female Voice Change   211
    Male Voice Change   213
    Choosing Music for Changing Voices   222
    Summary   236

Mini-Projects   239
References   239
Additional Reading   241

**12 Pop Ensembles and Musical
Productions**   243

Pop Ensembles   243
Musical Productions   252
Summary   256
Selected Repertoire for Pop Ensembles   258
Mini-Projects   262
Reference   263
Additional Reading   263

13 Management of a Choral Program   264

Teacher Burnout   265
Parent Organization   266
Student Leadership   268
Budget   270
Choral Library   272
Scheduling   280
Performance Attire   283
Instruments and Equipment   286
Using Technology in the Classroom   288
Selecting Hardware and Software   290
Awards   293
Professional Organizations   294
Summary   295
Mini-Projects   297
References   298
Additional Reading   298

Appendix: Selected Choral Repertoire   301

Choral Music for Mixed Choirs   301
Choral Music for Treble Choirs   304
Choral Music for Tenor-Bass Choirs   306

Index   309

Preface and Acknowledgments

This book was written primarily for use in choral methods courses for undergraduate music education majors. Church musicians, or students who are studying to become church musicians, will find most of the information applicable and helpful, and choral directors who have been teaching for a number of years may discover new repertoire, new materials, or a new idea.

Choral Music Methods and Materials offers an important balance between the practical and artistic components of successful choral music programs. Topics covered include developing a philosophy of music education, singer recruitment and retention, auditions, curriculum planning and education, repertoire selection, programming concerts, rehearsal planning and techniques, score study, classroom management, vocal techniques and musicianship skills, the changing voice, and pop ensembles and musical productions. The new National Standards for Arts Education are addressed, as well as fundraising, choral parent organizations, budgets, managing the choral library, choosing performance attire, avoiding teacher burnout, and the use of technology in the classroom. Suggested repertoire lists for classical and pop choirs are included, and mini-projects and a list of pertinent references are found at the end of each chapter. Real-life scenarios begin each chapter, and place the chapter's information into context.

The information and activities presented in this text will

enchance the college students' conducting classes, especially if taken simultaneously with their choral methods class.

I have sung in many choirs during my life, and every one of the directors with whom I sang began to shape my thoughts and feelings about the choral art and contributed greatly to my music education. These wonderful people include: Norma Dowling Green, Elizabeth Jenkins, Joe Groom, Fred Allen, Sylvia Ross, Anthony Palmer, David Stutzenberger, and the late Clayton Krehbiel. Although I never sang under her direction, Colleen Kirk had a profound influence on me as a doctoral student at Florida State University, and I am a great admirer of her vast contribution to choral music. My dear piano teacher, the late Alma McGee, believed in me, and helped to lay a firm musical foundation which I draw from every day.

The following colleagues have offered wonderful assistance, support, encouragement, and suggestions for various aspects of the creative process: David Mancini, Lloyd Pfautsch, Claire McCoy, Constantina Tsolainou, John Paul Johnson, Robert Stroker, Dennis Bowers, Rob Rucker, Walter Dick, Mollie McCollough, Michael O'Hern, Karen Mabry, Randy Hooper, Ron Banks, Andrew Anderson, and Thomas Tunks. I am deeply indebted to Southern Methodist University for granting me a sabbatical leave so that I could complete this project.

Three choral directors in the Dallas area graciously allowed their rehearsals to be disrupted so that photographs could be taken for this book. I am most grateful to: Lindy Perez and the Westwood Junior High School Choir (Richardson Independent School District); Karen Mabry and the North Garland High School Choir (Garland Independent School District); and Randy Hooper and the Garland High School Choir (Garland Independent School District). Thanks also are due to Mollie McCollough for offering a photograph of Espree, her pop ensemble at Lake Highlands High School (Richardson Independent School District).

Thanks are due to Nikki Horast who put me in touch with Thom Ewing, the photographer who took all but one of the beautiful photographs in this text. Thom worked extremely hard, was always pleasant, and showed a great commitment to this project.

I am grateful to Maribeth Payne, former editor in chief at Schirmer Books, who first believed in my project, and who guided its early stages. I wish to thank Richard Carlin, current senior editor, Jonathan Wiener, the editor in charge of my book, and James Hatch, production editor, for their invaluable assistance in guiding this project to a successful conclusion. I also appreciate the assistance of the people at Direct Choral Services (Arlington, TX) who helped to clarify publishing information on several compositions.

I am deeply thankful for every student I have had the privilege to teach during the course of my career in choral music. Through my work with them, I have learned so much, and to them, I owe much of this book. I am especially grateful to my conducting and methods students at Southern Methodist University for their interest, patience, and encouragement while I was writing, and for reading drafts of the manuscript and offering valuable feedback for its improvement.

Last, but by no means least, I wish to thank my dear parents for the love and support they have given to me so freely throughout my life, for the musical opportunities that they made available to me as a child, and for teaching me to do my very best in everything I undertake.

B. A. B.

Choral Music
Methods and Materials

CHAPTER 1

Philosophical Foundations

Ms. Barnes has a problem. Because of budget restraints, her principal has told her that one choir will have to be cut from her high school choral program next year so that she can be free to teach two freshman English classes in addition to her three remaining choirs. Ms. Barnes, her students, and the Choral Parents Organization have spoken to the principal about the value of music education in the lives of high school students, and a group even attended a school board meeting to plead their case. While sympathetic to their concerns, the administration was forced to stand firm with the decision to trim back its budget for the choral program.

Ms. Barnes has been contemplating her dilemma for some time. She has to choose among the following choirs, and is having great difficulty deciding which one to disband:

1. *Chorale: The most advanced group, this mixed choir is composed of thirty auditioned singers.*

2. *Concert Choir: This mixed choir is the largest group (seventy-five students) and is comprised of auditioned singers of intermediate ability.*

3. *Show Choir: This auditioned group sings popular music with choreography, and, in addition to being a fine musical organization that performs difficult music with finesse, the Show Choir is helpful in recruiting singers into the choral program.*

4. *Mixed Chorus: This group is the only unauditioned choir at the high school. Sixty students are presently enrolled in the Mixed Chorus, which serves as the training choir for beginning singers and musicians.*

Which group should be cut? What will dictate Ms. Barnes' choice? What do you believe?

The balance of this book deals with pragmatic issues designed to help choral directors manage and direct a successful choral program. However important and necessary this pedagogical information is, it will be most effective if based on a solid philosophy of music education. And while a book cannot dictate what you believe, ideas and issues can be presented for contemplation and discussion. Hopefully, through quiet reflection and by talking with professors, public school music teachers, and your fellow music students, your own personal philosophy of music education will emerge. As you have new experiences and grow as a teacher, this philosophy will likely change and grow as well.

Whether or not you are aware of it, your philosophy of music education will guide almost all facets of any choral program that you direct, for how you act is directly related to what you believe. In the scenario above, for example, if Ms. Barnes believes strongly in the importance of offering music for every student, she most assuredly will not do away with the Mixed Chorus, the only unauditioned group she directs. However, the Mixed Chorus would be the most logical choir to disband if she feels strongly that music is for the talented few and not for the masses. If music as entertainment is uppermost in Ms. Barnes' philosophy, she will maintain the Show Choir, because entertainment is a stronger focus for this group than for any other choir. In addition, the type of music that she chooses for all her choirs will reflect her philosophy. Granted, her decision is not an easy one, but by considering Ms. Barnes' dilemma, you can see how a philosophy of music education can and does affect decisions in your work.

Authors Charles Leonhard and Robert W. House, in their classic text, *Foundations and Principles of Music Education* (1972, pp. 85–86), cite three reasons for having a sound philosophical foundation:

1. *A sound philosophy can inspire and lighten the work of the music teacher.* To be the teacher in charge of revealing music's power and beauty to your students is an important responsibility and can be an exhilarating experience. Watching a young child totally abandon himself as he moves expressively to the mood of the music, seeing an adolescent's face light up as she hears for the first time the musical form of a listening example, or sensing the emotion in an audience's silence at the completion of a performance too beautiful to applaud or discuss are all examples of the rewards of teaching music.

These rewards often don't include enough financial remuneration to allow for fancy trips, a vacation home, or a new car every year. In addition, large class size, evening and weekend activities, "free time" spent in attending conventions, clinics, reading to keep current in the field, and constantly searching for new ways to bring a better learning experience to their students describes most music teachers' lives. Doing all this and more for limited monetary rewards, they continue to strive and struggle because most music teachers view their job as a *mission*. Underneath this commitment to their mission lies a strong belief in music and its power and importance in the lives of all people.

This mission can be very difficult at times. Some days the students aren't cooperative, the parents are unhappy, the school board is cutting the music budget, the administration adds more paperwork, and the after-school rehearsals are making the school day very long indeed. At times like these, having a sound philosophy in place can lighten the load and can serve as a major source of inspiration between "mountaintop experiences." Knowing why music is an important subject in the school curriculum, and knowing why you have chosen to teach music in the schools can provide that extra bit of energy required to weather the less rewarding times.

2. A sound philosophy can serve to guide and give direction to the efforts of the teacher. As part of a graduate course, a young teacher was asked for the first time in her career to write her philosophy of music education. She was puzzled as to how to begin until she made the connection between actions and beliefs. As she recalled her actions over a period of ten years of teaching in the public schools, she was able to formulate her philosophy of music education. In the decisions and choices she had made for her students and the choral program, she saw what she believed.

Sometimes, in addition to guiding actions, having a philosophy in place can be a time-saver. Since you have already thought deeply about what you believe, decisions or choices may come easier because you will simply apply your belief system to the situation in question. How often choirs perform, which choirs are offered, and the choice of music are examples of decisions that are guided by your philosophy.

3. A sound philosophy helps the music teacher clarify and explain the importance of music to colleagues and to the public in general. Unfortunately, this chapter's scenario could be happening right now in any school district across the country. When money is tight and budgets begin to shrink, music and other arts are often the first subjects to be cut from the school curriculum. More and more often, teachers, students, and their parents find themselves at school board meetings defending the inclusion of music in the schools. Having thought deeply about music's importance in the education of all young people can improve your communication with those who don't understand the value of music education.

Recently, the Music Educators National Conference, the National Association of Music Merchants, and the National Academy of Recording Arts and Sciences, Inc. have formed the National Coalition for Music Education, representing the entire music community in a national campaign to promote music education in the schools. The Music Educators National Conference (MENC) has available for distribution an *Action Kit for Music Education* (1991) that includes a wealth of excellent information and materials for mounting a campaign to ensure a balanced, sequential, high-quality education in music for all children. Included in the kit are:

1. A manual entitled *Building Support for School Music: A Practical Guide,* designed to help organize an advocacy group, analyze your school situation, and set and implement goals and strategies
2. Videotapes (*Let's Make Music, A Way of Learning,* and *School Music and Reverse Economics*) designed to help you in presenting your case to various groups
3. *Growing Up Complete: The Imperative for Music Education,* an inspiring and informative report from the National Commission on Music Education
4. Sample, low-cost brochures that can be handed out at meetings
5. *Issues in Music Education* that presents MENC's 1991 "Statement of Beliefs" on a variety of topics of concern to the music education profession
6. A window decal featuring the logo "Music Makes the Difference"
7. A resource flyer that includes a listing and order form for the complete *Action Kit* or for individual items.

These materials will inspire and educate any person or group charged to defend the inclusion of music as part of the core curriculum in the public schools, and the likelihood of this happening is, unfortunately, growing day by day. Facts reported in *Growing Up Complete* (1991, pp. 11–13) do not paint a healthy picture for the music education profession. Just to sample a few: "The federal government spends 29 times more on science education than on arts education"; "fifty-five percent of the nation's school districts are either unserved by a music specialist or served only part time"; and "the percentage of junior- and senior-high students taking music has declined by almost a third since 1950."

Formulating Your Philosophy of Music Education

Why Should Music Be in the Schools?

People today can be almost totally involved with machines on a daily basis. We talk to telephone answering machines as much as

or more than we talk to real people. We get money out of an auto-
matic teller machine rather than interacting with a human teller,
we pay for gasoline at the pump, and we talk to people through E-
mail on our computers rather than going to their homes or offices
to have a personal conversation. In such a world as this, efforts
must be made to stay in touch with those characteristics and qualities that make us human. Teachers must create opportunities for
students to be in direct contact with other students and where
interaction is necessary. In addition, now more than ever, provision must be made in education for developing students' feelings
as well as their minds and bodies. The study of music can make a
significant contribution in all these areas.

Participation in music can provide enjoyment and enrichment for
all humankind and provides a creative and socially acceptable manner in which to express feelings and to share them in community
with fellow human beings. People need other people, and because
the traditional family of the past has changed to include many broken homes where the parent or parents may have little time to
spend with their children, a musical organization can serve as a
healthy and enjoyable substitute for a family or as an extension of
the family unit.

In his book, *High School: A Report of Secondary Education in
America* (1983, p. 98), Ernest L. Boyer reports the findings of a
revealing study conducted in the early 1980s by the Carnegie
Foundation for the Advancement of Teaching. Of vital importance to music educators, one of the study's conclusions stated
that: "[T]he arts not only give expression to the profound urgings
of the human spirit; they also validate our feelings in a world that
deadens feeling. Now, more than ever, all people need to see
clearly, hear acutely, and feel sensitively through the arts. These
skills are no longer just desirable. They are essential if we are to
survive together with civility and joy." Failure to expose all students to this profound connection between music and the emotional life is, according to the National Commission on Music
Education, "a form of dehumanization by default" (*Growing Up
Complete*, 1991, p. 7).

Because all art may be perceived as a symbol of life, participation
in the arts may help us to understand ourselves, understand life,

Photograph by Thom Ewing.

and help us to cope more easily with life's demands. The composer Dominick Argento has said (1977, p. 18): "I do believe we all possess some untapped secret spring within us—it may even be synonymous with 'soul.' And I also believe that under normal circumstances we are unaware of this treasure or unable to utilize it, but in the presence of certain works of art we re-discover it temporarily—not in the work of art: in ourselves. Art itself merely unlocks the door or puts us in a proper mood to make the discovery. That, it seems to me, is the mystery and magic of music—music of all kinds, of all times."

The arts can make a difference between merely existing for survival's sake and living a full and meaningful life. In *Issues in Music Education* (1991, p. 1), the Music Educators National Conference (MENC) states that: "although formal instruction in music is very important in the development of those students who are gifted and talented in music, the primary purpose of music instruction in the schools is to improve the quality of life for all students through the development of their capacities to participate fully in their musical culture." Charles Hoffer (1993, p. 3) states that: "without music the quality of life in America would be less than it is now."

Several nonmusical benefits of music instruction in the public schools include the development of responsibility, cooperation, punctuality, and dependability. Music can be used to teach or enhance other subjects in the curriculum. Opportunities abound for critical thinking and creativity, and our history and culture can be transmitted from generation to generation through the study of music. In addition, administrators are pleased when the music program fosters school spirit or serves as a good public-relations tool.

MENC believes that music should be integrated into the school curriculum just as it is integrated into life: "Music can be used when appropriate to enhance the teaching of other subject matter, but in addition, it should maintain its integrity in the curriculum and should be taught for its own sake as well. The use of music as a means for the teaching of non-musical content should not diminish the time or effort devoted to the teaching of music as music" (*Issues in Music Education*, 1991, p. 2).

Who Should Learn?

Because education is a preparation for living in addition to a preparation for making a living, music has an important place in the education of *all* students. One of the eight assumptions illustrating the new vision of music in American education listed in *The School Music Program: A New Vision* (1994, p. 5) supports this view: "Every student at every level, PreK-12, should have access to a comprehensive program of music instruction in school, taught by teachers qualified in music." This belief is stated just as strongly in *Issues in Music Education* (1991, p. 1): "the finest possible education in music should be available to every student in the nation and . . . every student should have an equal opportunity to study music."

The Carnegie Foundation for the Advancement of Teaching study (Boyer, 1983) concluded that the arts are not a frill, and should be included in the core of common learning for every high school student. Their placement of the arts is in agreement with MENC's belief that the arts constitute one of the five fundamental components of basic education that should be at the core of every child's education.

Who Should Teach?

Teaching music is too important a mission to be left to those who are unqualified or only partially qualified to do the job. Because public school music will likely be the final opportunity for most students to have regular musical experiences, this opportunity must be offered and guided by qualified teachers. The young people of today need and deserve the brightest and best music teachers available.

According to the MENC "Statement of Beliefs," every student should have access to music instruction taught by teachers qualified in music. Just what does *qualified* mean? MENC believes that music teachers should be chosen from among those applicants having the greatest musical talent and the greatest gifts and skills for working with children. In addition, admission into a music teacher education program should be based on a variety of qualifications including musical, personal, intellectual, and instructional potential (*Issues in Music Education*, 1991, p. 3).

This means that music teachers must be good musicians first. Then, to their musicianship, they have added the skills and techniques necessary for working effectively with young people. This preparation includes knowledge of human development, techniques for behavior management, and interpersonal skills for building good relationships with students, parents, colleagues, and administrators. The old adage "Those who can't, teach" would certainly not apply to the type of music teacher described by MENC!

What Music Should Be Included in the Curriculum?

MENC believes that school music programs should "reflect the multimusical nature of our pluralistic American culture" and "include samples of the various musics of the world" (*Issues in Music Education*, 1991, p. 2). No longer can teachers include only Western art music and American folk songs in their music curricula and call it complete. Good educators always take into account the students they are teaching, and, today, these students reflect an increasingly pluralistic society. People from many different lands and cultures are currently living in America. Studying and performing music from the various cultures can not only provide enjoyment for all, but also may provide opportunities to understand one another better.

Many school districts place a ban on the singing of Christmas music because so many of their students hold different beliefs. To acknowledge these different beliefs and customs, a more representative program at Christmastime may include holiday music from various countries that would celebrate student's differences and help everyone to appreciate and understand a variety of traditions.

In the area of religious music in general, MENC believes it is an important component of the musical repertoire of all cultures. If the music is chosen for its musical quality, and the focus of the study and performance of the music remains on its musical characteristics, then the inclusion of religious music is certainly appropriate. Published by MENC, a pamphlet entitled *Religious*

Music in the Schools (1987, p. 1) begins with the following statement: "It is the position of the Music Educators National Conference that the study of religious music is a vital and appropriate part of the total music experience in both performance and listening. To omit sacred music from the repertoire or study of music would present an incorrect and incomplete concept of the comprehensive nature of the art." This pamphlet may prove useful to teachers who are experiencing conflict on this subject with parents or administrators.

You must remember that the quality of the music chosen for rehearsal and performance has an impact not only on the quality of your students' music education but also on the quality of music that is written and published. The publishing business is, after all, a business, and to remain in business, publishers must make a profit. If choral directors everywhere are buying a certain type of music, you can be assured that this type of music will be written and published. Music educators must recognize this fact of life and choose music that is worthy of rehearsal and performance and that will enhance their students' education. This will definitely have a direct impact on what is available for purchase.

What Is the Role of Performance in a Choral Program?

As part of their objectives for music education, MENC includes the importance of performing music alone and with others as well as being able to use the vocabulary and notation of music. No one would dispute that! Wisely, however, the objectives go further to include responding to music aesthetically, intellectually, and emotionally (*Issues in Music Education*, 1991, p. 1).

Performance education must be aesthetic education. Emphasis on perfecting the technical aspects of the music is simply not enough. To be truly successful, choral ensembles must be led beyond the technical aspects to experiencing the aesthetic qualities, for this is when music can make the most lasting and pervasive impact on singers and listeners alike. Bennett Reimer, in his book *A Philosophy of Music Education* (1970, p. 131) states: "The power of such experience is so great and its satisfactions so deep that those who have shared it are likely to be changed fundamentally in their relation to music. For such people music inevitably becomes a source of some of life's deepest rewards. This is no small matter, given the universal need for such satisfaction and its rarity in human life."

This is not to imply that technique and its mastery are unimportant, but rather a means toward achieving a greater end. When performers grasp fully the treatment of musical elements in each piece to be studied and performed, the potential for understanding the very essence of the music may be greater. In addition, these technical aspects are all vital and necessary to achieve the more important (and often more elusive) complete musical experience. Joseph Bassin (1991, p. 39) states: "[I]t is through attention to the components of the composition that one seeks the aesthetic experience." He goes further to say that conductors "must direct the students' attention toward encountering the music rather than diverting their attention by concentrating solely on technique." Opportunities must be provided at each rehearsal, even if only for a few measures, for singers to use their mastery of the technical demands to move toward experiencing the aesthetic qualities. Making beautiful music, even in small portions, will yield satisfaction along the way as well as provide motivation to persevere.

Performance education as aesthetic education presents lofty goals that take time to accomplish. Teachers, therefore, need to create a reasonable performance schedule for their choirs that will allow time for this to occur. Learning the notes as quickly as possible in any way that you can while you and your singers race from one performance to another will not only make aesthetic education a difficult accomplishment but will hardly offer time for education of any sort to be experienced. Kept in perspective, however, performance can serve as a showcase of student learning and musical understanding and can offer an exhilarating experience for performers and listeners alike.

The following creed was developed by MENC in 1991:

Music Educators' Creed*

As a music teacher, I devote myself to two important causes:
1. Helping all people to make music a part of their lives, and
2. Advancing the art of music.

I believe that all people have the right to an education in music that:

> Teaches them the lifelong joy of making music through singing and playing instruments
>
> Gives them a chance to express through music what cannot be expressed in words
>
> Helps them to respond to music intellectually and emotionally
>
> Teaches them the language of music notation and opens the door to improvising, composing and arranging
>
> Equips them to make informed judgments about musical works and performances
>
> Educates them in the music of all cultures and historical eras
>
> Allows them to discover and develop their special talents, including preparing to make music their profession, if they so choose
>
> Prepares them to be involved with music throughout their lives

I teach music because—music makes a difference in the lives of people.

Summary

A philosophy of music education will guide your actions in virtually every facet of your job as a choral director. Formulating answers to such questions as why music should be in the schools, who should learn, who should teach, what music should be included in the curriculum, and what role performance should play can provide a solid foundation on which to build a dynamic and successful choral program for your students.

In addition, knowing what you believe can inspire you during the difficult times as well as provide insight for colleagues, parents, and administrators as to the importance of music for every child. This is no small matter since school boards everywhere are being forced to make

* From *Soundpost*, Vol. 8, No. 3. Copyright © 1992. Published by Music Educators National Conference: Reston, Virginia. Reprinted with permission.

difficult decisions due to declining financial resources. Unfortunately, music programs are often among the first subjects to be cut, an action that places the total education of our young people in serious jeopardy.

Mini-Projects

1. Recall those teachers with whom you have studied in the past who have had a strong influence on you and for whom you have the utmost admiration and respect. What characteristics do

Figure 1.1   Philosophical points to ponder

Place a "T" beside any statement that you consider to be true. Place an "F" beside any statement that you consider to be false.

___The music teaching profession is just as important as a profession in business, medicine, or law.

___Music-related experiences are always beneficial to students.

___The importance of the music program is not really understood by many school administrators.

___A good music teacher always maintains composure, even in the toughest situations.

___A student who is not prepared for a concert is a liability to the ensemble and should not be allowed to perform.

___Aesthetic experiences are not likely to occur in elementary or middle school music classrooms or performances.

___When members of a performing ensemble know and like each other, they are likely to perform better together.

___Missing a concert for any other reason except personal illness or the death of a family member is cause for punishment.

___I feel confident as a future teacher.

___Students need not be evaluated in their music classes; they just need to have fun.

___Music festivals and contests are valuable experiences for ensembles and should be a major focus in a child's music education.

___I can make a real difference in this world by teaching music.

___Students can build self-esteem in their music classes.

___Teaching music is a good way to enhance your own reputation as a musician.

___The music classroom does not resemble real life.

___The most important component of a child's music education is learning self-expression.

___My performing skills are strong.

___Good music teachers don't need to enjoy working with people; they just need to be outstanding musicians.

these teachers possess? During your preparation for teaching, what additional characteristics have you discovered to be important for outstanding teachers to have?

Use the answers to the preceding questions to help you formulate your ideal teacher model. Include personal characteristics, musical characteristics, and teaching skills.

2. Based on an article entitled "Personal Skills: Passport to Effective Teaching" by Robert E. Fisher (1991), Figure 1.1 is a list of statements that will help you to discover what you believe about music education. Use your answers to stimulate your thinking and to provide topics for discussion between you and your classmates.

3. Write your philosophy of music education. Include in your paper answers to the following questions. Why is music important in the schools? Who should learn? Who should teach? What music should be included? What is the role of performance in the total curriculum of a choral ensemble? Mini-projects No. 1 and No. 2 should help you formulate your philosophy.

4. Pretend your methods class is the Board of Education from the school district in which you teach. They are discussing cutting back financially on the choral programs in all secondary schools in the district. Give a brief presentation, taking the stance that this would be a serious mistake.

References

Action Kit for Music Education. (1991). Reston, VA: Music Educators National Conference.

ARGENTO, DOMINICK. (1977). The composer and the singer. *NATS Bulletin, 13*(4), 18–31.

BASSIN, JOSEPH. (1991). A path to the elusive aesthetic experience. *Music Educators Journal, 77*(6), 38–40.

BOYER, ERNEST L. (1983). *High school: A report of secondary education in America.* New York: Harper and Row.

FISHER, ROBERT E. (1991). Personal skills: Passport to effective teaching. *Music Educators Journal, 77*(6), 21–25.

Growing up complete: The imperative for music education. (1991). Reston, VA: Music Educators National Conference.

HOFFER, CHARLES. (1993). *Introduction to music education*, 2nd ed. Belmont, CA: Wadsworth.

Issues in music education. (1991). Reston, VA: Music Educators National Conference.

LEONHARD, CHARLES, and ROBERT W. HOUSE. (1972). *Foundations and principles of music education.* New York: McGraw-Hill.

REIMER, BENNETT. (1970). *A philosophy of music education.* Englewood Cliffs, NJ: Prentice-Hall.

Religious music in the schools. (1987). Reston, VA: Music Educators National Conference.

The school music program: A new vision. (1994). Reston, VA: Music Educators National Conference.

Additional Reading

ABELES, HAROLD F., CHARLES R. HOFFER, and ROBERT H. KLOTMAN. (1994). *Foundations of music education*, 2nd ed. New York: Schirmer Books.

GLENN, CAROLE, ed. (1991). *In quest of answers: Interviews with American choral conductors.* Chapel Hill, NC: Hinshaw Music.

Guidelines for performances of school music groups: Expectations and limitations. (1986). Reston, VA: Music Educators National Conference.

JORGENSEN, ESTELLE R. (1990). Philosophy and the music teacher: Challenging the way we think. *Music Educators Journal, 76*(5), 17–23.

Music code of ethics. (1988). Reston, VA: Music Educators National Conference.

National standards for arts education: What every young American should know and be able to do in the arts. (1994). Reston, VA: Music Educators National Conference.

Opportunity-to-learn: Standards for music instruction: Grades preK–12. (1994). Reston, VA: Music Educators National Conference.

Summary statement: Education reform, standards, and the arts. (1994). Reston, VA: Music Educators National Conference.

CHAPTER 2

Recruitment and Retention of Singers

A group of middle school students are sitting at lunch discussing whether to audition for choir for the upcoming year. Ann has decided she will try out because she really likes the outfits the choir wears when they perform, and the T-shirts with the school name and mascot on them are great. Bryan agrees about the T-shirts, and adds that he has heard that the end-of-the-year trip to a nearby amusement park is fabulous. Donna mentions that all her friends are in choir, so she has decided to audition too. Manuel has been in choir for one year, and announces to the group that he is going to try out again simply because he loves to sing.

Motivation to Sing

Extrinsic Motivation

When students join choir for reasons like those cited by Ann, Bryan, and Donna in the scenario above, they are motivated extrinsically. The performance outfits, the choir T-shirts, the spring tour, the awards banquet with its potential trophies and certificates, or the chance to get out of the house and drive the car to an evening rehearsal are all examples of extrinsic motivation for participating in a choral ensemble. For adolescents, peer pressure can serve as an extrinsic motivator as well. The need to belong to a successful group where all the "popular" students are involved is a powerful force at this age.

Extrinsic motivation comes "from without," or, in this case, from attractions not directly related to the actual making of music. Until students have actually had a positive musical experience, their motivation for participating in choir may be almost totally extrinsic. The enterprising choral director will capitalize on this situation to attract new singers to the choir.

Intrinsic Motivation

Manuel chooses to join choir because he is drawn by the sheer joy of singing and making music with a group. Therefore, he is motivated intrinsically, or "from within." This type of motivation is the ultimate goal, and one that is the most meaningful and lasting. As singers get older and mature musically, they will likely become more intrinsically than extrinsically motivated to participate in musical activities. The choral director's job is to create consistent opportunities for music making to become the motivating force. The initial motivators (tours, outfits, awards, evening rehearsals) will remain, yet shift to a less important, peripheral position.

Many activities and organizations compete for students' time at the middle school/junior high and senior high school levels. This situation, coupled with the increasing number of credits required for high school graduation and the fact that a large number of students are employed part-time, suggests that an aggressive recruitment campaign for a choral program needs to be in operation at all times. For these reasons, smart choral directors are constantly considering new ways to attract new students.

Nothing Succeeds Like Success

A successful choir is the most important and effective aspect of recruitment and retention for a choral program. If the students sing a variety of quality music and sing it well, are happy to be in choir, and have positive comments to say to their friends, teachers, and family, a major portion of the recruitment effort is solved. If the choral program is perceived as an attractive activity in which to be involved, prospective singers will always want to join, and once they join, they will want to continue their participation.

The opposite is also true. If the choral program is perceived as an activity that is not fun, or if the teacher is difficult to get along with or is unfair, or whenever the choir sings for the school, the performance is an embarrassment, students will not want to participate. No amount of extramusical enticement will easily overcome a program that is unsuccessful at its very foundation.

What are the components that make up a successful choral program? The answers to this question will yield important information for recruitment and retention.

Obviously, the most important component is a choral director who has the necessary musical knowledge and skills for success. Without knowledge of music history, theory, good vocal technique, effective conducting skills, good rehearsal techniques, and the ability to choose and prepare appropriate music, the director will be operating at a distinct disadvantage and the entire choral program will suffer.

In addition to the necessary musical knowledge and skills, a director who has a positive approach toward the job to be done, no matter what difficulties are encountered, will do much to create a successful program. Singers will want to join and remain in such a group. "When life gives you lemons, make lemonade" is a good philosophy to adopt when you find yourself in charge of a program that needs building or major changes. Don't waste time and energy complaining about what you haven't got. Just get busy and make something out of what you *do* have while working toward a better choral program. Remember that change takes time.

An understanding of the age group with which the director is working is vitally important to a successful program. Students will sense immediately a caring and understanding attitude toward them as individuals and as a group. Word will spread quickly that choir is a place where students belong and feel important, and where their membership is valued. This does not suggest that the director attempt to be "one of the gang" by getting too close to the students, but rather suggests a warm, caring attitude within a professional approach.

Photograph by Thom Ewing.

Choral directors are group leaders and must recognize the need to nurture an *esprit de corps* among their singers. The following suggestions may help build student pride in choir, serve in rebuilding a failing choral program, enhance a successful choral program, and aid in recruitment and retention as well.

1. Organize a retreat at the beginning of the year. Whether it is held on a Saturday or is planned for an entire weekend, a retreat is an excellent way for students to get to know one another—and you—in a more casual atmosphere. Activities can include volleyball or baseball games, swimming, field-day competitions between choirs, election of choir officers, planning for the year, and rehearsals. If funds are limited, plan a Saturday in a local park and have students bring their own sack lunches.

2. Plan an end-of-the-year activity as well. A swimming party, a trip to a bowling alley or a skating rink, a supper together at a local pizza parlor, or any activity that the students enjoy can serve as a reward for hard work during the school year.

3. An awards banquet at the end of the year can also serve as a good culminating experience for the students—and for their parents as well. Make sure to honor every student in some way, so each person feels important to the overall success of the choral program. A certificate of participation can provide positive reinforcement to all singers regardless of whether they distinguished themselves by making All-State Choir or by earning the most outstanding student award. The banquet is also an excellent opportunity to honor publicly the parents and administrators who have contributed to the successes of the year. An inexpensive way to hold an awards banquet is to have it in the school cafeteria as a potluck dinner.

4. Order T-shirts, water bottles, key chains, hats, or anything the students think is "cool" and have the choir's name and school insignia printed on it. Students love to belong to groups and will welcome the opportunity to wear or use something that signifies they are a part of the choral program. Without the choir's name printed on them, these same items can be sold to all students in the school and serve as a fund-raiser for the choral program.

5. Keep a scrapbook of each year's activities and be sure to include lots of pictures, all concert programs, important correspondence, and news releases. Students enjoy seeing themselves in a book that will be maintained for years to come and eventually become part of the school's history.

6. Create a Choral Parents Organization. Parents can assist with fund-raising activities, telephoning, publicity needs, serve as chaperones, and provide transportation. In addition, when their parents are involved, students have more invested in the choral program, so they are likely to become involved more deeply and for a longer period of time than those students whose parents are not involved. (More details about parental involvement are given in Chapter 13.)

7. Involve students in leadership positions. Elect officers in each choir and give these students responsibilities to complete. Not only does this free the director to focus on the music rather than on nonmusical details of managing a choral program, but it also helps young people develop leadership skills and learn firsthand about responsibility. Students who are involved in this way feel more a part of the organization, and they also sense that the director places importance and trust in them as individuals.

8. Performances outside the school can build *esprit de corps* and school pride within the choral ensemble and are important for recruitment and retention. Not only is it fun for the students to leave campus to sing, but it also gives them a sense of who they are as a musical organization, especially if other choirs are participating in the event.

9. Performances on the school campus are equally important. The director must be careful, however, to choose an occasion when the choir will be heard and appreciated. School assemblies and evening concerts are better choices than performing at a pep rally or singing during lunch in the cafeteria. The choice of music to be sung at these on-campus performances is as critical as the occasion chosen. Make sure to select a variety of music that will appeal to, as well as educate, the student audience. Because peer pressure is a critical factor at the middle school/junior high and senior high school age, it is important that the choir be well received by friends, fellow students, and teachers.

10. Advertise the choral program. Advertisement means not only informing students about upcoming auditions, but also informing the entire school regarding the various successes of the choral program during the year. Ways to disseminate important information include: (1) congratulatory announcements over the intercom; (2) articles in the school newspaper; (3) articles in the city newspaper; and (4) posters in the halls or on bulletin boards.

Where Do You Find Students to Recruit?

Feeder Schools

Wise choral directors are aware that their particular school (at whatever level) is part of a school *system*; in other words, everything they do is related to where their students came from as well as to where they will be going. Therefore, establishing a good rapport with choral directors and students at your feeder schools is critical for recruitment. Visit their campuses frequently, offer to take sectionals or do a clinic, invite their choirs to share a concert at your school, and take your choirs to their campus to perform. Hold a "choir day" at your school on a Saturday and invite students (and their parents) from the feeder schools to come visit the choir room, observe rehearsals of the various choirs, have lunch or some sort of refreshments, and generally get to know one another. When it is time for auditions for the coming year, contact the choral directors at the feeder schools and have them announce to their students when you will be on their campus to conduct auditions.

Guidance Counselors

Guidance counselors are often the first people to see students who are transferring to your school and are frequently in charge of planning their schedules. If counselors are knowledgeable about the choral program, they are more likely to channel new students your way. Equally important, the choral director needs to inform the counselors about those choirs that require an audition, helping them to understand that the choral program is grouped by ability much the same as math and English classes. Just as they would not place a student into advanced trigonometry who is weak in math and who doesn't have the prerequisite skills to succeed in such a class, they must not place beginning choir students into the advanced choir.

Coaches

By attending athletic events and showing genuine interest in the athletic program in general, the choral director will likely build a good rapport with the coaches in the department. Coaches often serve as powerful role models, who, by showing support for the choral program, may cause athletes to participate in choir. By urging students to join, several "key" students may be recruited. By their own participation in choir, these students may bring other students with them. For example, football and basketball players who join choir may cause several cheerleaders to join, and friends of both players and cheerleaders will be eager to join as well because they will want to be involved in the same activities as their perceived leaders. Peer pressure is the key issue here, so capitalize on it.

Involve the Entire School in a Musical Production

Whether once a year or every few years, most schools will produce some sort of musical event that involves costumes, lighting, staging, sound, programs, and advertisement. Rather than limiting participation to the choral department, involve the entire school in various ways. For instance, the home economics department may be able to help with the costumes, the print shop can assist with the programs and posters for the advertising campaign, and the cosmetology classes may be interested in helping with makeup and hair. Students who understand lights and sound should be given the opportunity to be involved in the production. Students involved in these important nonmusical jobs will have an opportunity to observe you and the singers in rehearsal, and in this way, may find themselves interested enough in the musical portion to consider joining choir.

Likewise, make the auditions for the musical portion of the production open to the entire school. For those students who are not currently involved in the choral program, participation in a one-time event will allow them a chance to perform without a long-term commitment. Based on their experience, they can then decide whether they would enjoy being a part of choir on a regular basis.

Friends of Choir Members

If current choir members are pleased to be in choir, they may respond positively to the challenge that each choir member recruit one additional singer. If successful, this could double the enrollment! Offer an incentive by awarding a prize to the student who recruits the most new members, or to the choir that is most successful in this project.

General Music

If approached correctly, general music classes at any level can lay the foundation for a positive attitude toward singing as well as introducing students to the basics of note reading and proper vocal technique. General music is also an excellent place for the choir director to discover those students who have a special talent or interest in singing. Personally invite those students to audition for choir.

Church Choirs

Contact the youth choir director at several churches in the area to determine whether any of their choir members attend your school. Personally invite any church choir members who are not presently singing at school to audition for the school choir. Frequently, this interaction between school and church will serve to strengthen both music programs.

Private Piano Teachers

Piano students often make excellent choir members because their music-reading skills are being developed through their piano training as well as through their choral experiences. To locate these students, contact local piano teachers and ask them to provide you with a list of their students and the schools that they attend. You can then contact any students who attend your school and who are not involved in the choral program and invite them to join.

Study Hall

Locate all the study halls that meet at the same time as a choir rehearsal and arrange with the teachers in charge to allow those students interested in finding out more about choir to observe a rehearsal during their study hall. Depending on the number of students who come, try mixing the visitors in with the choir members and have them sing.

Summary

Recruiting students for the choral program is an never-ending process. The use of extrinsic motivators may be necessary to attract new singers, and may even be necessary for the overall retention of choir members. Once the students are in the choir, however, directors must create opportunities for the music-making to become the motivating force.

A successful choral program is your most powerful tool in the recruitment and retention of students. If the singers are proud to be in choir and enjoy the experience, they are likely to return year after year. Often, their pleasure will be so apparent that it will attract additional students into the choral program.

Establishing a strong rapport with your feeder schools is an extremely important aspect of recruitment. Go regularly to these schools to visit and perform, and invite them to your campus as well. Get to know the guidance counselors and coaches at your school, and plan a musical production every year or two that is open to involvement by the entire student body and faculty. Contact local piano teachers and church choir directors for recommendations for potential choir members. Be alert for good singers and musicians in general music classes and study halls, and challenge current choir members to recruit their friends.

Mini-Projects

1. Design and create a poster to recruit junior high/middle school singers into the choral program. Audition dates, times, and places should be included. Write a brief but catchy announcement to be given over the public-address system regarding the same audition and recruitment information.

2. Do the same activities listed in No. 1, but make the materials appropriate for a choral program at the high school level.

3. Suppose that you have been hired as the choral director of Mid-America High School where the choral program has suffered for many years. Specifically, the program had a total enrollment of fifty-six singers last year, and only twelve of them were boys. In addition, the overall morale is extremely low. The principal has offered both moral and financial support and has challenged you to build the choral program over the next few years. What steps would you take to accomplish this task? Be specific.

4. Make a list of at least five things that would serve as extrin-

sic motivators for potential singers in a middle school/junior high school choral program.

5. Make a list of at least five things that would serve as extrinsic motivators for potential singers in a high school choral program.

Additional Reading

SANDENE, BRENT A. (1994). Going beyond recruiting: Fighting attrition. *Music Educators Journal*, *81*(2), pp. 32–34.

SHERMAN, JOY. (1992). Recruiting—Boon or burden? *Choral Journal*, *33*(4), 29–30.

CHAPTER **3**

Auditions and
Placement of Singers

*The show choir is a highly select group that meets after school, three days
a week. Recently, one of the sopranos moved out of town, and her position needs to be filled. If the following students were the only three choices
to fill the soprano vacancy, which singer would be the best choice?*

*Kassie is an extremely talented soprano who has done outstanding
work in the traditional choir program for two years. Based on her audition, not only will she make an excellent musical contribution, but she
also dances well and could offer valuable help on choreography. The
problem is that Kassie works part-time. Her schedule varies so that she
works some weeks in the afternoon and some weeks in the evening. She
must keep this particular job, but she also wants to be in the show choir.*

*Mary gave an outstanding audition and she too dances well. She
doesn't work and has her own car to get to and from the afternoon
rehearsals. She has even volunteered to run a carpool for those students
who don't have transportation. One day in the teacher's lounge, however, the director overheard a discussion among several teachers.
Generally speaking, they all agreed that Mary was one of the brightest
and most gifted students they had ever had the pleasure to teach, but
her negative attitude toward school was really beginning to cause seri-*

ous problems, not only for Mary and her own work, but also for the entire class.

Jarnetha, a freshman, has been a dedicated member of the beginning girls choir for one year and has made wonderful progress both in vocal technique and musicianship skills. Her voice is adequate at this point, but it continues to grow and shows much promise. Because she loves to sing, she serves as a positive influence on the entire choir. She has not had any formal dance training, but her physical education teacher reports that Jarnetha works hard and always gets the task done.

Clearly, Kassie and Mary have the musical abilities, experience, and skill in dancing required for success in the show choir, but each has a major liability: Kassie cannot be at all rehearsals, and Mary has an attitude problem that has the potential to affect the entire group. Although Jarnetha is young and inexperienced, she seems eager to learn and shows much potential. Which soprano would be the best choice?

Because Kassie's work schedule varies and she would not be able to have consistent attendance at the after-school rehearsals, Kassie would not be the logical choice. Choosing Mary is definitely a risk, but her attitude may be helped by participation in the Show Choir. If you are willing to work with her as she grows as a person as well as a musician, and if you have reason to believe there is a good chance for success, Mary may be a good choice.

Jarnetha is inexperienced both in singing and dancing, but she has learned a great deal very quickly, is committed to hard work, has a positive attitude, and shows great potential. As a freshman, she is still adjusting to high school, but her youth may be a positive feature. If she joins the group during her freshman year, think how valuable a member she would be over the course of four years. Of the three sopranos from which you must choose, Jarnetha may be the best choice.

Obviously, the question asked in this scenario has no easy answer. The story was written to illustrate the point that many factors not related directly to musical ability and achievement can have a real impact on singers and their potential success as choir members. (This applies to prospective singers for traditional choirs as well as for pop ensembles.) In addition to the obvious characteristics of good vocal ability, sightsinging skills (or potential, in the case of a beginner), and a good ear for music, choral directors would be wise to consider such things as students' attitude, reliability, availability, and grades when formulating the type of singers they want in the choral program and in which choirs they will be placed.

Information to Be Gathered During an Audition

Personal Data Must Be Obtained for Every Student Who Auditions

As students are waiting to audition for choir, have them fill out a sheet such as the one shown in Figure 3.1. This information can be helpful if the singers are selected for choir, so, for future reference, the sheets should be kept in a file box or the information should be entered into the computer.

In case of important messages or mailings, home address and phone number are needed, and the parents' names (especially if different from the student's name) can be used for participation in the Choral Parents Organization. The student's class schedule is helpful when a message needs to be delivered during the school day, or when a performance occurs during school hours. Knowing whether students work after school or whether they are on an early-release program will be helpful as the choral director determines in which choir these students will be placed.

Musical information such as prior choral experience (both church and school choirs), the voice part usually sung, and whether the students play an instrument can be helpful not only as a means to initiate conversation at the beginning of the audition, but also will give the director some idea as to how to structure the audition. In addition, students can be identified as potential accompanists.

Use the personal data form in Figure 3.1 as a guide for creating one that will suit your own teaching situation.

```
Name:_____Grade:_____
Parents' Names:_____
Address:_____
Phone Number:_____

Do you work?                                          yes_____    no_____
        If "yes," what is your usual work schedule?_____
Have you ever sung in a choir?                        yes_____    no_____
        If "yes," for how long?_____
        What voice part did you sing?_____
        Was the choir a church choir_____or a school choir_____?
Have you taken private voice lessons?                 yes_____    no_____
        If "yes," for how long?_____
        Who was (is) your teacher?  _____
Have you played in an instrumental ensemble?          yes_____    no_____
        If "yes," For how long?_____
        If "yes," which instrument(s) did you play?_____
Have you ever taken private instrumental lessons?     yes_____    no_____
        If "yes," for how long?_____
        If "yes," who was (is) your teacher?_____
        If "yes," what instrument did (do) you study?_____
Class Schedule:
        Period 1:_____
        Period 2:_____
        Period 3:_____
        Period 4:_____
        Period 5:_____
        Period 6:_____
```

Figure 3.1 Personal Data Form

An evaluation of the musical abilities of the singers must be made so that they may be placed in the appropriate choir.

Evaluation of a student's musical abilities can be made within the sightreading and tonal memory tests. In addition, by asking singers to perform a prepared solo or to sing a familiar song (which has not been prepared), choral directors can observe the degree of breathing technique, posture, diction, and phrasing that the student has acquired.

Unless the singers study voice privately, a prepared solo may be a difficult requirement. In addition, if a solo is required, an accompanist will be necessary unless you are able to provide this service for the students, but even if you are an adequate pianist, playing the piano while the student is singing makes it difficult to listen attentively. Often just as revealing as a prepared solo is to ask the student, during the audition, to sing a familiar song such as "My Country 'Tis of Thee" or "America, the Beautiful." Most students are familiar with the melodies of these two patriotic songs. If the words present a problem, either provide students with a copy of the song or have them sing on a neutral syllable. Ask the student to perform the familiar song a second time, *a cappella*. This technique will show a singer's orientation to the tonal center, and will provide an opportunity for the choral director to hear the voice without accompaniment.

RANGE AND TESSITURA. So that they may be placed in the correct section of the choir, all singers must be tested for the range and tessitura. A series of vocalises such as those shown in Figure 3.2 can aid in determining this information. By listening to the speaking voice of every singer as he or she comes in to audition, you can choose an appropriate pitch on which to begin the exercises.

To find the outermost limits of the voice in question (the range), the exercises should be performed ascending and then descending by half steps. At the same time, the choral director must listen for where the beauty of the voice lies, where the singer becomes uncomfortable and perhaps lapses into poor vocal habits, and where a break in the voice occurs. This information will yield the tessitura of the voice and will suggest into which section of the choir the singer should be placed. (Note: In the case of boys whose voices are changing, choral directors will want to check periodically for range and tessitura throughout the school year, and not just at audition time.)

SIGHTSINGING. If students have had no musical training whatsoever, asking them to sightsing during the audition will only serve to prove the obvious, and may cause them to feel defeated. This situation can affect the remainder of the audition in a negative way, prohibiting the choral director from getting a true picture of students' abilities. For

Figure 3.2   Vocalises for determining range and tessitura

these beginners, the tonal memory test shown in Figure 3.6 will be a good indicator of potential. Asking them to echo clap various rhythmic patterns may yield additional information. For those students who have received instruction in sightsinging or who play (or have played) an instrument, a test of their sightsinging ability is strongly suggested.

If choral directors compose their own musical examples for the sightsinging portion of the audition, they are able to tailor these examples to meet the needs of their own particular situation. Sightsinging examples for a middle school/junior high choral program will obviously be less difficult than those for a senior high program.

To allow for varying ability levels among students, compose approximately six to eight examples ranging from very simple to very difficult (two to three examples for each difficulty level). Write clearly the single vocal lines so students will not be confused by vague notation, and be sure to write the examples in both the treble and bass clefs to accommodate both boys and girls.

When writing the easy examples, make sure that the music begins on beat one as well as on the tonic, use predominately stepwise motion, use 2/4 or 4/4 meter, and limit the rhythmic activity to whole notes, half notes, and quarter notes. These examples should be written in the keys of C, F, or G major. Study the easy sightsinging examples shown in Figure 3.3.

For the moderate examples, compose several examples that begin on a note other than the tonic and introduce simple skips (predominately triadic). Include more difficult key signatures, but avoid minor keys at this level. To make the examples more demand-

Figure 3.3   Easy sightsinging examples

Figure 3.4 Moderate sightsinging examples

ing rhythmically, write several in 3/4 meter, and introduce eighth notes as well as dotted quarter notes followed by an eighth note. Study the moderate sightsinging examples shown in Figure 3.4.

For the difficult sightsinging examples, write several in a minor key, and include several discriminating intervallic skips in the melody. Increase the rhythmic difficulty by using sixteenth notes as well as dotted eighth notes followed by a sixteenth note, and compose several examples that begin on an anacrusis. Meters for the difficult examples might include compound meters as well as asymmetrical meters. Study the difficult sightsinging examples shown in Figure 3.5.

TONAL MEMORY. Like the sightsinging portion of the audition, the tonal memory test will work best when a series of examples are played in order of difficulty. If students feel successful on the first

Figure 3.5 Difficult sightsinging examples

few examples, they may be more successful on the more difficult examples that come later, simply because they have gained a certain degree of confidence.

Suggestions to follow when composing the tonal memory examples include:

1. If a tonal center is suggested by the notes in the example, the example will probably be easier.
2. Beginning and ending on the same note is usually easier than having different starting and ending pitches.
3. The tempo at which the examples are played is important. Research in melodic perception suggests that very slow tempi (below quarter note = 100 M.M.) or very fast tempi (above quarter note = 260 M.M.) can affect a student's performance in a negative way (Tunks, Bowers, and Eagle, 1994).
4. The number of notes used in each exercise may affect student success. Generally, use examples containing five to seven notes.
5. To have a "purer" test for tonal memory, write the musical examples without the use of rhythm. To test rhythmic memory, have the student echo clap several rhythmic examples.

Especially important for the tonal memory portion is the use of a piano that has been recently tuned. Students will have difficulty singing in tune when the instrument to which they are listening is not in tune. Equally important is holding the audition in a place where the tonal memory test cannot be heard by those students waiting to audition. These students would obviously gain an unfair advantage by hearing repeatedly the examples before they go in for their turn. Study the tonal memory examples shown in Figure 3.6.

Figure 3.6   Tonal memory examples

Audition Form

The audition form shown in Figure 3.7 will serve as a guide. This form will be most useful when printed on the reverse side of the information sheet shown in Figure 3.1. This way, all information about each student may be considered when it comes time to make decisions. All information may then be entered into the computer for future reference.

Implementing an Audition

First of all, put the singer at ease! Most students are going to be nervous, so by visiting with them briefly (thirty seconds to one minute) at the beginning of the audition, you may help them to relax and, thus, to give a better audition. Answers to the questions on their personal data sheet can provide a place to begin the conversation. Listen carefully as they speak to get an idea of what voice part they may sing or on which pitch to begin the vocalises.

If a prepared solo is required and the student's voice is warmed up, you may want to hear the solo after the initial visiting time. If no solo has been prepared for the audition, ask the student to sing a familiar (but unprepared) song at this point. If the student hasn't warmed up before the audition, have him or her sing the range and tessitura exercises before the solo is sung. These exercises can serve the dual purpose of checking for range and tessitura while warming up the student's voice.

If the student has warmed up before the audition, listen to the solo first and then check for range and tessitura. If you (or the

```
Name:_____
Range:____to_____          Tessitura:_____to_____
Voice part assigned:_____
Sightsinging:            1      2      3      4      5
Tonal Memory:            1      2      3      4      5
Voice quality:
General comments:

Choir assignment:_____
```

Figure 3.7   Audition Form

Student auditioning for choir. *Photograph by Thom Ewing.*

accompanist) play the exercises as the student sings, be very careful to play the piano at a reasonable dynamic level so the voice can be heard accurately. Have the student stand where the piano keyboard cannot be seen. This will help to alleviate any potential vocal problems caused by the singer's knowing how high or low the pitches are.

To execute the sightsinging portion of the audition, give the singer a copy of the sightsinging exercises, communicate which example you would like to hear, and suggest singing on solfège syllables, numbers, letter names, or a neutral syllable. Then establish the key of the example by playing a cadence and/or arpeggio, give the starting pitch, and provide a maximum of thirty seconds for study. After thirty seconds, reestablish the key, give the starting pitch, and count off a full measure to establish a tempo.

The degree of success achieved on the first example will determine the direction for the remainder of the sightsinging portion of the audition. For instance, if the first example was obviously easy for the student, move directly to a moderate or difficult example. If the student experienced real difficulty with the first easy example, suggest a second easy example. To obtain an accurate picture of students' sightsinging abilities, however, you must ask them to sing examples that get more and more difficult until you determine that they have reached the limits of their current skills. If you have the time, work with the students on something with which they had difficulty. This will not only help the students, but will also give you an idea as to how quickly they can learn.

If students are unable to complete the example successfully the first time, give them an opportunity to try again. Perhaps a student's performance was affected by nervousness, and success will improve as composure is regained and a second chance is given. A slight deduction in the student's total sightsinging score may be taken to reflect this situation.

To carry out the tonal memory portion of the audition, have students stand where the piano keyboard cannot be seen. This will avoid potential vocal problems caused by knowing how high or low the pitches are, and, in addition, students will not be able to see the contour of the pitches as they are played. Tell them you will be playing a series of pitches and they are to sing these pitches back to you, like an echo. Suggest the use of a neutral syllable such as "lah" and encourage careful listening.

Give students an opportunity to try again if they are unsuccessful on their first attempt. Again, the student's performance may have been affected by nerves, and their efforts may improve after composure is regained. A slight deduction in the total tonal memory score may be taken to reflect this situation.

At the conclusion of the audition, be careful to choose carefully your parting words so that false hope will not be created in the student's mind. Comments such as "nice job" or "you did well today" can be misconstrued by a student who is nervous as well as eager to be accepted into a particular group. Simply thank students for their interest in choir, and let them know when and where the results will be posted. In addition, any information regarding the first rehearsal should be given at this point.

The entire audition process should be restricted to no more than ten minutes. This forces the choir director to be as efficient as possible and allows adequate time for everyone who is interested in choir to be heard. Be careful, however, to give each student a fair and similar audition. You want students to feel like they all were given an equal chance to join choir.

Which Choirs Should You Offer?

The number and types of choirs to be offered should be based on the number of students with which you have to work, the number of boys and girls, and the variety of talent and the perceived levels of commitment discovered through the audition process. After a choral program becomes established over a period of years, the configuration of choirs will be fairly easy to predict from year to year and may become stable.

An ideal choral program functions as a system that can begin as early as the elementary level. Through their general music classes and the opportunity to sing in an elementary school choir, students experience the joy of singing as well as learn very basic musical knowledge, skills, and vocal techniques. These experiences, if positive, can lay a good foundation for the more focused and sequential choral training beginning at the middle school/junior high level.

MIDDLE SCHOOL/JUNIOR HIGH SCHOOL. The middle school/junior high school choral program should contain several choirs that are training choirs. The students who sing in such groups will have had little or no vocal training, and are unlikely to be knowledgeable or skilled in sightsinging. Because the performance schedules will be less strenuous for these choirs, the choral director will have the opportunity to teach the basics of good vocal production and sightsinging technique, and to introduce or refine the ability to sing in parts. You may want to make these training choirs available, without a formal audition, to any student who is interested, but it is always a good idea to have everyone sing for you so they can be placed into the correct section of the choir, and also, so you will have some idea of their vocal and musical abilities.

Consider keeping the training choirs as groups of all girls or all boys, especially at the middle school/junior high level. At this age, the boys' voices are likely to have begun changing, and progress can sometimes be slow. In addition, without the presence of girls in the choir, the boys may be less inhibited as they learn to control and use their emerging voices. Remember, puberty will be an issue at this age, and everything possible must be done to encourage young boys to remain in the choral program! To satisfy both boys' and girls' growing interest in the opposite sex and to expand the range of literature that you rehearse and perform, you may want to consider having an after-school rehearsal on a regular basis where the boys' and girls' groups are combined to sing literature written for young mixed voices. Depending on the number of singers in your program, you may want to offer one or two intermediate-ability choirs in addition to the training choirs and the advanced group.

An advanced mixed choir at the middle school/junior high level is certainly desirable and appropriate. You may want to limit membership not only by ability but also by grade level, allowing only those students who are in the oldest grade in the school to audition. The oldest grade will vary by the configuration of grades in your school system, but is likely to be the eighth or ninth grade. An advanced girls' choir may be desirable and necessary at this age to accommodate the larger numbers of girls who may participate in choir (see Figure 3.8).*

HIGH SCHOOL. Even at the high school level, you will need to offer beginning choirs that teach the basics of sightsinging technique and good vocal production because, unfortunately, not all of your high school singers will have participated in a middle school/junior high choral program. These groups will also be a place

---

* The designation by ability level of the choirs listed here is for your information. In actuality, you will want to choose other names for the choirs.

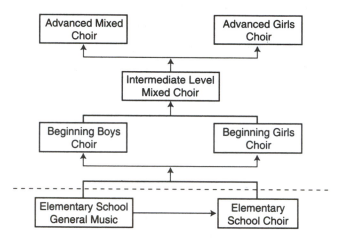

Figure 3.8   Possible choral offerings for the Middle School/Junior High School level

for those students who decide to join choir for the first time during their sophomore, junior, or senior years. You may consider keeping these beginning choirs all girls or all boys, with an occasional opportunity to sing together.

At the next step, you may want to offer a large mixed chorus that consists of singers of intermediate ability. These students have learned the basics of good vocal production and have acquired the basics of sightsinging technique, but, for some reason, they are not yet ready for an advanced choir.

The advanced mixed choir is often smaller than the mixed chorus and consists of a very select group of singers who are musically talented and knowledgeable, and who have shown strong commitment and loyalty to the choral program. For the most part, these singers have earned the right to sing in the advanced group by working their way through the ranks of the training choirs and/or the large mixed choir. The majority of these singers should be relatively independent, both musically and as individuals. From this group, various small ensembles may be formed that rehearse before or after school. Possibilities for smaller groups include a barbershop quartet, a girls' trio, a madrigal choir, or a pop ensemble.

To accommodate the larger number of girls than boys found in most choral programs, girls' choirs at both the intermediate and advanced levels may be necessary and desirable in addition to the

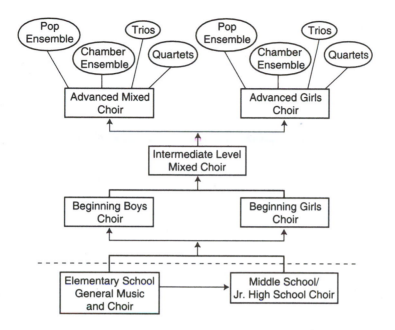

Figure 3.9　Possible offerings for the High School level

corresponding mixed choirs. A place must be found to accommodate all students who want to sing (see Figure 3.9).*

In addition to the traditional choirs discussed previously, a choir that specializes in popular music or jazz is often included in a choral program, especially at the high school level. Students in this type of choir need to be advanced singers as well as good musicians because this type of music can be quite difficult. Because choreography is often a part of the musical production of a pop ensemble, a portion of the audition needs to focus on movement. For more detailed information on pop ensembles, see Chapter 12.

Placement of Voices and Seating Arrangements

A choir director once had a bass section that quite frequently sang under pitch. One day during rehearsal, he changed the seating arrangement of the section and, much to everyone's surprise, the

---

* The designation by ability level of the choirs listed here is for your information. In actuality, you will want to choose other names for the choirs.

basses' pitch problem improved dramatically. This same director had a singer with a lovely soprano voice, but a very distinctive tone quality made it difficult for her voice to blend with the others. After days of frustration, the director finally decided to try various seating arrangements during rehearsal. He found a place for this soprano to sit so that her distinctive voice made a positive contribution to the choir by blending well with the other sopranos.

Placing Individual Voices

If singers are asked, they will frequently say that it is easier and more comfortable for them to sing beside some singers than beside others. This preference has less to do with how good or bad a voice is and more to do with the tone quality of each voice. The placement of individual voices within a choir can often make a tremendous difference in the way the entire choir will sound as well as improving the comfort level of individual singers.

As illustrated above, some voices have a very distinctive tone quality. Others can be classified as "buffer voices"—singers without soloistic qualities, but who are solid musicians with good voices that blend easily. Surrounding distinctive voices with buffer voices will often solve problems with blend.

In addition to improving the sound of the choir, careful placement of voices can improve sightreading abilities and confidence levels. Spreading strong readers throughout the section and pairing each one with a weaker reader will often strengthen the overall reading ability of the entire section. Also, pairing the more confident singers with those who are not quite as confident can cause these singers to feel secure enough to make a more positive musical contribution.

Seating the Sections of the Choir

Experimenting with placement of the various sections of the choir can often produce interesting results. For instance, if tuning is a persistent problem, try placing the soprano section beside the bass section, so the outer voices will be in close proximity as seen in Figures 3.10 and 3.11.

If you have fewer men than women in the choir, or if the men are the weaker sections, try placing tenors and basses in the front and center of the ensemble as seen in Figures 3.12 to 3.14.

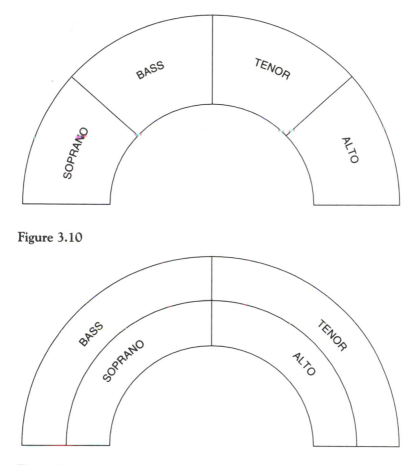

Figure 3.10

Figure 3.11

For advanced choirs, singing in mixed position (quartets, trios, quintets, and so forth) will sometimes improve tuning, and will usually have a positive effect on blend as well. In addition, singing in mixed position presents a challenge that serves to strengthen each singer and, therefore, the entire choir (see Figures 3.15 to 3.18).

For mixed choirs containing boys whose voices haven't changed and whose voice part is either alto or soprano, consider the following arrangement of sections. Place the boys with the unchanged voices on the outside of either the bass section or the tenor section, so that they are standing beside the part they sing but are also standing beside the other boys in the choir. Most boys would find it embarrassing to be placed in the middle of a section of girls (see Figures 3.19 to 3.20).

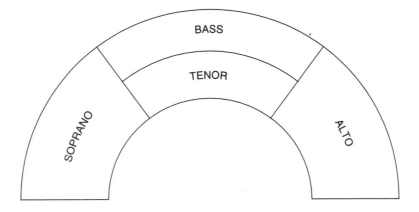

Figure 3.12

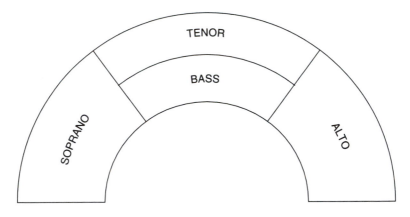

Figure 3.13

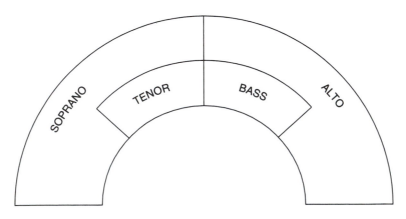

Figure 3.14

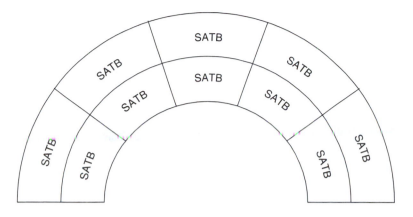

Figure 3.15

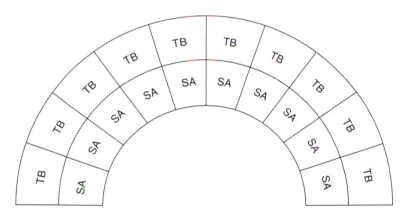

Figure 3.16

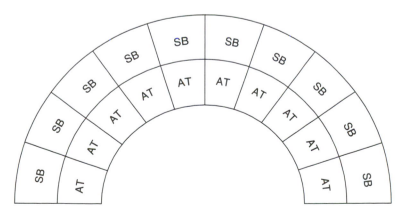

Figure 3.17

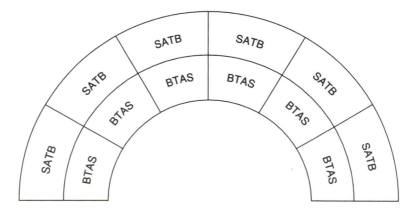

Figure 3.18

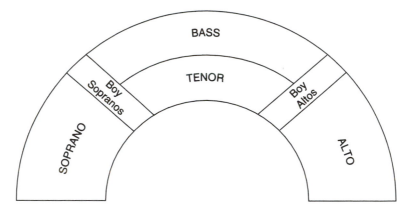

Figure 3.19

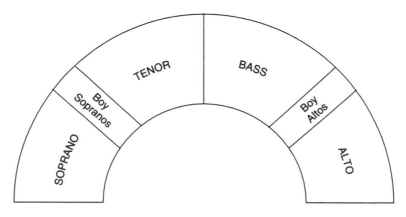

Figure 3.20

For treble choirs, try the arrangements shown in Figures 3.21 to 3.25. Figures 3.21 and 3.22 are widely used in choirs that have a strong and secure Soprano II section. Figures 3.23 and 3.24 may help a weak Soprano II section because they are removed from the alto part and are free to harmonize with the Soprano I section, the most usual harmonization. Figure 3.25, like Figure 3.24, places the outer voice parts (Soprano I and Alto II) beside one another, which may promote better intonation.

For male choirs, try the arrangements shown in Figures 3.26 to 3.29. Like the treble choirs, Figures 3.26 and 3.27 are widely used in choirs with stronger interior parts (Tenor II and Baritone). Figure 3.28 places these interior parts on the outside so they have to deal directly with only one nearby voice part. In addition, this arrangement, like Figure 3.29, places the outer voices next to one another, which may improve intonation.

The preceding list of seating arrangements is certainly not definitive. Every choir is different, and there are many possible variations available for you to consider. The important concept to learn is that changing the seating position of your choir is a possible solution to various musical problems, and each arrangement will create an entirely different sound. Be creative and experiment! The results are often well worth the time and effort required.

Summary

During a ten-minute audition, choral directors can discover information necessary for placing singers in the appropriate choral ensemble. The student's range and tessitura, sightsinging ability, and aural skills development must be checked, and the director can observe the degree of breathing technique, posture, diction, and sensitivity to phrasing that the student has acquired. Pertinent personal information must be obtained as well.

The types of choral ensembles offered should be based on the number of students who audition and their choral experience and abilities. At both the middle school/junior high and senior high levels, beginning choirs are needed so that the basics of vocal technique and musicianship skills can be introduced and stressed. Intermediate-level choirs are usually necessary to accommodate those singers who have

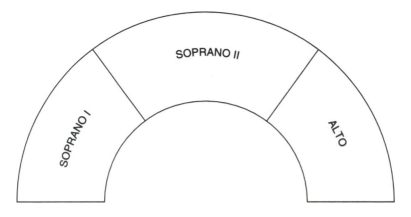

Figure 3.21

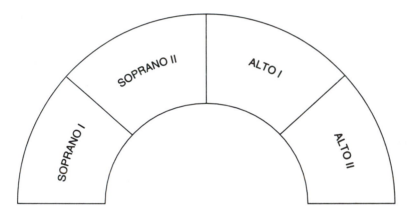

Figure 3.22

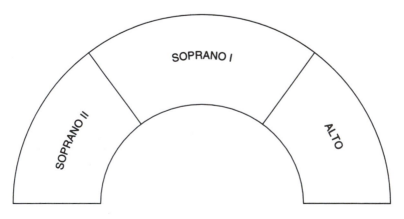

Figure 3.23

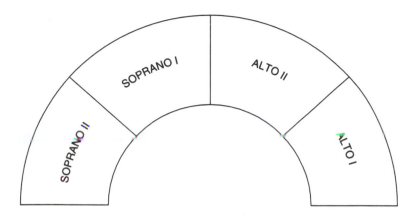

Figure 3.24

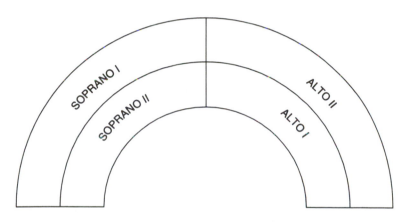

Figure 3.25

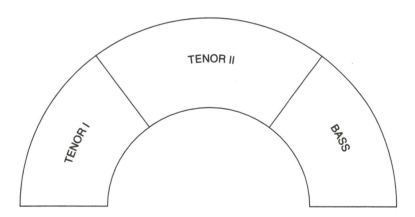

Figure 3.26

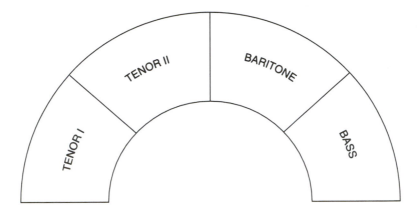

Figure 3.27

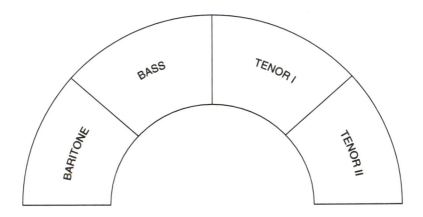

Figure 3.28

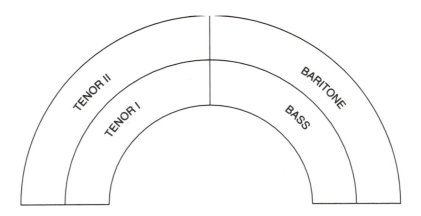

Figure 3.29

acquired the basics, but for some reason, are not ready for the advanced choir. The advanced choir may be small or large, but usually consists of a very select group of singers who are musically talented and knowledgeable. These singers have shown a strong commitment to the choral program and have earned the privilege of membership in the advanced choir. A separate group that sings popular music may be offered as part of the choral program, or a small group taken from within the advanced choir may be used for this purpose. At each ability level, both girls' and mixed choirs may be needed to accommodate the number of girls who participate in a choral program.

Experimenting with seating arrangements for the various sections of the choir can impact the overall sound of your choral ensembles in such areas as balance, blend, and intonation. Careful placement of individual voices within each section can improve the students' comfort level when they are placed beside voices that blend easily with their own voices. Sightsinging abilities and confidence levels may be enhanced as well.

Mini-Projects

1. Using the guidelines proposed in this chapter, compose your own easy, moderate, and difficult sightsinging exercises for use in an audition. Use these exercises in Mini-Project No. 3.

2. Using the guidelines proposed in this chapter, compose your own tonal memory examples to be used in an audition. Use these examples in Mini-Project No. 3.

3. Hold a mock audition. Prepare an information form, audition form, vocalises, sightsinging exercises, tonal memory exercises, and choose a familiar song. Each member of the class will then carry out his or her audition using fellow classmates as prospective choir members. The singers should act as though they are in the age group that you are auditioning (middle school/junior high or senior high). Hold each audition in front of the entire class so that your fellow classmates can observe and offer constructive feedback.

4. Select a group of five to eight singers from your methods class or choir. Choose a familiar song, and use it to determine the best sitting/standing arrangement for that particular group of singers.

As they sing and change positions, pay close attention to the slight variations in their sound. Follow these steps:

a. First, in a random position, have all singers sing the familiar song together.

b. Ask various pairs of singers to sing the song, and try to locate a pair of singers who sound really well together. Just one or two phrases of the song may be enough for you to make a decision. Often, just asking the two singers to exchange positions will make a difference in their sound together.

c. Begin to add singers on either side of the initial pair until all singers are placed in a straight line. Really experiment with various arrangements.

d. When you have placed every singer, have the entire group sing the song together again. Notice the difference in the sound. You may want to make a few minor adjustments at this point. (NOTE: This system of placing voices is similar to a system used by Professor Weston Noble at Luther College, Decorah, Iowa).

Reference

TUNKS, THOMAS, DENNIS BOWERS, and CHARLES EAGLE. (1994). The effect of stimulus tempo on memory for short melodies. *Psychomusicology*, *12*(1), 41–51.

Additional Reading

COMBS, RONALD, and ROBERT BOWKER. (1995). *Learning to sing non-classical music*. Englewood Cliffs, NJ: Prentice-Hall.

MICHELSON, STEVEN K. (1994). *Getting started with high school choir*. Reston, VA: Music Educators National Conference.

THOMAS, JANICE. (1995). Revisiting the madrigal ensemble. *Teaching Music*, *3*(2), 34–35.

4

Development and Evaluation of a Choral Curriculum

Joel enjoyed participating in choir during his freshman year, so he decided to sign up again and count it as his sophomore elective. His guidance counselor, however, is questioning the value of taking choir for more than one year. He feels that learning to sing and participating in performances are worthwhile activities, but after one year, what more is there to be learned? Wouldn't Joel just be doing the same things all over again?

Developing a Choral Curriculum

Choir directors eagerly prepare their students for outstanding performances when the power of music can be felt deeply by singers and audiences alike. This is no small matter, because these peak experiences are always significant, and may be the reason many students continue to participate in choir. In their quest for excellence in performance, however, novice choral directors may resort to a sort of drill-and-practice rehearsal style, often neglecting the very foundation for these peak experiences. Because this approach offers little to develop skills or musical independence, their students must endure this drill-and-practice regime over and over again as they prepare for each concert.

If directors broaden their focus to include a systematic study of music reading, vocal technique, style, history, aural skills, basic theory, and music terminology, students will gradually learn important skills and knowledge necessary to build a firm foundation for musicianship. When the preparation for performance is enhanced by this broader focus of instruction, and when it is placed within a sequential design of beginning-, intermediate-, and advanced-level choral ensembles, the guidance counselor won't need to ask "what more is there to learn? Wouldn't Joel just be doing the same things all over again?" More important, the students will be receiving a substantive, rich, and meaningful music education that will serve them now as well as in the future.

The National Standards for Arts Education

The content and achievement standards published in *National Standards for Arts Education: What Every Young American Should Know and Be Able to Do in the Arts* (1994) are cumulative skills and knowledge expected of students at the completion of grades K–4, 5–8, and 9–12.* Six of the nine content standards relate directly to students in choral ensembles and suggest appropriate activities. These standards are:

> Sing, alone, and with others, a varied repertoire of music. . . .
> Reading and notating music
> Listening to, analyzing, and describing music
> Evaluating music and music performances

* The National Standards for Arts Education were developed jointly by the American Alliance for Theatre & Education, the Music Educators National Conference, the National Art Education Association, and the National Dance Association under the guidance of the National Committee for Standards in the Arts. The United States Department of Education, the National Endowment for the Arts, and the National Endowment for the Humanities provided the grant that allowed these standards to be prepared. They were published in 1994 and are available from the Music Educators National Conference, Reston, VA.

Understanding relationships between music, the other arts, and disciplines outside the arts

Understanding music in relation to history and culture (pp. 59–63)

While this list does not represent a curriculum and does not suggest specific instructional activities to achieve the standards, the list can be used as a guide for both important endeavors. You can see that it is not only important to sing a wide variety of repertoire, but it is also important to read and notate music, listen, analyze, and describe music, develop skills in the evaluation of music performances, and understand music in relationship to itself, the other arts, and other disciplines as well as in relation to history and culture.

Content and Sequence

The curriculum of a choral program includes both the content of the instruction and the sequencing of that instruction (Whitlock, 1991, p. 39). This applies not only to the choir in which the student is currently enrolled, but also to that particular choir in relationship to the *system* of choirs in place within that particular school district. Content introduced at the elementary level will continue to be revisited throughout a student's entire music education, forming a spiral curriculum. Skills and techniques will be extended and refined, and knowledge will expand over the years. Don Collins (1993, p. 391) states rather emphatically that "students can become good musicians only through years of rehearsal and study that are persistent, consistent, organized, structured, and sequential in nature."

For example, Joel's basic musicianship training in performing, creating, and listening to music began in general music classes at the elementary school level. In the fifth grade, he decided to join the elementary school choir, which meets after school, twice a week. This performing ensemble experience built on the skills in singing and general musicianship that he acquired in general music classes. The knowledge and skills that were introduced to him at this young age were expanded and refined as he participated in choir during his middle school years. Exposure to increasingly difficult choral repertoire, as well as continuing development in the areas of vocal technique and musicianship skills, facilitated his musical growth. By the time he got to the high school and enrolled in freshman choir, he had acquired a basic foundation of musical knowledge and vocal skill, which he will continue to develop throughout his high school years.

When the system works, students like Joel emerge, and the level of musicianship can be incredible indeed. Unfortunately, in many situations, students like Joel are an exception to the rule. The system does not function as it should when, for instance, a student moves from one school system to another, the district decides to eliminate general music for grades one through three, the district has weak teachers at one particular grade level, or the student decides to join choir for the first time in his junior year in high school. In situations such as these, students will likely arrive in your classes without the entry-level skills necessary for success. For this reason, beginning, intermediate, and advanced-level choirs should be offered at both the middle school/junior high and high school levels.

Sample Curricula

BEGINNING CHOIR. A choir at the beginning level will have students who, for the most part, have not had any formal choral experience, although they may have sung for fun outside of school, and may have learned very basic vocal technique and sightsinging skills as part of their general music training. Most of their singing experiences have been in unison. The beginning choir, therefore, must continue to teach correct vocal techniques, introductory sightsinging skills, and offer experiences with choral literature which moves from singing in unison to two- and three-part music. (The latter must occur very quickly when the choir contains boys whose voices are changing. Due to the limited range and tessitura at this time in a boy's vocal development, unison music is usually not a good choice. More information about changing voices can be found in Chapter 11).

At the conclusion of the school year, students in a beginning choir should be able to:

1. Demonstrate the use of correct posture while singing.
2. Demonstrate the use of correct breathing technique while singing.

3. Sing with a pleasant and well-produced tone quality.
4. Sing in tune.
5. Sightsing music in major keys with melodic motion that is predominately stepwise but which may contain an occasional triadic leap; with rhythmic patterns comprised of whole, half, quarter, and eighth notes, using meter signatures of 4/4, 3/4, and 2/4.
6. Using correct musical terminology, describe the music that they have performed.
7. Using one or two facts about the composers and the periods of music history from which the pieces come, discuss the music that they have performed.
8. At least twice a year, perform with success a moderate number of pieces.
9. Sing, with success, music written in unison, two parts, and three parts.

INTERMEDIATE-LEVEL CHOIR. At this level, students will refine those skills learned previously as they develop new skills in sightsinging and vocal technique, and they will rehearse and perform more difficult music literature. Music terminology and music history as it relates to their music will be taught.

At the conclusion of the school year, students in an intermediate-level choir should be able to do the following with increasing skill and finesse:

1. Use correct posture and breathing technique while singing.
2. Sing in tune with a pleasant and well-produced tone quality.
3. Using correct music terminology, describe the music that they have performed.
4. Using one or two facts about the composers and the periods of music history from which the pieces come, discuss the music that they have performed.

In addition, students should be able to:

5. Sightsing music in major and minor keys containing triadic leaps as well as leaps of a fourth and sixth, with rhythmic patterns comprised of whole, half, quarter, and eighth notes (and

their corresponding rests) as well as the dotted quarter followed by an eighth note, and sixteenth notes, using meter signatures of 4/4, 3/4, 2/4, and 6/8.
6. At least three times a year, perform with success a moderate number of pieces.
7. Sing, with success, music that is written in four or five parts.
8. Sing, with success, several selections that are written in a language other than English.
9. Perform at one choral festival with adjudication.

ADVANCED CHOIR. Membership in the advanced choir requires singers who are on the road to musical independence. Their independence will be developed further through experience with challenging literature that requires excellent vocal technique and sightsinging skills. While they continue to refine skills learned previously, these advanced students will learn additional music terminology and history, and will develop a real sense of musical style. The performance schedule for this group will be more demanding than that of the beginning- and intermediate-level choirs. Singers may choose to audition for the All-State Choir, and participate in the Solo and Ensemble Festival, both of which require excellent musicianship and solid vocal training.

At the conclusion of the school year, students in an advanced-level choir should be able to do the following with increasing skill and finesse:

1. Use correct posture and breathing technique while singing.
2. Sing in tune with a pleasant and well-produced tone quality.
3. Using correct musical terminology, describe the music that they have performed.
4. Using one or two facts about the composers and the periods of music history from which the pieces come, discuss the music that they have performed.

In addition, students should be able to:

5. Sightsing music in major and minor keys containing both stepwise motion and leaps, with rhythmic patterns comprised

of whole, half, quarter, eighth, and sixteenth notes (and their corresponding rests), as well as the dotted quarter followed by an eighth note, dotted eighth followed by a sixteenth note, and triplets, using meter signatures of 4/4, 3/4, 2/4, 6/8, and asymmetrical meters.

6. Perform concerts during the year for both the school and the community.
7. Perform at one or two choral festivals with adjudication.
8. Perform a wide variety of music, including compositions in Latin, German, Italian, French, and Spanish.
9. Sing in small groups (such as trios, quartets, and octets) to encourage musical independence and sensitivity.
10. Rehearse and perform in a variety of seating arrangements, including mixed position, to encourage musical independence and sensitivity.

(For additional information regarding the sequencing of choral groups, refer to Chapter 3.)

The Time Factor

Teaching sightsinging skills, vocal technique, style, history, aural skills, basic theory, and music terminology involves the use of class time, which can impact the rehearsal and performance of music. If choral directors maintain a reasonable performance schedule, however, time will be available for this broader base of instruction. Music terminology, history, and style can be taught as it relates to the music in rehearsal, and a portion of the sightsinging exercises and aural skills can be designed to address potential trouble spots in the music. In this way, performance remains a primary focus of the choir, and rehearsal time is planned efficiently. In addition, because students are learning knowledge and skills to develop their musicianship, their performances are likely to be enhanced. Perhaps more important, however, their overall music education is more substantive and pervasive. (In Chapter 8, you will study a rehearsal plan that features much more than simply the rehearsal of music.)

Evaluation of Students

Evaluation of students in choral programs is necessary for several reasons. First, most school systems require that a grade be given for each course a student takes in middle school/junior high and senior high school. Second, evaluation provides communication to students and parents alike as to how successful the students' performances are and in what areas they need improvement. Third, evaluation holds the teacher accountable for what takes place in the classroom, and can provide data to guide improvements to the program. Finally, evaluation helps choir to be perceived as an important endeavor.

The choral experience is made up of a variety of important components that must be evaluated. Let's consider these components and see how they can be involved in the composition of an accurate grade for each student.

Attendance

Because singing in a choral ensemble is a group effort, students need to be present at rehearsals and performances. Fortunately, this portion of their grade is fairly straightforward to calculate and record because students are either present or they are absent. Encourage students who know of an upcoming absence to notify you in advance, and make sure you distinguish between excused and unexcused absences. You may want to consider having a more stringent consequence for a student's absence from a performance than for a rehearsal.

Students not only need to be at rehearsals and performances, but they also need to be on time. To encourage students to be on time, a system of dealing with tardies needs to be in place. Perhaps a predetermined number of tardies will equal one absence, or a notice goes home to the parents, or students have some sort of after-school duties to perform. Whatever the system, students should know that they are expected to be on time for rehearsals and performances, and, if they are not, they must deal with the consequences.*

---

* Some school systems do not allow attendance to be included in students' grades; therefore, in situations such as this, a citizenship grade must be given in addition to the grade for academic achievement. Make sure you understand fully the policy of your school system before you assign grades for your singers.

Attitude/Cooperation

No one would dispute the fact that a positive attitude and cooperation are critical aspects of choral membership, but their evaluation causes the choral director to wander into the subjective realm of evaluation. Especially in very large choral programs, where one choir can consist of seventy-five to one hundred students, observing accurately the level of cooperation and attitude of every student would be a difficult, if not impossible, task. And even if it were possible, the resulting evaluation would be the choral director's *opinion* of the student's behavior. If parents were to question this portion of their child's grade, would you be prepared to state specific instances in which cooperation was not evident or when the attitude was not positive?

If attitude and cooperation are to be included in the grade, however, a means of evaluating these components needs to be in place. First, it would be helpful to define a positive attitude and a willingness to cooperate. Paying attention, having all necessary music and a pencil at each rehearsal, coming to rehearsals and performances on time, following directions, not talking during rehearsal, and using good posture while singing would certainly provide evidence of those characteristics. The easiest method of keeping these records may be to give each student the benefit of the doubt and assume (expect) that they will do these things so that a notation in the grade book need only be made when they are negligent in some way. Still, in large choirs, this will be difficult. Hopefully, however, directors of large choral programs will have an assistant who can help.

Singing Accuracy

When students know they will be held accountable for knowing their vocal part for each piece of music in rehearsal, they are likely to be motivated to learn it accurately and more quickly. Because the amount of time involved in testing every student on every piece would be unrealistically high, you may want to consider testing only one piece (your choice at the time of the test), or small portions of several pieces (again, your choice at the time of the test). Modified in this way, the test will not be so lengthy, but students will still need to be prepared on all music.

Photograph by Thom Ewing.

Development of Musical Knowledge and Skills

Singers should not only sing quality music correctly and beautifully, but also should be able to speak intelligently about their music using correct musical terminology. In addition to the performance component, therefore, the choral experience should certainly include the development of musical knowledge and skills. Tests on sightsinging technique, skill at rhythmic and melodic dictation, and knowledge of musical terms and pertinent factual information learned through the study of the music will provide tangible evidence for this portion of the students' grades. John Grashel (1993, p. 46) suggests that, with an increasing emphasis on accountability, tomorrow's school music teachers "will unquestionably be held responsible for the content as well as the technical skill development taught in their performance classes."

Aptitude or Achievement

When the choral director decides to include tests of singing accuracy and musical knowledge and skills in the grading process, a new issue comes into play: whether to grade on aptitude, achievement, or a combination of the two. In choirs where membership is determined by audition, grading will be somewhat less difficult because the singers will usually possess the musical aptitude necessary to achieve a high level of success in all aspects of the choral experience. In unauditioned choirs, however, where singers can display a wide variety of ability levels, grading can become a real challenge.

Simply stated, aptitude refers to a person's natural abilities, talent, and capacity for learning. Achievement, on the other hand, refers to the degree of success achieved and depends in part on how hard a student works toward various goals. Achievement is also dependent on aptitude. Consider the following two students and see how difficult it would be to assign a grade to their work.

Ingrid has a beautiful (yet untrained) alto voice, but has very limited aural skills. Because of this, she has great difficulty on melodic dictation tests, and her grades are consistently low on any tests of singing accuracy because she cannot always hold her part. On the other hand, Ingrid has a very positive attitude and works harder than anyone else in the entire choral department. She meets the choir director before and after school for extra help. Because of her limited aptitude, however, Ingrid's grades usually hover around a C or C-minus. Should some provision be made for her limited abilities because of how hard she works? Should she be penalized on her level of achievement because her musical aptitude is low?

Susanne is the most talented student ever to participate in the choral program. She has a beautiful voice, an ear for foreign languages, and a real talent in the area of aural skills. Yet Susanne rarely puts forth any effort and seems content to achieve whatever she can achieve without doing much work at all. In addition, she is frequently the cause of behavior problems during rehearsal. Even if Susanne, because of her high musical aptitude, can achieve an A in choir, should she receive an A if she is obviously not working up to her potential?

The answers to these questions are not easy, and for the conscientious choral director, decisions on grades will frequently be difficult and sometimes heart-wrenching. In the final analysis, arriving at a grade based on a blend of achievement and aptitude may be the best approach, but the answers will never be easy.

The Right Percentage

After deciding on which components will make up your students' grades, you will need to decide what percentage of the grade each component will take. For example:

Attendance, attitude, and cooperation	40%
Development of musical knowledge and skills	30%
Singing accuracy	30%

After making your decision, give this information to students and perhaps, even to their parents. Informing everyone, before the grading period begins, about how the students' grades will be calculated, allows students to know what is expected of them.

Musicianship Sheets

To help keep track of each student's progress every grading period, consider the use of musicianship sheets similar to the four levels printed in Figures 4.1 through 4.4. You may want to use the sheets to create a contract for a grade with each student (using a designated portion of each sheet for the various grades earned each grading term). This system can serve as a powerful motivator, and may encourage your students to work harder, both inside and outside of class.

Working this closely with individual singers will certainly keep you informed of their progress as well as their difficulties, but this system involves a large amount of time. As your advanced students progress to higher levels, however, they can help you by listening to the students at the first and second levels as they attempt to demonstrate various skills. The blank in front of each activity is for your initials (or those of an advanced student who is serving in your place). When everything has been performed correctly at each particular level, you may want to award the student with a certificate of achievement.

Notice that students must demonstrate a positive attitude and a willingness to work. If they have been successful at all other activities on the sheet but have an uncooperative attitude or cause problems during rehearsal, they cannot achieve that level until this problem is corrected. The musical skills and cognitive information that are tested at each level are things taught and reinforced in class.

First Level Musician

_____ 1. Demonstrate a positive attitude and a willingness to work.

_____ 2. Demonstrate the proper breathing technique for singing.

_____ 3. Demonstrate the proper posture for good singing.

_____ 4. Sing a major scale.

_____ 5. Sing your part correctly from any song currently in rehearsal (Director's choice).

_____ 6. Perform with no errors any two of the eight rhythmic exercises on page 3 of the sightreading booklet (Director's choice).

_____ 7. Perform with no errors the first ten interval patterns on page 1 of the intervals handout.

_____ 8. Sightsing a simple melody.

_____ 9. Define with 100% accuracy the following terms:
Soprano, alto, tenor, bass, sharp, flat, treble clef, bass clef, time signature, measure, interval, double bar line, _a cappella_, accompaniment, unison.

(attach a sheet of terms and definitions)

STUDENT'S NAME:_____

DATE COMPLETED:_____

Congratulations!

Figure 4.1

Second Level Musician

_____1. Attain the First Level Musician Award.

_____2. Demonstrate a positive attitude and a willingness to work.

_____3. Sing your part correctly from any song currently in rehearsal (Director's choice).

_____4. Sing a natural minor scale.

_____5. Perform with no errors any two of the eight rhythmic exercises on page 5 of the sightreading booklet (Director's choice).

_____6. Perform with no errors any interval pattern from Nos. 11–30 on page 2 of the intervals handout (Director's choice).

_____7. Demonstrate the ability to sing at sight a melody using stepwise motion as well as simple skips and rests.

_____8. Define with 100% accuracy the following terms and/or symbols: Crescendo, decrescendo, repeat signs, accent, fermata, first and second ending, 8va, D.S., D.C., ritard, sforzando, coda, staccato, legato.

(attach a sheet of terms and definitions)

STUDENT'S NAME:_____

DATE COMPLETED:_____

Congratulations!

Figure 4.2

Third Level Musician

_____1. Attain First and Second Level Musician Awards.

_____2. Demonstrate a positive attitude and a willingness to work.

_____3. Sing your part correctly from any song currently in rehearsal
(Director's choice).

_____4. Perform with no errors any rhythmic exercise from page 7 of the
sightreading booklet (Director's choice).

_____5. Perform with no errors any interval pattern from Nos. 31–50 on pp.
3–5 of the intervals handout (Director's choice).

_____6. Sightsing a melody using stepwise motion as well as skips and rests.

_____7. Demonstrate ability to sightsing your part within a small group (SATB
or SSA).

_____8. Demonstrate your knowledge and ability to *perform* the following:

> a. *Crescendo* and *decrescendo*
> b. *Staccato* and *legato*
> c. Accent
> d. *Sforzando*
> e. *p, mp, mf, f*

_____9. Take rhythmic dictation with at least 80 percent accuracy.

STUDENT'S NAME:_____

DATE COMPLETED:_____

Congratulations!

Figure 4.3

Super Musician

_____ 1. Attain the First, Second, and Third Level Musician Awards.

_____ 2. Demonstrate a positive attitude and a willingness to work.

_____ 3. Sing your part correctly on any song currently in rehearsal (Director's choice).

_____ 4. Name all notes on bass and treble clefs.

_____ 5. Try out for All-State.

_____ 6. Participate in Solo-Ensemble Festival.

_____ 7. Perform a solo for the class.

_____ 8. Conduct the class on one of the songs currently in rehearsal.

_____ 9. Perform with no errors any interval pattern from Nos. 50–70 on pp. 6–8 of the intervals handout (Director's choice).

_____10. Sightsing a melody.

_____11. Sightsing your part within a group (SATB or SSA).

_____12. Take melodic dictation with at least 80 percent accuracy.

STUDENT'S NAME:_____

DATE COMPLETED:_____

Congratulations!!!

Figure 4.4

Summary

A choral curriculum includes both the content of the instruction and the sequencing of that instruction. Each choral ensemble is a part of a *system* of choirs which begins with elementary school and progresses through high school. Directors at every level must broaden the focus on performance to include a systematic study of music reading skills, vocal technique, style, history, aural skills, basic theory, and music terminology. When the preparation for performance is enhanced in this way, and when everything is placed within a sequential design of beginning-, intermediate-, and advanced-level choral ensembles, students will gradually learn important skills and the knowledge necessary to build a firm foundation for musicianship, and a valid choral curriculum will be in place.

The evaluation of choir members helps choir to be perceived as an important endeavor, and provides communication to students, parents, and administrators as to the student's successes as well as areas that need improvement. Evaluation holds the teacher accountable for what takes place in the classroom, and can provide data to guide improvements to the program. The evaluation process must be systematic and objective, not only to ensure that students' grades are an accurate reflection of their success, but also, that the grades can be justified to parents and administrators. The make-up of a students' grades should be a reflection of what has taken place in the classroom.

Mini-Projects

1. Visit your local school district offices and request copies of their curriculum guides for choral music at the middle school/junior high and high school levels. Discuss the contents with your classmates.

2. Compare and contrast the curriculum guides from your local school district to the National Standards for Arts Education found in the booklet *National Standards for Arts Education: What Every Young American Should Know and Be Able to Do in the Arts* (published by MENC).

3. Ask several choral directors to share with you their method of grading. Compare the various methods, and decide which aspects of each would be effective, appropriate, and fair.

References

COLLINS, DON L. (1993). *Teaching choral music.* Englewood Cliffs, NJ: Prentice-Hall.

GRASHEL, JOHN. (1993). Research in music teacher education. *Music Educators Journal, 80*(1), 45–48.

WHITLOCK, RUTH. (1991). Choral curriculum as it affects performance at the secondary level. *Choral Journal, 32*(3), 39–45.

Additional Reading

DETTWILER, PEGGY DIANE. (1995). Grading the choral ensemble . . . No more excuses! *Choral Journal, 35*(9), 43–45.

RICHMOND, JOHN W. (1990). Selecting choral repertoire as pre-curriculum: Planned serendipity. *Choral Journal, 30*(10), 23–30.

Teaching choral music: A course of study (1991). Reston, VA: Music Educators National Conference.

The school music program: A new vision. (1994). Reston, VA: Music Educators National Conference.

National standards for arts education: What every young American should know and be able to do in the arts. (1994). Reston, VA: Music Educators National Conference.

WILLMAN, FRED. (1992). New solutions to curricular problems. *Music Educators Journal, 79*(3), 33–35.

CHAPTER *5*

Repertoire

Otis had just been hired as the choral director at Shaw High School, and the time had arrived to order music for fall. Even though he was a first-year teacher, he wasn't worried about choosing music because he had kept a list of repertoire that his college choir had sung, eagerly anticipating the day that he could direct this music with his own choirs. Otis found his list, ordered the music, spent many hours in preparation for the first rehearsal, and introduced each piece with enthusiasm to his advanced choir. After just one rehearsal, however, Otis began wondering whether they were wise choices for his high school choir.

Selection of Repertoire

The music to be rehearsed and performed by your choirs comprises the very core of the choral curriculum, and, because the choice of music has the potential to affect all else that transpires during the entire year, decisions must be made with much thought and consideration. In the scenario for this chapter, Otis ordered quality music that he loved and which he carefully prepared for his high school choir, and he presented it with enthusiasm. However, it became apparent very quickly that the pieces were inappropriate choices because he had chosen the music with no consideration whatsoever of such things as the ability level and size of the choir, as well as his singers' ages, ranges, and vocal limitations.

The number and type of concerts (holiday, pop, patriotic, spring) planned for the year can offer guidance for music selection, and lists of choral music by voicing and difficulty level are provided in most states for use in contest participation. Little else, however, is available to guide the choral director's choices. Without guidelines to limit the endless variety and quantity of music available, choosing music can be a tremendous challenge as well as a time-consuming task, and many factors must be considered for this all-important responsibility.

Choose Repertoire from Which Students May Grow Musically

First and foremost, students need to be better singers and more intelligent musicians as a result of working on the repertoire chosen for their music education. Therefore, an important question choral directors need to ask as they select repertoire for their choirs is: "What will the singers *learn* from their experience with this selection of music?" Will students experience Baroque performance practice or jazz stylistic traits? Will they have an opportunity to improve their ear by working on music that features close harmonies, to improve their execution of smooth, flowing legato lines, or to work for better breath support during *pianissimo* singing?

To help your choirs grow as musicians and singers, you will want to choose several selections that will cause them to stretch their abilities. Students will respond to a challenge, but remember, also, that students may be overwhelmed and frustrated by too many challenges. A good balance would include a majority of music right at or very slightly beyond the choir's ability level, one or two selections that are difficult (*for that choir*), and one or two selections that can be perfected with relative ease.

Choose a Variety of Music

Because you may be the sole person in charge of regulating your students' exposure to choral music, you must accept the challenge and responsibility for them to experience the "whole picture." In a single year, it may be impossible to sing all styles of music, but over two, three, or four years in choir, students should have the opportunity to rehearse and perform a balanced repertoire representative of the vast heritage that choral music provides.

This balanced repertoire includes music from the various periods of music history as well as spirituals, vocal jazz, music of other cultures, and good arrangements of popular and folk music. Languages other than English should be explored. A balance should be struck between *a cappella* and accompanied selections, and, whenever possible and appropriate, instrumental accompaniments other than piano should be used. In addition, choir members should experience music suitable for small ensembles as well as for large choral groups.

For example, if the choral program has the resources (both musical and financial), consider combining all choirs at a concert to perform a larger work with members of the school orchestra providing accompaniment. Performing in combination will provide a large-group experience with appropriate repertoire for those singers in smaller choirs, as well as provide an opportunity for all choir members to perform with an orchestra. School choir may be the only chance some students will have to experience such a special occasion. A nonmusical benefit derived from such an opportunity is the building of an *esprit de corps* among the entire choral department. Such a unified spirit often spills over into musical performance, and in this way, becomes a *musical* benefit as well.

Choose Music About Which You Are Excited

A large dose of enthusiasm is often necessary to "sell" choir members on a selection of music. Even with enthusiasm, this task may feel insurmountable at times. Imagine attempting it when you yourself aren't sold on the music! Students will sense the lack of excitement and will respond (or rather, not respond) accordingly. If you aren't excited about the music, the choir will rarely be! This is not to suggest that if the director does not particularly enjoy Baroque music, he or she should avoid all contact with selections from this era. Directors should strive continually to broaden their level of comfort to include a variety of styles, eras, and composers.

Sometimes a choir won't respond positively to a particular selection even when the director is rehearsing it with enthusiasm. If this happens often enough, the novice choral director may become concerned and perhaps put the piece aside. At this point, the *choir* is selecting the repertoire, not the director. Students will learn that if they don't like a particular selection, all they have to do is let you know (often in rather creative ways!) and the music will be dropped. Remember that, while it is important to consider student requests for music (and you certainly don't want to choose music that the students will dislike), the director is the one with the education and experience required to make these very important decisions.

*Ranges and Tessituras of Each Voice Part**

The *range* of a particular voice part may be defined as the compass of its music from the lowest note to the highest note. *Tessitura* may be defined as the area within the range where most of the notes occur for that voice. Therefore, tessitura is concerned with the part of the range most used and not in any extreme notes that define the range of a voice part.

For example, the lowest note in the soprano part of a particular selection is c^1, and the highest note is g^2. Therefore, the range for the soprano is c^1 to g^2, or an octave and a fifth. Closer inspection of the music reveals that the majority of notes that the sopranos have to sing fall between e^1 and e^2. This octave is the tessitura for the soprano part.

Obviously, your choir will sound its best when singing music that falls within the tessitura of the singers, but unfortunately, not all music will always fall neatly into these prescribed parameters. In searching for repertoire, you will find music (or a section of the music) that falls outside the ranges/tessituras appropriate for the various sections of your choir. Should this music be put aside? Perhaps, but ask yourself several questions:

1. What vowel is sung on the extreme note(s)? If the answer is an open vowel (such as "ah"), you may want to consider choosing the selection. If the extreme notes are sung on a closed vowel, problems may occur.

---

*   The pitch notation system used in this book is as follows:

C   c   c¹   c²   c³

2. What is the duration of the extreme notes? Do the sopranos sing a^2 for four measures on a closed vowel sound? Obviously, this situation may present problems for an inexperienced choir.

3. How are the extreme notes approached? If these notes are preceded by a wide and awkward leap, singers may have difficulty executing the notes with the proper vocal technique. If, however, a stepwise motion leads naturally to the extreme notes, the choir may not experience a problem.

4. What is the dynamic level of the notes in question? Extreme dynamics (*pp* or *ff*) coupled with notes outside a comfortable range may cause difficulty.

5. Are the notes in question exposed or are they supported by the other sections of the choir? If the tenor section has a limited range and the music in question features several g^1's in an unaccompanied soloistic passage for the tenors (which also serves as the emotional climax of the piece), you may want to put this piece aside for another year.

Text

In writing choral music, a composer usually selects the text before writing the music. In fact, text alone will often suggest to the composer such factors as the form, character, style, texture, harmonic language, and melodic structure of a musical composition. Because text plays such an important part in the choral art, you must look carefully at the words of a composition as well as the composer's setting of them as you select repertoire. Questions to be asked include:

1. Is the text of such value that it can stand alone as a selection of quality literature in its own right? A quality piece of choral literature will not likely emerge from an inferior text.

2. Did the composer do justice to the text in the musical setting or does the musical setting move contrary to the intent of the text? In other words, does the musical composition feature a careful wedding of text and music?

3. Was the composer sensitive to word stress? Do musical and textual accents fall simultaneously or do they work against one another?

4. If the original language is not used, does the translation retain

the meaning, character, and similar word stress of the original? Unfortunately, when a translation is used, the music will often lose its unique national flavor.

5. Will the choir that has the musical ability to perform the piece also have the emotional maturity to understand the text and deliver it in a convincing manner? Young choirs may have difficulty relating to a text simply because they don't have the real-life experiences from which to draw.

6. Will the text *appeal* to the choir members? This is a critical issue, especially with young choirs. Junior high boys will not be very comfortable with or tolerant of songs about flowers, elves, or birds.

7. Will the text be acceptable according to the guidelines set forth by your school district? For example, Christmas texts may not be allowed, so songs of a more general, holiday nature will need to be substituted. Choral directors must be aware of the policy in their own district, whether or not they agree with it. Failure to comply may cause legal problems—or worse, the loss of your job.

Accompaniment

When choosing music, keep in mind accompanimental forces available for rehearsal and performance. If an accomplished pianist from the community is willing and able to serve as the accompanist, this fortunate situation obviously opens up literature with more difficult piano accompaniments. More likely, however, a student (or several) will serve as an accompanist, so make an accurate appraisal of their abilities and choose music accordingly. The accompanist is a critical part of the choral program—both in rehearsal and performance.

When considering performance of a larger work that calls for instrumental accompaniment, check with the band and/or orchestra director at your school to see if players are available both for rehearsals and performance(s), and if they are able to perform the parts. If the budget allows, fill in crucial or missing parts with players outside the school while filling a majority of the parts with school band or orchestra players.

If a larger work is chosen and the piano reduction of the orchestral parts is to be used as accompaniment, look carefully at the

Student accompanist. *Photograph by Thom Ewing.*

reduction. Does it retain the character of the music? Is it written awkwardly so that the pianist will have great difficulty? Many reductions may prove nearly unplayable, so look at several editions of the music (when available).

Likewise, when considering choral music originally written for organ accompaniment, but a piano will be substituted, look carefully at the accompaniment. Is it adaptable to the piano? Is the organ's wide variety of timbre a necessity? Does a large portion of the piece feature long, sustained sections that could be performed better on the organ? Unless the basic nature of the piece is retained and the accompaniment is easily adaptable to the piano, put the music aside until you have opportunity to perform it with organ accompaniment.

Arrangements and Transcriptions

In choosing choral arrangements or transcriptions for choirs, ask these questions:

1. Does the arrangement remain true to the intent of the original tune? For example, spirituals will often be overarranged,

and some arrangements of popular music can prove frustrating when the music in the students' hands is just different enough from the rendition they have heard on the radio to cause problems.

2. When a piece is transcribed from a choir of one voicing to a choir of another voicing (SATB to SSA, for example), does the transcription change the essential nature of the piece? Does the text still work? Is the harmonic structure still intact when one voice part is deleted?

Size of Choir

The size of the various choirs should be taken into consideration when selecting repertoire. Small ensembles (twelve to twenty-four singers), by their very nature, will exhibit a more transparent sound than ensembles of larger size; therefore, the selection of Verdi's *Requiem* would certainly be inappropriate for your chamber choir, even if the singers had the ability to perform it. The nature of the piece requires larger forces to do it justice. Likewise, the lightness and intimate nature of English madrigals will suffer if performed by a choir of large proportions. Consider the circumstances around which the piece was originally written. This will serve as a guide in selecting appropriate music for the appropriate choir.

Vocal Maturity of Choir

Just as the text must be appropriate for the emotional maturity of the choir, the music must be appropriate for the vocal maturity of the singers. Music should be selected that will allow the students' voices to develop naturally without making potentially harmful demands of them. Extreme dynamics, extreme ranges over a long period of time, and excessive length of a selection are examples of characteristics that should be considered when choosing appropriate music for the vocal maturity of your choir.

Texture

Especially for those choirs just learning to sing in parts, the texture of the music may be an important consideration. In simple polyphonic music, the melodic nature of the imitative vocal lines may be easier to grasp for young, inexperienced singers than the often unmelodic, block harmonies found in more homophonic music.

Potential Audiences

As music is selected, keep in mind the potential audiences who will hear the performances. This is an area often neglected when choosing music and planning concerts. Remember that the listener is a part of the choral experience along with the composer, the director, and the choir. In any given audience on any given occasion, a wide variety of listeners will be present, and each will come to the concert with different expectations. In addition to entertaining them, you will want to educate the audience members and broaden their musical experiences so that they will leave the concert feeling more comfortable with a wider repertoire.

While both serious and light selections have their place in most concerts, the occasion itself can serve as a guide in selecting the type of music that should predominate. A performance for a convention of the American Choral Directors Association suggests quite a different focus than a performance for a local civic club luncheon at Christmas. The former is a formal concert on a stage and would feature music of a more serious nature. The latter is an after-dinner holiday performance where the audience is sipping coffee and finishing their desserts. This audience would probably expect and enjoy a lighter program featuring familiar holiday music.

When to Order Music

The Ideal Timetable

Auditions often occur at most schools in the spring of the year at preregistration. This timetable allows the choir director to have a reasonable idea of the ability levels and sizes of next year's groups in adequate time to make wise repertoire decisions. Enough time is allowed for music to be ordered and received well in advance of the following school year.

If you secure a new position in the spring before you will actually begin teaching, you may even have the luxury of attending auditions for the following year. After hearing each student, you should have enough information to place singers in appropriate groups. In addition, each group's potential strengths and weaknesses may be suggested at this point. This information should guide the choice of repertoire for the year.

For example, if an unusually large number of beginning choral students have auditioned for choir, you may safely assume you will have at least one beginning choir whose sightreading abilities and vocal techniques will probably not be developed. In this case, choose music at an easy to moderate difficulty level and take into account the ranges and tessituras discovered for each student during the audition. The number of selections ordered for this choir will probably be fewer than for more advanced choirs, simply because it will take more time for beginners to learn and perfect each piece.

An adequate number of advanced sopranos, altos, and basses may have auditioned for choir, but the tenor section, while not lacking in quality, is lacking in numbers in comparison to the other sections. In this case, avoid music that calls for the tenor part to divide. Likewise, if the alto section is lacking in substantial voices and depth, choose music that does not feature the alto section in its lower range.

If you are unable to attend auditions in the spring, information about the choirs you will direct must be obtained from other sources. If the former choral director is available, make an appointment with him or her to discuss ability levels and past repertoire. If this is not possible, secure tapes of the choirs' performances during the past several years and listen carefully to determine strengths and weaknesses of each group. Peruse the choral library at the school to get an idea of the type and difficulty level of music that the choirs may have sung in years past. Any information gleaned from these suggestions will help in making wise repertoire choices for your choral groups.

If music has been ordered too late to be in the students' hands on the first day of class, consider beginning the year with several selections of music already in the choral library that haven't been sung in several years. While you should continually challenge yourself and your choirs with new and different music, there is value in revisiting literature that has been performed in years past. Fortunately, the longer the director is at a school, the larger the choral library will become. This wealth will provide quality literature when time (or money) prohibits the ordering of new music.

Where Do You Find Music?

The search for choral literature is an ongoing process that will continue throughout your teaching career. Conscientious choral directors constantly have their eyes and ears open for new and interesting music for their choirs. Just where can you look and listen?

Concerts

The best and easiest way to find new literature is to attend as many choral concerts as possible. Not only listen carefully, but also write notes about the music right on the programs and keep them for future reference. This process allows the luxury of hearing the music performed by a choir. Even a less-than-desirable choral performance can offer a more accurate idea about the music than a run-through at the piano.

Conventions

A music convention often seems like one glorious ongoing concert and can offer a wealth of music from which to choose. The wealth doesn't stop at the concert stage door, however. Make sure you attend interest sessions and workshops on various aspects of the choral art. Often a packet of free music is provided for all those in attendance. In between the concerts and interest sessions, schedule several visits to the exhibits where you can put your name on publishers' mailing lists, peruse the music on display, and often gather free single copies for your files.

Music Publishers

By placing your name on the mailing list of several music publishers, you may periodically receive brochures containing a list and/or excerpts of their new releases. Some publishers will include a demonstration recording, allowing you to hear the music in performance. For a small annual fee, many publishers will send groups of single copies several times during the school year.

Local and Regional Music Retailers

Many local music stores are willing to carry single copies of choral music if they are asked. Larger music stores may offer music reading sessions several times a year. This provides another good opportunity to sing the music rather than having to play it on the piano. In addition, a reading session offers the opportunity to interact with your colleagues about choral literature that works. The fee for the reading session may include a large packet of music to take home and add to your single-copy file.

Colleagues

Make friends with fellow choral directors who may have a teaching assignment similar to yours, and schedule time to share literature with each another. This sharing should include music that has worked successfully with your choirs as well as those pieces that have presented problems. Knowing what hasn't worked with other groups is as valuable as knowing about successful literature.

Radio

If you live in an area that has a classical radio station, listen frequently for choral performances. Stations often publish a radio guide that will list the music (with composers) played on their programs. If no guide is available, call the station, tell them the day and time you heard the music in which you are interested, and ask them for the title, composer, and recording information. The recording may lead you to additional choral literature as well.

Recordings

Build a good personal library of recordings. In addition to building your repertoire list, this practice will continually surround you with performances by different choral groups. Listening such as this may help to shape and refine your concept of choral tone and will often present varying interpretations of music to consider. Occasionally, you may want to play one of your recordings for your choir to illustrate a certain interpretation or tone quality.

Professional Journals

Publishers often advertise in professional journals, announcing "What's New for Fall" or "the latest music from this composer or that composer." Especially helpful is the section in each issue of the *Choral Journal* devoted to music reviews. Choral directors study new releases and write brief comments about selected music to help readers make wise choices for their choirs.

Textbooks

A repertoire list, arranged by voicing and difficulty, appears in the appendix for this book. Other textbooks on various aspects of the choral art often contain lists of literature as well. Refer to texts such as:

LAMB, GORDON. (1988). *Choral techniques*, 3rd ed. Dubuque, IA: Wm. C. Brown.

DECKER, HAROLD A., and COLLEEN J. KIRK. (1988). *Choral conducting: Focus on communication.* Englewood Cliffs, NJ: Prentice Hall.

DECKER, HAROLD A., and JULIUS HERFORD, editors. (1988). *Choral conducting symposium*, 2nd ed. Englewood Cliffs, NJ: Prentice Hall.

COLLINS, DON. (1993). *Teaching choral music.* Englewood Cliffs, NJ: Prentice-Hall.

Anthologies

Several anthologies are available that feature collections of music for choirs of various voicing and ability. These include:

Something to Sing About (Levels 1, 2, and 3). Each book contains music for mixed, treble, and male choirs; published by G. Schirmer, 1982.

Something New to Sing About (Levels 1, 2, and 3). This collection has separate books for mixed, treble, and male choirs by difficulty level with student text; published by Glencoe Publishing, 1989.

Something New to Sing About (for Young Voices). Two volumes (SAB/SATB/SACB and 2-part/SSA/Male Ensemble) with student text; published by Glencoe Publishing, 1987.

Five Centuries of Choral Music. Volumes I and II. This collection features music for mixed choir only; published by G. Schirmer, 1963 (Vol. 1), and 1988 (Vol. 2).

Essential Elements for Choir. (Grades 7–12). This series contains over 200 time-tested choral works in four levels for mixed, treble, and tenor-bass ensembles (student text and teacher edition). Also available are a student text and teacher edition in four levels designed to teach vocal technique, theory, and sightreading skills. Objectives are based on the National Standards for Arts Education. Published by Hal Leonard, 1995, 1996.

Contest and Festival Lists

Most states print lists of choral music for use in their annual choral festivals or contests. These lists are extremely helpful because the music is listed by voicing and difficulty level. Often, publishing information is included as well.

Choral Music in Print

Choral Music in Print is found in most college and university libraries as well as in some music retail stores, and is an exhaustive listing of available choral music. It is divided into sacred and secular volumes, and indexed by title and by composer. Updated frequently, these volumes provide such helpful information as editor or arranger, language, voicings, and publisher.

Creating Music Files

Single Copy File

As you collect single copies of choral music, file them in an organized manner. This will save you many hours of leafing through stacks of music to find the piece you need.

The most basic method of organization is by voicing. Putting the music in file boxes or folders will help preserve the life of the music as well as allow for even further organization. Possibilities include arrangement by difficulty levels, by historical periods, music for the changing voice, music for chamber ensembles, holiday music, sacred and secular music, and so forth. After a substantial amount of music has been collected, consider organizing by composer.

Choral Music Card File

Instead of, or in addition to your single copy file, you may want to keep a card file on music that your choirs have performed as well as music that you have discovered and may perform in the future. You will need to organize it at least by voicing and may want to arrange it further according to the suggestions under "Single Copy File." The cards in this file will contain helpful information including publishing information, ranges/tessituras, specific difficulties, dates performed, accompaniment, language, and source of text. You may want to put this information on a computer database rather than on cards to be stored in a box. Regardless of your choice, the card printed in Figure 5.1 will serve as a guide for the information needed for each musical selection.

Summary

Because you may be the sole person responsible for the music your students study and perform each year, you must take this responsibility seriously and spend the time required to choose carefully and wisely. These musical selections and the learning that takes place as a result of your students' contact with them forms the basis of their education in choral music. A variety of quality music must be cho-

(Front of Card)

Composer/Arr./Ed._____
Title_____
Voicing_____Solo(s)?_____Language_____
Publisher_____Edition No._____
Source of text_____Sacred_____Secular_____
Accompaniment_____
Number of copies on hand_____

Range and tessitura:

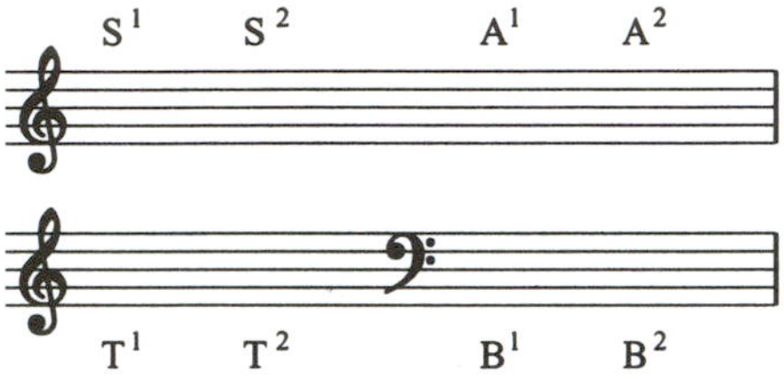

(Back of Card)

Dates performed: _____   _____   _____   _____

Specific difficulties
found:_____
_____
_____

Difficulty level   1   2   3   4   5

Period or style of composition:
      Medieval _____   Renaissance_____   Baroque_____
      Classical_____   Romantic_____   20th C._____
      Folk_____   Popular_____   Jazz_____

Large ensemble_____   Small ensemble_____

General comments _____
_____
_____

Figure 5.1   Choral Repertoire Card

sen from which students can become better singers and more intelligent musicians. In addition, your selections must be appropriate
for the size of the choir, as well as for the singers' vocal abilities and
maturity level. Other aspects to be considered include the ranges
and tessituras of each voice part, the text, the accompaniment, the
texture, and the potential audiences for which the group will perform. Consider the difficulty level of each piece and choose music
that will challenge your singers but not overwhelm them. Always
remember that *nothing*—not enthusiasm, hard work, or good inten-
tions—can overcome the wrong choice of literature, so choose
carefully and wisely.

The search of quality literature for your choirs should be a process
that continues throughout your teaching career. Places to locate
music include concerts, conventions, music publishers, local and
regional music retailers, colleagues, classical radio stations, recordings, professional journals, textbooks, anthologies, contest and festival lists, and *Choral Music in Print*. Begin and maintain a single
copy file of music and organize it well. Keeping a choral music card
file on a computer database will place pertinent information on
each piece virtually at your fingertips.

Mini-Projects

1.   Using questions asked on the choral repertoire card printed
in this chapter, study five pieces of music with which you are not
familiar. Use this information as you complete Mini-Project No. 2.

2.   Refer to a current issue of the *Choral Journal* and read several reviews of new music. Then select two or three pieces from the
music you studied in Mini-Project No. 1. Using the journal reviews
as a guide, write a review of each piece as though you were writing
for the *Choral Journal*. Include in your review: ranges and tessituras;
vocal demands; difficulty level; text; appropriate age group; etc.
This project will help you go through the same process as you would
when you choose music that will be appropriate for your choirs.

3.   Using any music available to you (such as music from your
school's choral library, any single copies you may have collected,
and any anthologies), choose three to four selections that would be

appropriate literature for the following choir. Give specific reasons
for your choices.

> The Park Manor High School Concert Choir consists of forty
> singers who are either juniors or seniors. Their ability level is
> moderate, and their accompanist is quite good. The sopranos are
> strong in number (thirteen) and ability; the altos are not as strong
> in ability and smaller in number (nine); the tenors are the weak-
> est section, both in ability and number (five); and the basses do
> good work and consist of thirteen singers.

4.   Select two pieces that would be appropriate literature for a
mixed chamber choir of twenty-four voices, and two pieces that
would be appropriate for a mixed choir of seventy-five singers.

5.   Locate *Choral Music in Print* in your college or university
library. Familiarize yourself with its organization by looking up several musical selections.

Additional Reading

BRUNNER, DAVID L. (1992). Choral repertoire: A director's check-
list. *Music Educators Journal, 79*(1), 29–32.

DUPERE, GEORGE H. (1991). Sacred choral repertoire for mixed
voices: A recommended listing. *Choral Journal, 32*(3), 25–37.

KEAN, RONALD M. (1993). Multicultural and ethnically inspired
choral music: An annotated list. *Choral Journal, 33*(10), 45–54.

MAYHALL, BRUCE. (1994). The quest for high-quality repertoire.
Choral Journal, 35(2), 9–15.

Religious music in the schools. (1987). Reston, VA: Music Educators
National Conference.

RICHMOND, JOHN W. (1990). Selecting choral repertoire as pre-
curriculum: Planned serendipity. *Choral Journal, 30*(10), 23–30.

WHITLOCK, RUTH. (1991). Choral curriculum as it affects performance at the secondary level. *Choral Journal, 32*(3), 39–45.

CHAPTER 6

Programming Music

Mr. Chen, a local high school choral director, is puzzled. He has attended three concerts this week by three very outstanding choirs. All three groups sang interesting music that was carefully prepared, and the singers performed with finesse and enthusiasm. Why then, Mr. Chen muses, did only one of these three concerts prove to be a truly musically satisfying evening?

Taking a closer look at the programs for the three performances helped to explain his feelings. He discovered that all the music performed by Choir No. 1 featured slow tempi and a homophonic texture. In addition, several successive selections were written in the same key. No wonder he began to nod off after the first few pieces!

Mr. Chen had left the concert for Choir No. 2 feeling restless and unsettled. On closer inspection, he found no real continuity in the program order for this concert. The first portion of the program was in the following order: a pop arrangement of a familiar tune followed by a Renaissance motet, a rollicking spiritual, a very quiet, contemporary piece, and finally, a selection from the Bach Magnificat in E-flat. Listening to this program was similar to riding on a roller coaster!

The answer to Mr. Chen's question was obvious when he looked at the program for Choir No. 3. The director had given careful consideration to the placement of every selection on the concert program. Variety was certainly present, but the contrasting selections were placed in a musical sequence that made sense from beginning to end. Rather

*than jumping from one point to another, the audience felt like they had
"traveled" with the singers between the various points of interest in the
concert.*

*Now he understood. What created the difference in these three
concerts wasn't the quality of music performed, the choir's abilities and
preparation, or the enthusiasm with which each choir performed. The
difference was in the programming—the order of music for each concert—that made the concert for Choir No. 3 an outstanding performance and a musically satisfying evening.*

Obviously, this scenario portrays two rather drastic examples of
poor programming, but the story was written to illustrate an issue
that you will experience, either as the choral director of your own
programs or as a member of an audience. Programming does make
a difference! Unfortunately, the job is one that is often performed in
a haphazard manner.

In Chapter 4, the responsibility for choosing appropriate music
was discussed. Countless hours will be spent in the selection process
by reading music at conventions, talking to colleagues to find out
what has been successful with their choirs, and playing through
stacks of music at the piano. Ranges, tessituras, texts, and difficulty
levels will be checked to assure that the music selected will be well-
suited to your choirs. Deciding the order of the music that will be
performed is an extremely important step in the process. Spending
adequate time to create a meaningful program may affect the quality of the performance and will help ensure the audience's enjoyment of your concerts. Listed below are several suggestions that
may facilitate the task.

General Programming Tips

Consider Programming When Selecting Music

The time to sketch out the order for concerts is during the music
selection/ordering process itself. When planning in this manner, you

won't find yourself needing "one more piece" to complete the program two weeks before the concert. Because concerts will have been planned in detail well in advance, smarter choices can be made. This is an important issue, especially when choral budgets may not be large enough to accommodate any unwise purchases.

Choose a Variety of Music

Choosing a variety of music is certainly a worthy goal for any concert program and can help sustain audience interest if programmed properly. Variety can be achieved through selecting music from different periods of music history that illustrate various styles and textures as well as the inclusion of folk music from America and other cultures, and good arrangements of popular music. Creating a balance between *a cappella* and accompanied music, and between sacred and secular compositions will also provide interest. In addition, a program that includes both serious music as well as music in a lighter vein can create variety.

Vary Keys and Tempi

Singing several selections in the same key will soon prove boring to the audience and can affect the pitch and enthusiasm of the choir. Likewise, too many successive pieces in a similar tempo may have the same effect. Interestingly enough, the impact on the concert is so subtle that the audience may not know why they are bored or restless, and the singers (and you) may be puzzled as to why things aren't going well musically. Careful attention to key and tempo may help to avoid these problems.

Vary the Difficulty Level

Careful programming helps singers maintain a more consistent level of performance throughout the concert. After several pieces with demanding tessituras and dynamics, for example, insert a composition that gives the choir an opportunity to recuperate. In addition, if several selections require intense listening, the audience will appreciate the insertion of a composition that is less difficult to follow.

Choose Several Transitional Pieces

The term "transitional piece" is not a reflection on the quality of the music, but rather refers to a composition chosen to serve an important function—that of helping the concert move from one point to another. Therefore, a selection that serves as a transitional piece in one concert will not necessarily serve the same function for another concert.

Suppose a set of sacred, *a cappella* pieces are programmed at the beginning, while the remainder of the concert consists of a variety of folk-song arrangements. To bridge the gap between the two contrasting sets of music, one or two compositions will be necessary to serve as a transition to the lighter focus. In a long concert featuring only one or two performing ensembles, a well-placed intermission and/or the use of Roman numerals in the printed program to designate a new set of musical selections can serve the same function as a transitional piece.

Choose Carefully the First Selection

The first selection on any program is critical, for it serves not only to capture the audience's attention, but also provides an opportunity for the singers to gain confidence as they adjust to the acoustics of the performance area, to the lights, and to standing in front of an audience. For these reasons, the first selection is not the place to program the most difficult or demanding music. The first selection should be a piece with which the choir feels extremely secure, and one in which the difficulty level, dynamics, and ranges/tessituras are moderate. Relatively short compositions that feature a moderately fast tempo are often good choices for the opening selection.

Carefully Place Any Unusual Compositions

Concerts will often contain one or two selections that are outstanding in some way. For example, suppose a twentieth-century composition has been selected, containing atonal harmony, choral speech, and a variety of vocal sounds. The compositions with which you surround this unusual piece can make a real difference in the flow of the program.

Move from Sacred to Secular, and Serious to Light

Moving from sacred music to secular music is a good, general rule. However, when the secular music selected is of a serious nature, you will have more freedom to mix sacred and secular within the program. Moving from serious to light is always a good idea. Singing a medley of Broadway tunes right before a Renaissance motet obviously doesn't make good sense.

Plan with Care When Each Choir Performs

When more than one choir will be performing on the same concert, attention must be given to the order in which each group performs. Issues to be considered include the ability levels of the choirs involved as well as the logistics of the entire concert program.

Programming the beginning-level choirs first and moving to the more advanced groups is usually a good idea. This way, each group will be shown to its best advantage, and no group will feel embarrassed by sensing that their choir is not as good as the one that sang before them.

Logistics of the concert include such things as processionals and recessionals, instrumental accompaniments needing advance set-up time, changing the arrangement of the risers, and selections sung by a combination of choirs. A good rule to follow is: arrange the choirs in an order such that a minimum of time is required to move from one group to the next.

Include an Intermission

If the entire program will last over an hour, plan to include an intermission. In addition to providing a rest for both the audience and singers, this time can be used to solve a large number of logistical problems. For example, if a show choir or vocal jazz ensemble will perform on the concert, a good place to program this group is after intermission, because of the advance set-up time often necessary to change the configuration of the risers (or to remove them altogether), to set up an instrumental ensemble or microphones, or to allow singers to change performance outfits.

Photograph by Thom Ewing.

Several Programming Ideas

Arrange the Music in Chronological Order

When representative music from various periods of music history has been chosen, arranging the program in chronological order can offer the audience and singers alike a vivid illustration of the differences among periods.

Plan the Concert Like Planning a Dinner

If a larger work is planned, a sensible program order places the highlight of the concert toward the middle of the concert. Begin the concert with music that serves as an appetizer and salad, and then present the main course. The audience will have been led to this point in the program and the singers will be well adjusted and warmed up by this time. After the main course, move gradually to a lighter focus by presenting the audience with music that will serve as dessert and coffee. An after-dinner mint might even be offered (an encore, or a very brief, catchy selection that the singers enjoy).

Plan a Concert around a Theme

A patriotic concert, a variety of music set to texts by Shakespeare, music with a common textual theme (love songs or songs of nature, for example), a holiday concert, and a program featuring music by one composer or one period of music history are all examples of concerts planned around a theme. If text is the common theme, be careful to choose selections on their musical merit as well as for textual appropriateness. In concerts of music by one composer or from one period of music history, program unity will automatically be in place because of the similarity of composing style. Make sure the issue of variety is addressed as well.

Sample Programs

The following mini-concert programs and accompanying comments illustrate several of the suggestions discussed in this chapter.

ADVANCED HIGH SCHOOL OR COLLEGE CHOIR

Venite, exultemus Domino	Jan P. Sweelinck
In the Midst of Life	Henry Purcell
Notre Père	Maurice Duruflé
My spirit sang all day	Gerald Finzi
Haste on, my joys!	Gerald Finzi
Embraceable You	George Gershwin, arr. Steve Zegree
Over the Rainbow	Harold Arlen, arr. Kirby Shaw

Explanation of Program Order

1. *Venite, exultemus Domino*, Jan P. Sweelinck, ed. Colton (SSATB, Concordia No. 98-1938).

This selection is moderately fast and in a joyful mood to capture the audience's attention. In addition, the ranges and difficulty level are moderate to allow the singers to warm-up and to adjust to the performance setting. The key is C major.

2. *In the Midst of Life*, Henry Purcell, ed. Boepple (SATB, Mercury Music Corp., 352-00034).

This piece will serve as a good contrast to the first selection on the program. Written in C minor, the tempo is slow, and the music creates a high level of tension through the use of chromaticism with several cross-relations. The English text contrasts with the Latin of the first piece, and a continuo accompaniment offers further variety. This selection is difficult for the singers as well as for the listeners.

3. *Notre Père*, Maurice Duruflé (SATB, Durand S.A., 362-03307).

After the intensity and chromaticism of the Purcell, this piece will serve as a respite for singers and audience alike. This selection, written in F major, features very moderate ranges, a moderately slow tempo, and warm, lush harmonies. In addition, the homophonic texture and the French language offer variety. Because of its placement within the program, this selection may be the highlight of the evening as well as serving as the transition between the sacred and secular portions of the concert.

4. and 5. *My spirit sang all day*, Gerald Finzi (SATB, Boosey and Hawkes) and *Haste on, my joys!*, Finzi (SATB, Boosey and Hawkes).

These two secular selections are from a cycle of six songs with text by Robert Bridges. Highly lyrical and featuring unusual harmonies and fast tempi in the key of G major, these pieces will help propel this concert toward its final portion. After the Duruflé, the choir will be ready for the technical and range demands as well as the energy required for delivering the text and mood of these delightful pieces. These secular selections also serve as a transition from the preceding sacred pieces to the two vocal jazz numbers that follow.

6. and 7. *Embraceable You*, George Gershwin, arr. Steve Zegree (SATB, Warner Bros., 43509052) and *Over the Rainbow*, Harold Arlen, arr. Kirby Shaw (SATB with Sop. solo, EMI Feist Catalog, Inc.).

While an upbeat, flashy ending is a good way to end a concert, a nice warm and quiet closing can often be just as effective. These two vocal jazz pieces will serve such a purpose here. They are both *a cappella*, moderately slow, and feature the keys of E-flat (Zegree) and C modulating to D-flat (Shaw).

SUMMARY OF CONCERT PROGRAM. Featuring music from three historical periods, this particular concert works well when placed in chronological order, moving from sacred to secular as well as from serious to light. Attention was given to choosing different keys, tempi, languages, and moods, and transitional pieces were employed to ensure a smooth flow from beginning to end.

The audience at this mini-concert will feel as though they have "traveled" with the choir from one musical point to the next without any real abrupt changes in destination. The singers in this concert will have had ample opportunity to warm up and adjust with the first selection, and will have experienced opportunities within the concert to recuperate due to the placement and variety of difficulty, ranges, and technical demands of the music.

MIDDLE SCHOOL/JUNIOR HIGH TREBLE CHOIR

Sound the Trumpet	Henry Purcell
Kikkehihi	Johann H. Schein
Schön Blümelein	Robert Schumann
The Cuckoo	arr. Gregg Smith
Margaret has a milking pail	Gerald Finzi
Bandicoot (from *A Menagerie of Songs*)	Carolyn Jennings

Explanation of Program Order

1. *Sound the Trumpet*, Henry Purcell, ed. James Erb (SA, Lawson-Gould, No. 787).

This festive setting is a vivacious duet from the Birthday Ode, *Come Ye Sons of Art*, and will serve to capture the audience's attention as well as allow opportunity for the singers to adjust to the performance environment. This selection features moderate ranges, a moderate tempo, and keyboard accompaniment. The key is D major.

2. *Kikkehihi*, Johann Hermann Schein, ed. William D. Hall (SSA, Boosey & Hawkes, No. 6103).

This Renaissance madrigal will appeal to young singers and audiences alike with its imitation of a hen's and rooster's morning cries.

Written in three parts and performed *a cappella*, the music will present a challenge to the singers. The texture is polyphonic, and in the B section, the tessitura for soprano I is rather demanding. Aspects of the music that will provide contrast with the first selection include the tempo (marked "spirited"), key (A-flat major), language (German), and length of the composition (very brief).

3. *Schön Blümelein*, Robert Schumann, ed. William D. Hall (SA, National Music Publishers, WHC 61).

This duet is written in strophic form with a codetta, so the repetitious vocal lines coupled with moderate ranges/tessituras will offer the singers a rest following the challenging second selection. The German language, however, will present a challenge to the singers. Contrast is found in the style of composition, the two-part homophonic texture, key (C major), and moderate tempo.

4. *The Cuckoo*, arr. Gregg Smith (SA, G. Schirmer, No. 11695).

This American folksong arrangement features a creative piano accompaniment, long flowing vocal lines, soprano solo, and a moderate tempo. This selection will serve as a transition to a lighter focus for the remainder of the concert. The key is F-sharp minor, and the melody has a mournful quality.

5. *Margaret has a milking pail*, Gerald Finzi (SS, Oxford University Press).

This delightful song for two equal voices and piano accompaniment is very brief, taking approximately 20 to 30 seconds to perform. The tempo is quick and the key is F minor. Interesting and worthwhile in its own right, this selection will also set the stage for the final number on the program.

6. "Bandicoot" from *A Menagerie of Songs*, Carolyn Jennings (unison, G. Schirmer).

"Bandicoot" (an animal from Australia) is the first of seven imaginative musical settings of poetry by Maryann Hoberman. The choir will need to invest a great deal of energy to deliver the text at a very fast tempo, but the piece is fun to sing. With three opportunities within the piece for the singers to whistle a portion of the melody, this selection will end the concert with a happy feeling for choir and audience alike.

SUMMARY OF CONCERT PROGRAM. This program for a middle school/junior high school treble choir illustrates that a non-chronological order can create a satisfying concert. The program begins with a selection from the Baroque period, moves back to the Renaissance period, and then skips to the Romantic era for the third selection. The remainder of the music is from the twentieth century.

All music for this concert is secular. Featuring an upbeat, flashy composition to complete the program, the selections move from serious to light. Attention was given to choosing different keys as well as different tempi, and the difficulty levels were varied to help the choir maintain a consistent level of performance throughout the concert.

HIGH SCHOOL CHORAL CONCERT

I.
Male Choir

As Beautiful as She	Eugene Butler
The Water Is Wide	arr. Luigi Zaninelli
Amo, Amas, I Love a Lass	arr. Marshall Bartholomew

II.
Advanced Girls Ensemble

Lift Thine Eyes (*Elijah*)	Felix Mendelssohn
Nigra Sum	Pablo Casals
Three Selections from *Winter Cantata*	Vincent Persichetti
(flute and marimba accompaniment)	
God's Bottles (from *Americana*)	Randall Thompson

III.
Chamber Choir

Fair Phyllis I saw	John Farmer
Phyllis, farewell	Thomas Bateson
Ce moys de May	Clément Jannequin

*** INTERMISSION ***

IV.
Concert Choir

Cantate Domino	Hans Leo Hassler
In memoria aeterna	Antonio Vivaldi
In These Delightful Pleasant Groves	Henry Purcell

Alles hat seine Zeit	Franz Joseph Haydn
The Evening Primrose	Benjamin Britten
Ching-A-Ring Chaw	Aaron Copland/Irving Fine

SUMMARY OF CONCERT PROGRAM. The four choirs presented in this concert are listed in order by ability level. The Male Choir is the least advanced, so they sing first. After the first three groups perform, it will be time for a brief intermission. During this break, the marimba and music stands used on the Persichetti selections will be removed from the stage. The risers will not have to be changed because the number of sections needed for the largest choir were set up before the concert began.

The most advanced choir will sing after intermission, and will present the longest portion of the program. Because several of the members of the Chamber Choir are also in the Concert Choir, the intermission will provide adequate time for them to change outfits and reassemble with the advanced choir before the program continues.

In addition to details regarding when each choir will perform, attention was also given to each group's presentation with regard to good programming techniques discussed previously. For example, the first selection for each choir features moderate demands, keys and tempi are varied, and the music moves from serious to light.

COLLEGE CHOIR WITH GUEST CHOIR

I.
Guest Choir

Adoramus te	Giovanni Palestrina
Ave verum corpus	Wolfgang A. Mozart
Festival Te Deum	Benjamin Britten
Alleluia	Randall Thompson

II.
Host Choir

Regina Coeli	Giovanni Palestrina
Deposuit potentes	Giovanni Pergolesi
Psaume 146	Salamone Rossi
In memoria aeterna	Antonio Vivaldi
Sancta maria, mater Dei	Wolfgang A. Mozart
Selected Chamber Music	Wolfgang A. Mozart

Ecco quel fiero istante
Se lontan, ben mio, tu sei

Luci care, luci belle
Grazie agl'inganni tuoi
(accompanied by two clarinets and a bassoon)
III.
Combined Choirs

Regina Coeli, K. 276   Wolfgang A. Mozart

EXPLANATION OF CONCERT PROGRAM. This program features music by two choral groups in a "Mostly Mozart" concert commemorating the 200th anniversary of his death. Each choir will sing a separate program and then combine at the end to perform the *Regina Coeli*.

The guest choir performs first on the program and will sing selections from three periods of music history arranged in chronological order. The "main course" of their performance (*Festival Te Deum*) falls third on the program so the choir will be adequately warmed up. Attention was given to selecting music in different keys, and further variety was achieved through accompanied and *a cappella* selections.

The host choir's program also features music from three periods of music history arranged in chronological order. Attention was given to varying tempi and keys. During the chamber music portion of the concert, each of the four selections will be performed by small groups of singers with the accompaniment of two clarinets and a bassoon. This provides a timbre difference as well as a difference in the size of performing ensemble.

Logistically speaking, the host choir remains on stage following their separate performance, and the guest choir simply joins them. During this time, the director of the host choir will speak briefly to the audience and guest choir regarding how well they performed and how nice it was to have them as a part of the concert program. By the time these brief remarks are completed, the choirs will be in place, and they will proceed immediately to the final Mozart selection.

Summary

If planned carefully, the order of the music to be performed can have a positive impact on the quality of your choral concerts. Creating a meaningful program at the time you are selecting and ordering the music can save you from making any unwise or unnecessary choices or needing to order an additional piece at the last minute.

The interest of both singers and audiences alike can be sustained by choosing a variety of music as well as by varying keys, tempi, and difficulty levels. Selecting several transitional pieces can help the concert flow smoothly from one point to another. When presenting a concert consisting of more than one choir, plan carefully the order in which each ensemble will perform. Consider each group's ability level and logistical needs to make this decision. A well-placed intermission can help make musical transitions as well as provide time for changes of costume or stage set-up.

The first selection in any concert is an important one, for it is during this time that the choir makes an adjustment to the performance area. Any unusual compositions should be placed carefully within the program. Moving from sacred to secular music as well as going from serious compositions to music written in a lighter vein is always a good idea. Placing the concert in chronological order or planning a concert around a theme can provide interest. When performing a larger work in addition to smaller pieces, you may want to plan the program like you would a dinner, placing the "main course" toward the middle of the concert.

Mini-Projects

1. Attend several choral concerts with a fellow classmate and be attentive to the program order for each concert. Discuss with your friend what, if any, changes you would make in the order of the music or the order of the choirs (if the concert featured several groups.)

2. Choose five to seven selections of music, and, using the suggestions discussed in this chapter, place them in an appealing order for a mini-concert.

3. Choose five to seven selections for a program to be planned around a theme. Using the suggestions discussed in this chapter, place the selections in an appealing order for a concert.

4. You have invited the Mixed Choir from a nearby middle school to perform on your spring concert. Consisting of thirty-six singers, this advanced group will sing music requiring only one piano for accompaniment. The three high school choirs that you direct will also perform on the concert:

   a. Chamber Singers (advanced group, twenty-one singers). All the music for this group is sung *a cappella*.

   b. Treble Choir (beginning group, forty-three singers). This group is singing a group of pieces that requires a flutist and a clarinetist.

   c. Concert Choir (intermediate group, sixty-eight singers). This choir needs two pianos for one of their selections.

Plan the order in which these four choirs will perform on the concert. Your decision should be based not only on the age and ability levels of each choir, but also on the logistical demands required by each group. These demands include (but are not limited to) the number of riser sections and any accompanying instruments they may need. Your plan should include exactly when these items will be moved on and off the stage. If necessary, you may have a ten-minute intermission. Be very specific.

Additional Reading

BRUNNER, DAVID L. (1994). Choral program design: Structure and symmetry. *Music Educators Journal*, 80(6), pp. 46–49.

CHAPTER **7**

Musical Analysis and Score Preparation

Mrs. Gomez is reflecting back on her third period's rehearsal, trying to decide what had gone wrong. The Girls Ensemble had been extremely frustrated while rehearsing the new piece she had selected for them to perform at the graduation ceremony in two weeks. In fact, things had gone so badly she wonders whether the choir's cool reception of the piece can be overcome.

Mrs. Gomez had not had time to study the music before the rehearsal, but she wasn't particularly worried. She figured she could just learn the piece along with the girls. As she thought back over the rehearsal, however, she was surprised to realize that her lack of preparation had made a difference! Because she couldn't provide the guidance necessary to lead the choir through its first experience with the new music, Mrs. Gomez was frustrated with herself. And because of this lack of leadership from their director, the choir was unsuccessful musically and equally frustrated. The rehearsal had almost been a total waste of time.

Unfortunately, situations such as this one happen more frequently than they should. Because of an unrealistic schedule or an unforeseen event or emergency situation, choral directors may have to go into a rehearsal without adequately studying the music. Of course, emergencies do happen, but these circumstances should be the exception and not the rule. Careful preparation of the music to be rehearsed will yield benefits ranging from rehearsal discipline all the way to the final performance of the music.

Aural and Visual Study of the Music

The first thing most directors want to know when they find a new piece for their choir to perform is how the music sounds. Listening repeatedly to recordings of various performances of the music is always helpful in formulating a concept of the work as a whole. So you will have a variety of interpretations to consider as you formulate your own interpretation, listen to several different performing groups if available. If no recordings are available, playing the piece on the piano will give you a good idea how the music sounds. Remember, however, that the music will have a slightly different sound when a choir sings it than when you play it.

After establishing a holistic concept of the piece, more detailed study at the piano or by singing each individual line yourself will help you become familiar with each part and its relation to the other parts and to the accompaniment, if any. First, take the time required to play or sing each individual part from beginning to end to locate any difficult intervals or rhythmic patterns singers will encounter. After studying, listening to, and singing each individual line, play various combinations of parts together to discover how the different voices relate to one another, any difficult intervals between parts, if the voice parts cross each other at any point, and potential rhythmic difficulties created by all parts singing together. Finally, play the accompaniment to discover its relationship to the vocal parts. Is it independent or supportive?

Listening to recordings, playing the piece on the piano, and singing each individual line will help to create an *aural map* of the music to be rehearsed and performed. An aural map is a model in the director's mind and ear of the way the music should sound when performed correctly. This sound is so securely in place that the director can evaluate the choir's success without the aid of the

Conductors studying the music prior to rehearsal. *Photograph by Thom Ewing.*

piano. As the singers rehearse the piece, their efforts will be measured against the director's expectations. Obviously, if the aural map is not in place by the first rehearsal, the director will not know whether the choir's efforts are correct, and consequently, will have little idea as to how to help the singers improve. This was part of Mrs. Gomez's problem in this chapter's scenario.

In addition to the aural study, you must make a detailed visual study of the score prior to the first rehearsal. Aspects of the music to notice include tempo, text, dynamics, important entrances, repeated motives, potential rhythmic, harmonic, and melodic difficulties, diction problems, and so forth.

The questions and their answers shown in Figure 7.1 will serve as a guide to show just how thorough a choral director's study of the music should be. This study needs to happen before the first rehearsal. The questions on the form may be used for any piece of music, but what will be a significant question for one musical selection may not be significant for another.

Because this study is intended for the director's preparation for rehearsal, answers to the questions should have a direct impact on how you will approach the piece with the choir as well as what teaching strategies you might use. Through your study, you may dis-

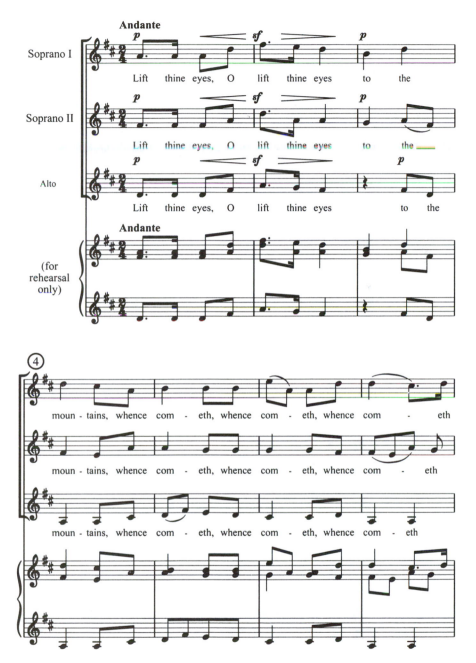

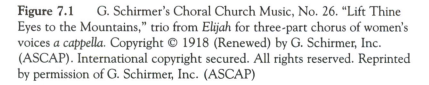

Figure 7.1   G. Schirmer's Choral Church Music, No. 26. "Lift Thine Eyes to the Mountains," trio from *Elijah* for three-part chorus of women's voices *a cappella*. Copyright © 1918 (Renewed) by G. Schirmer, Inc. (ASCAP). International copyright secured. All rights reserved. Reprinted by permission of G. Schirmer, Inc. (ASCAP)

Figure 7.1   Continued

Figure 7.1 Continued

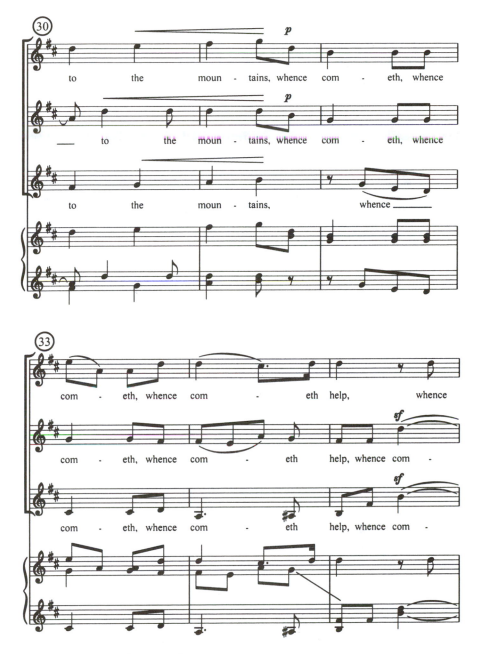

Figure 7.1   Continued

Figure 7.1   Continued

cover potential difficulties within the music that can be solved easily by creating warm-up or sightsinging exercises to deal with the problem. Locating these potential trouble spots in the music and contemplating possible solutions to the problems before rehearsal will save valuable rehearsal time.

Title: "Lift Thine Eyes"
Composer: Felix Mendelssohn
Publisher: G. Schirmer (Hal Leonard) HL 50292660

TEXT

1. **What (who) is the source of the text?** Psalm 121:1–3.

2. **What meaning and/or mood does the text convey?** The text is an inspirational and uplifting one that suggests God will offer help throughout our lives.

3. **Is there any word painting? If so, where?** Yes. The melodic line ascends on the text "Lift thine eyes"; high ranges for the words "Lord" (measure 13) and "mountains" (measure 31); the melodic and harmonic movement is minimal on the words "Thy keeper will never slumber" (measures 21–24), suggesting the steadfast and faithful nature of God's promise to be with us throughout our lives.

4. **Are there any potential diction problems? If so, where?** Yes. The words "lift Thine" (pronouncing the "ft" followed by "Th"); singing through the "l" of "help"; a deep enough "ah" in the diphthong of "mountains"; and the final vowels in "mountains," "cometh," and "heaven."

5. **Does the text present potential problems with word stress? If so, what words and where?** Yes. Singers will have a tendency to stress the final syllables of "cometh," "mountains," and "moved," and will possibly want to do the same type of thing on the second note for the word "earth" (measure 16).

FORM

1. **What is the overall form of the composition?** The form of the piece is ABA', with the B section containing three smaller sections within it (*a* from measures 8–16, *b* from measures 17–20, and *c* from measures 21–27).

2. **During which section does the climax of the entire piece occur (if there is a climax)?** The climax occurs on the words "never slumber" in the B section, right before the return of A, measures 25–27.

MELODY

1. **Does (do) the melody(ies) consist predominately of short or long phrases?** The phrases are predominately long ones.

2. **Is the melody predominately conjunct or disjunct?** The melodic movement in Section A is predominately disjunct, while the melodic movement in Section B is more conjunct.

3. **Is there a short melodic motive on which much or all of the piece is based? If so, what is it?** No.

4. **Are there any problem intervals (within one part or between parts)? If so, what and where?** Generally, no. In measure 31, Soprano I may have difficulty controlling the descent from g^2 down to d^2 with the change in dynamics required, and all parts will have to listen and tune carefully during the harmonic changes within the subsections of the B section.

HARMONY

1. **In what key is the music written? Does it modulate? If so, to what key(s) and where does it happen?** The A section is in the key of D; the B section is written in A major and E minor, and concludes with a dominant seventh chord in the key of D major to set up the return of the A' section.

2. **Is the harmonic rhythm predominately fast, medium, or slow?** The harmonic rhythm is medium during the A section, and medium fast in the B section.

3. **Describe the harmonic language.** The harmony in the A sections is diatonic. Related to the brief modulations, the harmony is more chromatic in the B section.

4. **Are there any significant points of dissonance?** No.
5. **Are there places where the chord movements may be difficult or awkward for the choir? If so, where?** No.

RHYTHM

1. **Is there one rhythmic motive on which much or all of the rhythmic
   structure is based? If so, what is it?** No.
2. **What is the tempo? Does this make any rhythmic execution difficult?
   If so, what and where?** The tempo is marked "andante" and will not
   make any rhythmic execution difficult.
3. **Are there any meter changes? If yes, what note value will remain constant?** The meter remains in 2/4 throughout.

TEXTURE

1. **Is the texture generally thick or thin or does it change? If it changes,
   where does it change?** The texture is generally thick, with all three parts
   singing together most of the time.
2. **Is the composition predominantly monophonic, polyphonic, homophonic, or a mixture? Describe.** The A sections are homophonic, while
   the B section is more imitative.
3. **Characterize the accompaniment and its relationship to the choral
   parts.** The piece is unaccompanied.

DYNAMICS

1. **What is the overall dynamic scheme of the piece?** The dynamic
   scheme for Section A: *p sfz p*; Section B: *p* $<$ $>$ *p; p* $<$; *sub. pp*
    $<$ *f* $>$; Section A': *p sfz p sfz p*.
2. **Are there any places where dynamics are "written into the music"
   (through the addition of voices or use of range, etc.) If so, where?** Yes.
   The use of range helps to create the *sforzando* in measures 2, 29, and
   35–36. "Thy keeper" begins *pianissimo* and the voice parts adding on to
   the Soprano I help to create a *crescendo*. Range helps to create the climax
   in measure 25.

RELATIONSHIP OF PARTS

1. **Are there places in the music where one section of the choir is more
   important than the others? If so, where?** Due to the homophonic texture in the A and A' sections, the melody (Soprano I) is very important.
   In the B section, all entrances are important. In measure 30, the syncopation in the Soprano II part will need to be brought out.

2. **Are there any groupings of choir sections into duets, trios, or other textures? If so, where?** In measures 21–24, the Soprano II and Alto move together as they answer the Soprano I's preceding statements.

3. **Are there rhythmic or melodic similarities between parts that could be taught at the same time? If so, where?** Yes. "Thy help cometh" (measures 9–11) and "Thy keeper will never slumber" (measures 21–24) are similar.

HISTORICAL BACKGROUND

1. **During what period of music history was the piece written?** The piece was written in the early Romantic period.

2. **What characteristics of the period are found in the music you are studying?** Characteristics include an emotional setting achieved chiefly through the use of extreme dynamics, sudden changes in dynamics, and soaring melodies.

3. **What performance practices would be applicable to the study and performance of this piece?** "Lift Thine Eyes," a trio from the oratorio, *Elijah*, was written for three solo voices. To be faithful to Mendelssohn's original intent, the piece should be performed by three soloists. Frequently, however, this trio is included in choral anthologies and on music contest lists, and is often sung by choirs of girls or women. A full-bodied sound would certainly be appropriate since, during the Romantic period, women rather than boys would have sung this piece.

4. **What circumstances (personal, musical, and/or historical) surrounded the composer at the time this piece was written?** Mendelssohn (1809–1847) was a German composer whose music was influenced more by Bach, Handel, and Mozart than by his Romantic contemporaries. *Elijah* was composed in response to an invitation from the city of Birmingham, England, to be performed at its annual music festival where Mendelssohn had previously conducted his oratorio, *St. Paul.* Written between 1844 and 1846, *Elijah* was performed just fifteen days after its completion. (Mendelssohn died in 1847 at the age of thirty-eight).

The original language is German, and the text of *Elijah* is based on I Kings 17–19. Authorities claim that the English translation, which is most often heard, is far more popular than the German original. "Lift Thine Eyes" falls right before the equally popular and well-known chorus "He, Watching Over Israel," which is also written in the key of D major.

CONDUCTING CONSIDERATIONS

1. **Check the meter and tempo of the composition. What conducting pattern will you use?** Since the tempo is marked *andante* and the meter is 2/4, the piece should be conducted in a 2 pattern.

2. **Check the text and tempo of the composition. What style(s) of conducting (legato, marcato, etc.) will be appropriate? Will this style**

change? If yes, where? In the A sections, the pattern should be legato. In the B section, the pattern should be slightly less legato.

3. **Locate important entrances and cutoffs. Mark them in the score** (see Figure 7.2).

4. **Locate any rhythmic values that will need to be shortened to allow for breathing. Mark them in the score** (see Figure 7.2).

Marking the Score

An important part of your music study is marking the score. So that you can remind yourself of important occurrences by taking a quick glance at the music, use a colored pencil (preferably the erasable kind), and choose carefully what you mark so the score will not look cluttered.

Where each voice part will breathe throughout the piece is an important aspect to consider and mark in the music. Often, a note value will need to be shortened by an eighth note or a quarter note to allow for a breath or lift. A breath signifies a cessation of sound as well as allowing enough time for the singers to take a breath, while a lift also signifies a cessation of sound but is often so quick that no breath can be taken. Being this specific will lead to a cleaner performance. Require choir members to have pencils at every rehearsal so that they can mark breaths and lifts in their scores as well. Alleviating frustration and boredom and saving valuable rehearsal time, this method usually allows problems to be fixed once rather than having to repeat the same thing every time you sing the piece (see Figure 7.2).

For an example of shortening note values for releases and breaths, look at measures 8 and 16. In measure 8, Soprano II must take a breath before coming in on "Thy help"; to hear clearly the Soprano II entrance on beat two, all voice parts will release at the same time. Notice that the quarter note on the word "help" has been made into an eighth note followed by an eighth rest to allow for all parts to release together. A similar situation occurs in measure 16 because of the Alto part. They need to breathe before coming in on "He" in measure 17. To make their entrance clearly heard, all voice parts will release together in measure 16 with the second quarter note of "earth" shortened to an eighth note followed by an eighth rest.

The changes in measures 8 and 16 involve a personal decision on the part of the director, and could be done another way. In measure 8, the Soprano I and Alto parts could release as written on beat 2, and

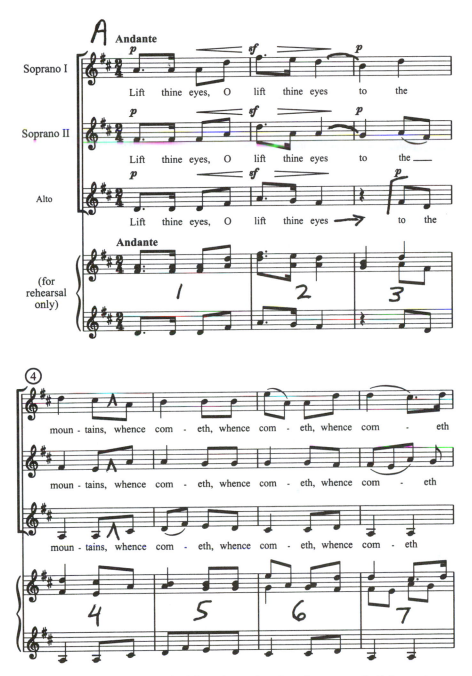

Figure 7.2 Music marked for rehearsal and performance. G. Schirmer's Choral Church Music, No. 26. "Lift Thine Eyes to the Mountains," trio from *Elija* for three-part chorus of women's voice *a capella*. Copyright © 1918 (Renewed) by G. Schirmer, Inc. (ASCAP). International copyright secured. All rights reserved. Reprinted permission of G. Schirmer, Inc. (ASCAP).

Figure 7.2   Continued

Figure 7.2 Continued

Figure 7.2   Continued

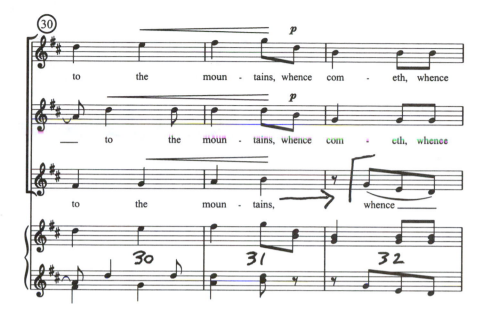

Figure 7.2 Continued

Figure 7.2 Continued

in measure 16, the Sopranos I and II could carry their release across the bar. This way, the new entrances may be blurred somewhat, but it is certainly an option. The point is that you, the director, must go through the music and make decisions such as these before the first rehearsal, so that you can inform your singers what they are to do.

Another important part of score study and preparation is the identification of places where the choir will want or need to breathe and shouldn't, for various reasons. Such a place exists between measures 2 and 3. Using the symbol that resembles a slur will help remind you to remind your singers, through your conducting gesture, that they are not to breathe here. Having them mark the same thing in their music will help as well.

Important entrances can be marked by placing a bracket wherever they occur. This way, when you glance down quickly at the score, these events will be highlighted and can be seen clearly. Look at measures 8–10 and note the markings for each part; the same thing occurs in measure 17, and in measures 20–25. Notice how the brackets call attention to the entrances and make them easier to see.

Circling dynamic changes and tempo changes is often a good idea, and writing in the letter scheme for the form of the piece can serve as a helpful reminder as well as facilitate rehearsal procedure. Rather than identifying the place to start by giving the page, score, measure, and beat, you can simply say "Begin at the B section."

Connecting Your Study with Rehearsal Activities

The preceding study of Mendelssohn's "Lift Thine Eyes" is not simply an isolated intellectual exercise, but rather a preparation that can and should have a direct impact on what happens in rehearsal. What you discover during a study of this depth will provide a guide for teaching the music to the choir.

For example, the mood of the piece was described as inspirational and uplifting. This character should be reflected both in the director's conducting gesture and facial expressions. A discussion of the text and its mood will facilitate the singers' understanding of the words they are singing and may encourage an inspired expression on their faces as they sing. This expression may have a positive effect on the entire musical performance.

The formal structure of the piece (ABA') may suggest to the director that the final A' section be learned immediately after the beginning A section to highlight similarities and differences. The medium-fast harmonic rhythm discovered in the B section may suggest that the director rehearse slowly, out of rhythm, each chord so that the choir can hear clearly the harmonic changes. In measure 30, the syncopation in the Soprano II part will need to be brought out. In rehearsal, the director may want to rehearse the Soprano I and Alto alone before adding the Soprano II. This way, the beat is solidly in place in the outer voices before adding the syncopation. In addition, the choir, and especially the Soprano II part, has the opportunity to hear just how interesting and important those two syncopated notes really are.

Summary

Nothing can substitute for the careful preparation of music prior to the first rehearsal. Studying the music both aurally and visually can yield valuable information that impacts the entire rehearsal process including your level of confidence, the efficient use of time, and your choice of teaching strategies.

Singing each individual voice part, playing the piece on the piano, and listening to various recordings will help create an aural map of the music against which your singers' efforts in rehearsal will be measured. A visual study of the score will further your understanding of such aspects as tempo, text, diction, important entrances, form, dynamics, and the relationship of parts. A study of this magnitude will also reveal potential difficulties within the music so that you can mark them in your score and plan several remedies prior to rehearsal.

Mini-Projects

1. Select two compositions with which you are not familiar but which are likely to be recorded. Listen carefully and repeatedly to at least two different recordings of your selections. Decide which performances you prefer and why.

2. Take the music selected in No. 1 to the piano and play through each part individually and then in various combinations. Mark in pencil any potential trouble spots that you discover.

3. Analyze both selections using the questions on the form used for "Lift Thine Eyes."

4. After listening to and analyzing the two pieces, use a red pencil to mark the music for rehearsal.

Additional Reading

COOK, NICHOLAS. (1987). *A guide to musical analysis*. New York: G. Braziller.

DUNSBY, JONATHAN. (1988). *Music analysis in theory and practice*. New Haven: Yale University Press.

LaRUE, JAN. (1992). *Guidelines for style analysis* (2nd ed.). Detroit Monographs in Musicology, No. 12.

WHITE, JOHN DAVID. (1994). *Comprehensive musical analysis*. Metuchen, N.J.: Scarecrow Press.

CHAPTER 8

The Rehearsal

The rehearsal was going badly, and Mr. Friedman was getting more and more frustrated. The choir's attention span had long since expired, and he was at a loss as to what to do next, but the class period wasn't over for twenty more minutes and he couldn't just leave the students idle. What could he do to recapture their attention?

I. Planning the Rehearsal

The mental discipline required of directors to plan the details and sequence of events for the day can allow them the freedom to run a more efficient and effective rehearsal. At first glance, this statement may seem like a contradiction in terms when *discipline* is mentioned as allowing *freedom*! On closer scrutiny, however, you may see that studying the music and planning the events for rehearsal can give you freedom of focus; that is, your attention can remain almost entirely where it should be: on the singers and their efforts, rather than on yourself and what will happen next. Mr. Friedman would have certainly benefitted from a carefully-constructed rehearsal plan. In fact, his rehearsal may not have deteriorated into the shape it was in if he had given some thought to the day's activities.

Because of the element of the unknown that is present in every rehearsal, however, a rehearsal plan should be exactly that: a *plan* that remains flexible and that may be modified slightly according to what happens in rehearsal. Novice conductors often feel that, because they planned it, they must carry out every detail regardless of what happens during rehearsal. Don't be afraid of modifying your plans as singers achieve objectives faster or slower than predicted.

For example, the choir may not have as much trouble with a section of the music as you had anticipated. Because of their success, you can move quickly on to the next step without having to isolate individual parts as you had planned. The opposite may be true as well. The choir may have extreme difficulty with a portion of the piece that you believed would give no problem at all, and you will either need to spend more time than you had anticipated in this section or abandon this portion of the rehearsal until you can study the music further. The singers may come to choir right from a pep rally one day, and, instead of spending approximately eight minutes on warm-ups, you will need to spend additional time to focus their attention and calm them down. Having a plan in place in all three situations will prevent activities from veering too far from the tasks at hand, yet will provide the flexibility to adapt activities as needed.

Where to Begin

A careful study of the music is the first step in planning any rehearsal for choirs of all ages and maturity levels. Not only will studying the score prepare you to conduct the music, but it will also suggest how to rehearse the music with the choir. For example, if your study revealed that a canonic section begins one of the compositions, your rehearsal plan will probably include teaching the melodic line to all sections in unison before an attempt at the canon is made. Or, if you observed that the form of another composition is ABA', the A' section can be rehearsed directly after the A section so that their differences and similarities can be discovered and experienced. If the music to be rehearsed features singing in close and sometimes dissonant harmony, planning a warm-up exercise to work on this technique would be helpful. Each time you revisit the music for study and preparation, further insights will be made, which, in turn, will have an effect on any subsequent rehearsal plans. (A more detailed discussion of music analysis and score study is found in Chapter 7.)

Warm-up Exercises

When students come into the choir room for rehearsal, they bring with them all that has happened to them up to that point in the day. Some may have had an argument with their parents, or their boyfriend or girlfriend, some may have gotten into trouble in their last class, and some may be ecstatic about a high grade on a geometry test. Somehow, the choir director needs to focus the energy and attention of all these singers on the activities of the rehearsal! This is not an easy task, but it can be done through carefully planned warm-ups designed to benefit the choir not only vocally, but also mentally and physically.

1. *Physical preparation*. A good way to begin rehearsal is to have choir members massage the shoulders of their neighbors. During massages, allow students to visit quietly with their fellow singers. This brief time can not only loosen tight muscles, but can also help the members make friends with other people in the choir, bringing the group closer together. This closeness can have a positive effect on everything from rehearsal discipline to actual music-making. After the massages, have the choir do a few stretching exercises, neck and shoulder rolls, and finish with good singing posture. At this point, the body should be better prepared for rehearsal.

2. *Mental preparation*. Directors often employ the same vocal exercises each day, and singers learn to perform them without any involvement whatsoever. This practice may result in a choir that is vocally prepared for rehearsal, but whose minds have not been focused. The easiest way to focus the minds of your singers, therefore, is to vary the exercises you do at each rehearsal. When students need to listen carefully and think about the new or varied exercises, they are likely to be more involved in the activity and their minds will be challenged and focused.

3. *Vocal preparation*. To warm up the voice, you will want to begin with an exercise of a somewhat limited range. For example, humming on a descending five-note scale or singing "yah-hah-hah" on the scale degrees of 1–3–5–3–1 would be good ways to start the vocal/mental warm-up. To extend the range both up and down, repeat the exercises ascending and/or descending by half steps, and then proceed to exercises of a wider range that require more flexi-

Physical preparation for singing. *Photograph by Thom Ewing.*

bility. Include at least one exercise that deals with a problem to be encountered in the music to be rehearsed that day.

If you are working on a piece that features many chromatic passages, for example, design an exercise to help singers tune carefully when moving by half steps. This is not only an efficient use of time, but also shows students a connection between the warm-up portion and the remainder of the rehearsal. So often a director will warm up the choir, and then say "Okay, now let's get started," when in reality, the rehearsal began when the students first walked into the choir room (more about warm-up exercises in chapter 10).

The warm-ups (physical, mental, and vocal) should take from eight to ten minutes, depending on how many exercises you choose, the choir members' ages and attention spans, and at what time during the day the choir meets. Obviously, a choir that meets at 8:30 in the morning will likely need to vocalize longer than a choir scheduled at 2:00 in the afternoon.

Sightsinging

Sightsinging skills, like vocal techniques, are as much a part of the training of singers as are the rehearsing of pieces to be performed at a concert, and a choir must be given opportunities on a regular basis and in a systematic fashion to gain knowledge and skill in this area. To teach a choir to sightsing is definitely the longer, slower route to take, but one that will provide singers with a degree of independence and skill. If this job is left undone, you and your singers will be reduced to learning pieces by rote, with limited understanding of the music to be performed. Sadly, singers in this situation will be forever dependent on a teacher to teach them their part, perhaps limiting their successful participation in music performance long after they have left your classroom. To say that this is a disservice to your students is a huge understatement.

When you are introducing a new piece to a choir that has at least moderate sightsinging skill, their first reading of the music can serve as the sightsinging portion of the rehearsal on that particular day. Creating sightsinging exercises based on a potentially troublesome melodic or rhythmic figure found in a piece to be rehearsed is yet another way to help students understand the vital connection between learning to sightsing and the rehearsal/performance of music. Again, this is an efficient use of rehearsal time. By using these practices, students are not only learning to sightsing, they are also solving problems found in their music, and they may see more clearly that sightsinging skills have a direct connection to the rest of the rehearsal.

The warm-up exercises, by their very nature, need to be at the beginning of the rehearsal, but the sightsinging portion is more flexible and can be moved to various positions within the period. For example, if the choir will be rehearsing a piece that features syncopation, and you have created a sightsinging exercise to facilitate their success in this area, it would make good sense to place the sightsinging exercise right before rehearsing the piece. Wherever the sightsinging portion of the rehearsal is placed, however, it should last approximately five to ten minutes (more about sightsinging in Chapter 10).

The First Piece

The first piece to be rehearsed can often set the tone of the entire rehearsal, so choose it carefully. A piece with a moderate to moderately fast tempo can help propel the rehearsal forward. Choosing a work with moderate ranges to allow the choir time to warm up further is always a good idea. And directors will often work on the "bigger picture" (style, memorization, endurance) during the first piece rather than work on tedious details, because not only is the choir still warming up vocally, they are still working on mental focus as well. The first piece may be a good time to review an aspect of a selection that was mastered by the choir in the preceding rehearsal. Five to ten minutes spent on the first piece is usually a good plan.

Middle of the Rehearsal

Because singers' voices and minds are warmed up and still fresh at this point, the pieces requiring the most tedious work should be placed second and third during rehearsal. For example, a highly dissonant piece would work well here if notes and rhythms are still a problem, and where a lot of starting and stopping with much repetition may be necessary. This is also the place where singers will be likely to sustain energy and attention for longer periods of time (ten to twenty minutes for each piece), so a selection requiring lengthy rehearsal would work well in the second or third spot.

Necessary at this point is a reminder about the importance of being sensitive to your singers' fatigue and frustration levels. If, after ten minutes, you notice the choir has reached its limit, you will need to leave the selection and return to it tomorrow, even if the amount of work you had planned to do on this piece required more time. Twenty minutes on one piece may really stretch singers of junior high/middle school age (and occasionally, some high school students), so use your knowledge of the choir when planning the rehearsal to accommodate successfully their attention span, and then heed their unmistakable signals during rehearsal and modify accordingly.

Ending the Rehearsal

After tedious and lengthy work during the middle of the rehearsal, it will be a good idea to begin tapering off the demands, both vocally and mentally, as you and your singers move toward the conclusion of your time together. The length of time spent on pieces toward the end of a rehearsal should be shortened as well (five to ten minutes each). The end of a rehearsal is a good time to look at the big picture again, such as working on a more animated delivery of the text, or attempting in its entirety a selection that has been rehearsed only in its various sections. Try to plan something that will not only provide closure for the day's work, but will also create anticipation and excitement about the next rehearsal.

Sample Rehearsal Plan

Figure 8.1 is presented as a guide to planning your own rehearsals. Notice the amount of detail included at each step, from an estimation of time required for each piece or activity to exactly which voice parts will rehearse together. Outline form is a clear and concise way to write out plans for the day, but other methods may be just as effective. The important thing to learn is, no matter what the format, planning a rehearsal in detail will make the time more productive and pleasant for everyone concerned.

The music to be rehearsed includes *Revecy venir du printans* by Claude Le Jeune (CPP/Belwin, Inc., DMC 1203), *Fire, fire, my heart* by Thomas Morley (G. Schirmer, No. 2266), *Chanson on "Dessus le marché d'Arras"* by Adrian Willaert (Associated Music Publishers, NYPM Series, No. 31), and *Sing we and chant it* by Thomas Morley (E. C. Schirmer No. 1183). The choir for which the rehearsal is planned is a high school chamber choir, and the rehearsal is one hour and twenty-two minutes long (block scheduling).

This rehearsal addresses six of the nine content standards presented by the National Standards for Arts Education. These six standards will be cited briefly in the explanation of the rehearsal plan.

Figure 8.1. Sample Rehearsal Plan

I. Warm-ups *(ten minutes)*

    A. Massages and stretches

    B.

yah hah hah hah hah;

Note: Encourage diaphragmatic breathing; ascend by half steps; vary vowels and work for unification.

    C.

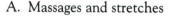

I love ____ to sing!

Note: Ascend by half steps; raise arms slowly upward as the vocal line descends.

    D.

fa la la fa la la   fa la la fa la la   fa la la fa la la   fa la la la fa

Note: Sway back and forth as you sing to feel the exercise in "one" (for *Sing we and chant it* and *Fire, fire, my heart.*)

    E. Exercise D in a 3-part canon

II. Sightreading exercises *(twelve minutes)*.

   A. Three new exercises from the sightreading booklets

      1. Study each one silently.

      2. Chant the solfege syllables in rhythm.

      3. Sing on solfege.

III. *Revecy venir du Printans*—Claude Le Jeune *(ten minutes)*

   A. Listen to a recording of "America" (from *West Side Story*) to hear the shift from 3 + 3 to 2 + 2 + 2 as needed in this piece.

   B. Sing first phrase of "America"

   C. pp. 3–4 (refrain)

      1. Give divisi for this section (SSATB)

      2. Speak in rhythm on "doot," tapping the quarter note on your leg (relate to *West Side Story* experience)

      3. Work notes and rhythms on "dah" with piano playing parts

         a. SSATB

         b. S1 S2

         c. SSA

         d. TB

         e. SSATB

         f. SSATB (without piano playing parts)

IV. *Fire, Fire, My Heart* *(eighteen minutes)*

   A. Work pp. 6–8 (a "fa la la" section) on text with piano playing parts

      1. SSATB

      2. TB

      3. ATB

      4. S1 S2

      5. SSA

      6. SSATB

B. Notes, pp. 9 to end

    1. SSATB on text without piano playing parts

    2. Work on notes in final three measures (codetta) with piano playing parts

        a. S1 S2

        b. SSA

        c. SSAT

        d. SSATB

        e. SSATB without piano playing parts

C. p. 6 and p. 8—work on the transition into and out of this "fa la la" section

D. p. 5 to end on text without piano playing parts

V. *Chanson on Dessus le marché d'Arras" (twelve minutes)*

A. pp. 3–4

    1. Review notes from the monophonic model (SATB in unison) on "dah" and remind them of breaths

    2. Speak French for them, phrase by phrase and have them echo

    3. Speak French in unison and in rhythm

    4. Sing on French, slowly

    5. Sing at a slightly faster tempo

B. pp. 5–6

    1. S and T sing S line on "dee"

    2. A and B sing A line on "dee"

    3. Sing as written (pp. 5–7) on French

VI. Brief discussion with choir about sixteenth-century madrigals and relate the discussion to the music currently in rehearsal *(ten minutes)*

A. Musical considerations

    1. Text painting

    2. Predominately homophonic

    3. Often had fa-la-la refrains

    4. Intended for small group performances, sometimes for after-dinner entertainment

    5. Texts often dealt with pastoral settings, nymphs, fairies, shepherds, unrequited love

6. Sung in vernacular

7. Often used lively, spirited rhythms which would have been out of place in the church services of the day

8. Performed without accompaniment or with instruments doubling or substituting for the voices

B. Name several important English and Italian composers

C. Highlight the paintings displayed around the room from the sixteenth century.

VII. *Sing we and chant it (ten minutes)*

A. Sing entire piece on text, swaying to feel one beat per measure

B. If they are unsuccessful on A, ask them, as they sing, to hit lightly into the air an imaginary beach ball on beat one of every measure to get the same effect.

C. Divide choir into two equal groups. Have each group sing the piece for the other and have the listeners evaluate whether the performers have achieved the feeling of one pulse per measure.

Explanation of Rehearsal Plan

Warm-ups

Physical preparation will be achieved by massages and stretches. Using the limited range of five notes, the first exercise will help with vowel unification and diaphragmatic breathing as the voice begins to warm up. In addition, if a moderately fast tempo is chosen, energetic involvement will be encouraged, setting the tone for a well-paced rehearsal.

The second exercise extends the range to an octave and requires a more fluid line. Use of physical movement to encourage accurate tuning is helpful and blends the physical warm-up with the vocal warm-up. The third exercise is a variation of a major scale sung frequently in rehearsal, but the slight melodic and rhythmic differences will engage the singers' minds as well as their voices. As students sway, they will continue to wake up their bodies, involve themselves on a deeper level, and perhaps solve a problem expected in *Sing we and chant it*. The final exercise really gets the choir singing.

National Standards for Arts Education (p. 59): "Singing, alone and with others, a varied repertoire of music" is the content standard. The achievement standard deals with singing with expression and technical accuracy.

Sightreading Exercises

Devoting ten to twelve minutes during each rehearsal to strengthen sightreading skills will result in choir members who not only sing well, but who are also learning to be knowledgeable musicians. The sightreading portion can be moved to other positions in the rehearsal to provide variety in rehearsal procedure. When the exercises are designed to solve a potential problem in a particular piece of music, you may want to place the exercise just before that piece is to be rehearsed.

National Standards for Arts Education (p. 61): The content standard is "reading and notating music." The achievement standard deals with sightreading accurately and expressively.

Revecy venir

The first piece was chosen carefully because of its moderate ranges and a moderately fast tempo. The choir has sightread this piece before today, but no work has been done to secure notes and rhythms. Listening to and singing a portion of a familiar song from *West Side Story* may serve to engage their attention in addition to solving a similar rhythmic problem found in this piece. Speaking the rhythm first will likely enhance the choir's later success with notes as well. The syllable "dah" was chosen for singing because of its open nature (the French text will be added at a later date when the notes are more secure). Notice that the parameters of this piece are limited to the refrain. On another day, when this piece is placed later in the rehearsal, a longer time will be spent using much larger parameters and perhaps incorporating more work on details. Today, a short introduction (only ten minutes) to a portion of the piece was the intent, in addition to continuing the vocal and mental warm-up.

National Standards for Arts Education (p. 61): The content standard is "listening to, analyzing, and describing music." The achievement standards deal with analyzing aural examples of music, and describing how the elements of music are used in a specific piece that make it expressive, unique, and interesting.

Fire, fire, my heart

Note the highly detailed plan that calls for eighteen minutes to be spent on this selection. Remember that this is the place to spend longer amounts of time on more tedious work. The ranges for each vocal part are more extreme for this selection, but the singers should be warmed up by this point in the rehearsal.

Notice that the rehearsal plan calls for all voices to sing pp. 6–8 before the section is broken down into one or two voice parts at a time. This holistic experience will serve several purposes: (1) students will have an opportunity to sightsing; (2) the experience will establish the parameters within which the day's work is planned; and (3) the initial reading can serve as a "pretest" for students and director alike, perhaps highlighting where the most severe problems will be.

After intense work is complete on pp. 6–8, the choir moves on to p. 9 to the end where a repeat is found of the same music from pp. 6–8, only this time a three-measure codetta must be rehearsed. In addition to learning the codetta, the choir will have an opportunity to sing this "fa la la" section without the aid of the piano playing the parts.

After these two repeated sections are learned, the choir must experience the transitions into and out of them. They know the music preceding the "fa la la" sections, so it is simply a matter of reviewing and then continuing into the newer section. The final experience for this piece is an attempt to sing from p. 5 to the end to see how it all fits together. This will serve as a "post-test," will show singers and director alike where problems may still exist, and will provide closure for this portion of the rehearsal.

Chanson on "Dessus le marché d'Arras"

Welcomed by the singers as they move toward the end of the rehearsal are the moderate ranges as well as the shorter amount of time planned for this composition (twelve minutes). Reviewing notes on the monophonic model will provide a momentary rest for the choir after the tedious rehearsing of the preceding piece, and learning the French during the unison portion will be easier than learning it during the chanson that follows. Although the polyphonic nature of the chanson requires that the sections sing their parts at different times on pp. 5–6, it makes good sense for the sopranos and tenors, and altos and basses to learn their parts at the same time because they have the same material. This is an efficient use of rehearsal time, and also leaves fewer singers idle.

Brief Discussion of Madrigals

The majority of music that the choir is rehearsing for the upcoming concert is either a sixteenth-century Italian or English madrigal. Therefore, the director will spend a short amount of time (ten minutes) during today's rehearsal to introduce the singers to characteristics of this musical form and how they are shown in the music they are studying. Several composers will be named, and their attention will be drawn to the sixteenth-century artwork that is on display around the room. This brief discussion on madrigals comes at a time when the singers will need a change of pace, and they are likely to listen more carefully.

National Standards for Arts Education (pp. 62–63): The content standards are "understanding relationships between music, the other arts, and disciplines outside the arts" and "understanding music in relation to history and culture." The achievement standards deal with a comparison of the characteristics of two or more arts from the same historical period or style, and classifying by genre, style, and historical period representative examples of music.

Sing we and chant it

Because the notes and rhythms are secure, the director is attempting to put some finishing touches on the musical interpretation of this selection. Working on the bigger picture at this point in a rehearsal is always a wise choice because voices are getting tired and attentions spans are getting shorter. The amount of time planned for this portion of the rehearsal is only eight minutes.

The swaying activity was used in the warm-up exercises, and

should now help the singers' success. Notice that an alternative is planned in case the choir has difficulty achieving the feeling of one beat per measure. The choir is then divided in half and each group sings for the other. The listeners are asked to evaluate the performers on whether they achieved the feeling of one beat per measure. This activity will extend their attention spans, encourage careful performing and listening, and will help develop in the choir members the skill of critical evaluation. If things go as planned, this experience will conclude the rehearsal in a very positive way, and the choir will look forward to the next rehearsal.

National Standards for Arts Education (p. 62): The content standard is "evaluating music and music performances." The achievement standard deals with evolving specific criteria for making informed, critical evaluations of the effectiveness of performances, and applying that same criteria to their own performance of music.

As you can see, a rehearsal planned in this manner has a certain shape to it, resembling a musical phrase that begins softly, builds to the middle, and tapers off at the end. This shape reflects the need to prepare not only vocally, but also physically and mentally, and takes into account the singers' attention spans and fatigue levels. Planning every rehearsal is as important as planning a concert program. You will find that the results will far outweigh the efforts required.*

II. Rehearsing the Choir

Mark, a junior music education major in his second semester of conducting, is about to rehearse a group of singers for the first time. As he looks out at the sea of faces in front of him, many questions are racing through his mind. Will I hear the mistakes? Have I studied the music thoroughly enough? What if I forget my beat pattern? What do I do if the basses aren't paying attention? Will my preparatory beat be clear to the singers?

---

* Nineteen prototype lessons that could serve as a guide in planning rehearsals are found in *Teaching Choral Music: A Course of Study.* (1991). Reston, VA: Music Educators National Conference, 18–49.

Making the transition from conducting the music to rehearsing the music can be difficult—even overwhelming at times. Prior to rehearsal, the music is studied carefully, appropriate conducting gestures are practiced, and a rehearsal plan is prepared. Then, for the first time, you find yourself in front of a group of singers with whom you must *rehearse* the music! Things are complicated further as soon as the choir begins to sing, because your developing error-detection skills must be used to determine what in the music needs to be corrected. Trying to comprehend so much information at once can prove to be a frustrating experience, and may cause the novice choral director to be unsure of which direction to take.

Flowchart for Choral Rehearsal

To help alleviate this frustration, the flowchart shown in Figure 8.2 and the accompanying comments are offered as a guide for use in developing rehearsal techniques and acquiring listening skills. By providing a visual image of what transpires within a choral rehearsal, this step-by-step plan may prove helpful in organizing rehearsal time as well as sorting out the wealth of musical information a conductor must perceive when directing choirs.

STEP 1. STUDY THE SCORE. Before the first rehearsal of any musical selection, the conductor must carefully study the music that has been chosen for the choir. Spending sufficient time to complete this task creates a firm foundation on which all else is built—from the first rehearsal to the performance. Aural study of the music will create an aural map of the composition for the conductor, and both visual and aural study of the music will yield insights for rehearsing the composition with the choir. Potential problem spots should be noted and possible solutions planned before the first rehearsal. Nothing can substitute for this careful preparation!

STEP 2. PLAN THE REHEARSAL. As discussed in detail at the beginning of this chapter, a plan for each rehearsal provides a musical focus for the time shared by choir director and singers. Planning details such as the order of pieces to be rehearsed, what will be done, and approximately how long will be spent on each piece, when the announcements will be given, and exactly which warm-up and sightsinging exercises will be used can have a positive impact on every aspect of the rehearsal. Each rehearsal plan should be based on a careful study of the music.

STEP 3. CHOOSE A SECTION OF MUSIC TO REHEARSE. The third step in the sequence calls for establishment of parameters or boundaries within which the music will be rehearsed. The size of your parameters will vary according to what you are working on and

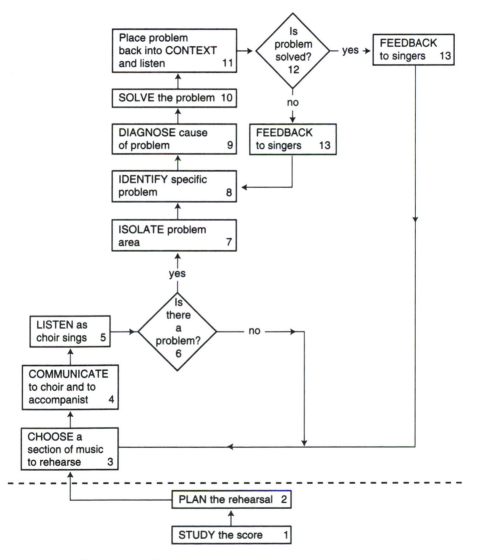

Figure 8.2   Flowchart for Choral Rehearsals

how close you are to the performance. Within whatever size parameters you choose, however, you must always have something specific in mind to rehearse. Establishing parameters within which to work toward a specified goal will eliminate the tendency of novice conductors to sing through the piece at each rehearsal and to correct whatever goes awry. This "hit-or-miss" approach is haphazard and inefficient at best, and often results in overrehearsing the beginning of the music while the remainder is neglected.

Using larger boundaries for the choir's initial contact with the piece will give the singers an overview of the composition. Sightsinging the entire work may serve as a good introduction if the choir's sightreading skills are sufficient for the task. Other ways to introduce a new composition include playing a recording or having the accompanist play through it. These experiences, using large boundaries, will provide an initial impression and a holistic view for the singers.

After the first experience, establish more limited parameters and focus on a specific aspect of the composition to rehearse. For example, focus attention on learning notes and rhythms in Section A only, or rehearse the various sections in the piece that feature a similar musical problem. Perhaps you will want to work on the crescendo occurring across six measures on page 4, or help the choir make a smooth transition from duple to triple meter in the B section. If the piece is the first selection of the rehearsal, choosing a section of the music that features moderate ranges in all voices until the choir is adequately warmed up is always a good idea.

As various sections of the composition are learned and polished, your rehearsal parameters will begin to enlarge somewhat to include the linking together of various sections until the entire piece is complete. Larger boundaries are necessary to rehearse such aspects as style, memorization, and endurance.

STEP 4. COMMUNICATE TO CHOIR AND TO ACCOMPANIST.
Communication is one of the most important aspects of a rehearsal and can be nonverbal as well as verbal. The most obvious aspect of nonverbal communication is the conducting gesture, but more subtle nonverbal factors also can communicate messages to the choir. For instance, facial expressions can show the mood of the piece in addition to revealing how you feel about the music, about the singers, and about their efforts in rehearsal. Body language can sug-

gest tension, fatigue, or excitement about the music. These messages are communicated to the choir whether or not you want them to be, so wise conductors pay attention to nonverbal aspects of their rehearsal demeanor.

Verbal communication indicates any information, instructions, or corrections the conductor may give to the choir and accompanist, and because the choir came to sing and not to listen to the conductor talk, verbal communication must be kept to a minimum. This implies speaking in the most concise and efficient manner possible. You may know precisely what you want to do and where you want to do it, but if you cannot communicate this information to the choir and accompanist, very little will be accomplished.

Careful preparation before rehearsal will yield detailed information about the music, the composer, and the historical period within which the music was composed. This information is very important, and will serve to guide and enlighten the conductor as well as the singers; however, the choice of what is actually communicated during rehearsal must be limited to information that is relevant to the music currently in preparation. A good guide to follow is to share only that which will enhance the choir's understanding and performance of the composition. This is *not* to diminish the importance of such information, but rather to serve as a reminder that a choir rehearsal is not a music history or theory class. Students participate in choir to sing, so be selective about what you share.

For example, if the choir is rehearsing a Bach chorale, they should know when and where Bach lived and composed, a brief background on chorales and their function in the Lutheran church service, and Baroque characteristics that are found in and are pertinent to their particular piece. The choral rehearsal is not the place to make a chord-by-chord analysis of the harmony or give a lecture on the entirety of Bach's life. Detailed study such as this is the focus of a music theory class or a music history/appreciation course.

Perhaps the most effective manner in which to impart pertinent information to the choir is not at one time, but carefully spread out over the time the music is rehearsed. Some information will help provide an overview of the composition and would be appropriately given at the time the music is introduced. Additional information to enhance the understanding of a particular aspect of the music should be given when that aspect comes up during rehearsal.

To communicate instructions regarding where you want to begin, use the following order: page, score (system), measure, beat. Another technique that makes communication easy between director, choir, and accompanist is for everyone to number the measures of the composition so that this is the only information required other than on which beat within the measure you will begin. Rarely do you need to waste time telling the choir where you will stop, because you will stop them yourself when you get there. In addition, you need to indicate which section(s) of the choir will be singing as well as on what aspect of the music they will be working (notes in measure 4, intonation, crisp rhythm, diction). And don't forget the accompanist. He or she plays a vital role in the music-making and can often make or break the success of a rehearsal. The accompanist needs to know "where, what, and who," as well as whether to play parts, the accompaniment, or simply to give initial pitches.

Speak these directions clearly, efficiently, and in a voice that can

Photograph by Thom Ewing..

be heard by the group. Allow a reasonable length of time for the choir and accompanist to find the place in question, and when their eyes are up (signifying they are ready), begin.

STEP 5. LISTEN AS CHOIR SINGS. Listening accurately is probably the most important task a conductor does, and is a skill that develops and improves with experience. In addition, good listening requires careful aural and visual study of the music *before* rehearsal. If you don't know what the piece should sound like, how can you determine whether the choir is singing it correctly?

As novice directors develop error-detection skills by working with choirs, they may be overwhelmed frequently with the amount of musical information that must be heard and acted on—right on the spot! Rather than "listening in general," try focusing attention on the specific aspect being rehearsed at the moment (alto part, dynamics, rhythmic accuracy in measure 34, or intonation, for example). By listening for the aspect in question and placing other aural information in the background, frustration caused by "information overload" may be alleviated. As better skills in listening are developed, a larger number of things will be heard at once.

STEP 6. IS THERE A PROBLEM? As the choir sings the section of the music you have selected and communicated, determine if a problem exists. If there is no problem (or the problem is one to be corrected at a later date), go back to Step 3 on the flowchart and begin the same sequence again using a different section of music. If there is a problem, proceed to Step 7.

STEP 7. ISOLATE THE PROBLEM AREA. Once a problem is discovered, isolate the area in which it was heard while working toward the identification of the *specific* problem (Step 8), diagnosis of the cause of the problem (Step 9), and its solution (Step 10).

Isolation can mean many things. In general, it refers to working with less than the whole. For example, if the entire choir is having difficulty with notes, rather than continuing to sing the section with all voices, work quickly with one voice part at a time to discover which section(s) is(are) having difficulty; or isolate the notes and rhythm by taking away the text and have the choir sing on a neutral syllable. Asking the choir to speak the text in rhythm isolates the rhythmic aspect of the music as well as provides opportunity to focus on diction.

Isolating will help the director as well as the choir, especially if the director is inexperienced. Attention can be focused on one or two aspects at a time by breaking down various components of the composition to seek the identification and cause of, as well as the solution to a problem. More careful listening can occur. In addition, this approach broadens the choir's awareness of the music, because the singers become familiar not only with their own part, but also with all components that make up the construction of the composition. As directors become more experienced and error-detection skills improve, the *degree* of isolation needed may diminish, but the technique of isolation in general is a useful and necessary one.

STEP 8. IDENTIFY THE PROBLEM. Often, problem identification is an area in which novice conductors have trouble. A problem will be heard—that is, the conductor knows that *something* is not right—but to state specifically what is wrong is often difficult.

For example, the choir has just sung measures 3–10 and the harmonic sequence didn't sound correct. At this point, however, you are not aware of the *specific* problem. To facilitate identification of the problem, isolate the sections of the choir, asking each to sing their part alone. If no problems exist at this point, begin to combine the sections. Perhaps you will discover that the dissonance between the soprano and tenor parts is causing difficulty, or the problem is occurring when the alto and soprano parts cross. Now you have identified the *specific* problem. Proceed to Step 9.

STEP 9. DIAGNOSE THE CAUSE OF THE PROBLEM. Through careful study of the music prior to rehearsal (Step 1), directors will have located *potential* problems in the score. Possible causes of and several remedies for these potential troublespots will have been considered as well. At this point, valuable rehearsal time and frustration will be saved in the sequence because of the conductor's careful score study prior to rehearsal.

The cause of a problem will often suggest the remedy. For example, you have heard the sopranos continue to sing below pitch a particular group of very high notes (*the problem*). The *cause* of this problem may be: (1) a closed vowel (remedy: vowel modification); (2) poor breath support (remedy: work on breathing); (3) a very long line for the sopranos (remedy: have them stagger their breathing); or (4) poor vocal production (remedy: stop and work on whatever aspect you determine is causing the trouble). You can see the potential for frustration—and resulting discipline problems—if you focus exclusively on one cause to the exclusion of other possibilities. Several remedies may be necessary before the problem is corrected.

STEP 10. SOLVE THE PROBLEM. You have heard a problem, isolated the area, identified the specific problem, and determined its cause. Now the problem must be corrected. Correcting the problem includes not only informing the choir about the problem but also having them work on the solution. As obvious as this sounds, many novice conductors will hear a problem and simply tell the altos to "sing in a more legato style in measures 5–6" or tell the tenors and basses to "sing an F natural instead of an F sharp in measure 18." Simply telling the choir what the problem is does not necessarily assure that it will be corrected! After stating the problem, the director must have the singers actually work (sing) toward the solution. As the choir sings, the members' efforts will provide tangible evidence as to whether they understand and can do whatever needs correction.

Be certain that the choir is secure with the solution before placing it back into context. Remember that several remedies may be necessary before the problem is solved.

STEP 11. PLACE THE PROBLEM BACK INTO CONTEXT AND LISTEN. After isolating a problem to identify it, diagnose it, and solve it, the problem must be placed back into context before continuing the sequence. Listen carefully to determine if the problem really has been corrected.

Placing the problem area back into context is similar to an organ transplant. During the operation, doctors remove the poorly functioning organ and replace it with a new one. The job is not complete, however, until the doctors reattach the vital *connections*

of the body to the transplanted organ. Choral directors must do
the same thing in the music! The musical problem is not completely solved until all the connections that were severed to solve
the problem have been reconnected. In addition, placing the
problem area back into context will give a sense of closure for
both the choir and director.

STEP 12. EVALUATE WHETHER THE PROBLEM IS SOLVED.
If the problem is solved, move back to Step 3 and begin the
sequence again with another section of music. If the problem is not
solved, return in the sequence to Step 8 and proceed, perhaps after
reevaluating the cause of the problem. Remember, isolation may
again be necessary.

At this point in the rehearsal, choir members may be frustrated
due to a lack of success, and it may be wise to put the music aside.
Leaving a problem unresolved rather than wasting rehearsal time
"beating a dead horse" will prove less frustrating for all concerned.
Try approaching the problem from a different angle at the next
rehearsal when both you and the singers are fresh, and you have
studied the music further.

STEP 13. FEEDBACK TO THE SINGERS. After working through
Steps 3–12, the director will need to provide some form of feedback
to the choir regarding its progress. Feedback, of course, has been
offered along the way, but some sort of summative statement is
needed at this point. Often, when success has been achieved, all
the director needs to say is an enthusiastic "That's right!" or "That's
what we want!" So often, not having to sing the problem area again
is all the positive reinforcement given to a group that has been
working very hard. Singers need to hear positive comments, and
will often be willing to work harder if they know that their efforts
are appreciated. This is a step often neglected by directors, but one
that is critical to establishing a healthy rapport and a positive
atmosphere in which to work.

If the the singers have been less than successful, they need to
be informed. Often they will know, but an informative evaluation from the director will help explain why they were unsuccessful as well as suggest what the choir needs to do next to
correct the problem. Negative evaluation can be couched in a

positive manner with comments such as: "Your tone quality was much better in this section that time, but we still need to work on the diction in measure 6." Statements such as this will not defeat a choir that has been working hard to correct a problem, but the group has been informed that there is more work to be done.*

Summary

The discipline required to study the music and to plan each rehearsal gives conductors the freedom to focus almost totally on the singers and their progress. A plan should remain flexible, however, and should be modified according to what happens in rehearsal.

Warm-up exercises include physical, mental, and vocal preparation for singing, and obviously need to be at the beginning of rehearsal. The development of sightsinging skills is also an important portion of your students' music education, so regular opportunities must be given to gain knowledge and skill in this area. Both the warm-up and sightsinging exercises can be designed to solve problems found in the music. This practice is not only an efficient use of time, but also shows students that there is a strong connection between warm-ups, sightsinging, and the rehearsal of music for performance.

A rehearsal should have a definite shape to it, and may often resemble a musical phrase that begins softly, builds to the middle, and tapers off at the end. A good beginning includes the warm-ups, perhaps the sightsinging exercises, and a piece which should be moderate in its demands, both vocal and mental. Because students' voices and minds are warmed up and still fresh, the middle of the rehearsal contains the most tedious work. During this portion of the rehearsal, the amount of time spent on each piece can be somewhat longer than at the beginning or the end. After such tedious work, singers will appreciate a tapering off of both vocal and mental requirements toward the conclusion of class.

---

*   This sequence of events takes much more time to read and discuss than it takes when it actually occurs during a rehearsal. Working through steps 3 through 13 may require as little time as one minute, although more complex problems can take much longer.

The flowchart in this chapter provides a visual image of what transpires within a choral rehearsal and may prove helpful in organizing rehearsal time as well as sorting out the wealth of musical information a conductor must perceive when directing choirs. Steps 1 and 2 advocate a careful study of the music and the creation of a rehearsal plan, and Step 3 deals with establishing parameters in the music within which you will rehearse. The critical issue of communication is discussed in Step 4. Listening, probably the most important task a conductor performs, appears in the chart as Step 5. In Step 6, the conductor determines whether a problem has been heard, and, if not, a return to Step 3 is suggested. If a problem is perceived, the conductor then isolates the area to work toward the identification of the *specific* problem (Step 8), diagnosis of the cause of the problem (Step 9), and its solution (Step 10).

Solving the problem is discussed in Step 10, while Steps 11 and 12 deal with placing the problem back into context and listening to determine whether the problem is actually solved. If the problem persists, a return to Step 8 in the sequence along with a reevaluation of the cause of the problem is suggested. The importance of providing the singers with accurate and honest feedback is discussed in Step 13.

Mini-Projects

1. The Concert Choir is made up of forty-five high school singers with above-average ability. The rehearsal period is 12:00–12:50, which is right after lunch for thirty-five of the members, so they often come in rather loud and boisterous. The singers are predominately freshmen and sophomores. The choir room has several practice rooms off the main rehearsal area, making sectional rehearsals a real possibility if needed.

Plan three consecutive rehearsals for this choir using the following music found in *Something to Sing About*, Level 1 (G. Schirmer, 1982). If this anthology is unavailable to you, find four other selections of music, decide on the status of the music, and plan three consecutive rehearsals for the choir described.

Include warm-ups for each rehearsal. One warm-up for each rehearsal needs to be related to a piece on which you will work that day.

Write your plans in outline form. Give enough information so that you know what to do but don't give so much detail that you are unable to understand it by a quick glance at the rehearsal plan. Indicate the amount of time you intend to spend on each piece or activity (fifty-minute rehearsals). Be as creative as possible.

THE MUSIC

Fa una canzona (p. 78)—Orazio Vecchi
I Walk the Unfrequented Road (p. 235)—arr. Lee Kjelson
Never Tell Thy Love (p. 104)—Houston Bright
Three Hungarian Folk Songs (p. 138)—Matyas Seiber

THE STATUS OF THE MUSIC

1. *Fa una canzona:* The notes/rhythms are learned but are not absolutely secure yet. The choir does not know the Italian text at all.
2. *I Walk the Unfrequented Road:* The notes/rhythms are secure, but the choir is having a difficult time achieving a legato line.
3. *Never Tell Thy Love:* The choir has read the entire piece once and has learned the notes/rhythms on p. 104 (Section A) only.
4. *Three Hungarian Folk Songs*
   a. "The Handsome Butcher": The choir knows notes and rhythms, but the diction and interpretation (dynamics, accents, etc.) need work.
   b. "Apple, Apple": The choir can sing the notes/rhythms correctly but is still dependent on the piano playing their parts. They are having trouble achieving a legato line and are not watching you carefully as you attempt to use rubato throughout the piece.
   c. "The Old Woman": The choir has never read it or worked on it.

2. Observe at least two choir rehearsals in local schools. Pay close attention to the connection between the order of pieces rehearsed and the students' behavior and level of participation.

3. Choose two pieces with which you are not familiar. Study them carefully, and locate potential problems. Create three warm-up exercises for each piece that will solve these problems discovered in your study.

Reference

National standards for arts education: What every young American should know and be able to do in the arts. (1994). Reston, VA: Music Educators National Conference.

Additional Reading

BARROW, LEE G. (1994). Programming rehearsals for student success. *Music Educators Journal, 81*(2), 26–28.

Choral music packet: Supplement to teaching choral music. (1991). Reston, VA: Music Educators National Conference.

CLARK, BUD. (1990). Humor in the classroom. *Choral Journal, 31*(1), 15–18.

DEMOREST, STEVEN. (1993). Customizing choral warmups. *Choral Journal, 33*(7), 25–28.

DOERKSEN, DAVID P. (1990). *Guide to evaluating teachers of music performance groups.* Reston, VA: Music Educators National Conference.

FREER, PATRICK K. (1992). Education research: Practical implications for the rehearsal. *Choral Journal, 33*(5), 29–34.

Teaching choral music: A course of study. (1991). Reston, VA: Music Educators National Conference.

ULRICH, JERRY.(1993). Conductor's guide to successful rehearsals. *Music Educators Journal, 79*(7), 34–35, 68.

9

Behavior Management in Rehearsal

Allison is late to rehearsal again, and disrupts the announcements by getting her music from the top of the piano and crawling over the entire alto section to get to her seat. Soo Mee is chewing gum, Nicole and Marie are talking about the homecoming dance, and Kristen can't seem to stop playing with an old piece of construction paper that is hanging off the bulletin board near her seat.

Mrs. Jensen, the choral director, is getting anxious and frustrated because the Spring Choral Festival is only one week away, and the choir is simply not ready to perform. She can't understand how this has happened because she carefully chose this year's selections, and has studied the music and practiced her conducting gestures every night for weeks. She knows she is an excellent musician, and she is pleased with her choir's potential, but she is continually frustrated by the choir's general lack of musical success. She feels the problem is directly related to student behavior. Why do they act this way? What can be done to encourage cooperation and positive behavior patterns?

Choral directors who are fine musicians with outstanding conducting skills, and who have selected appropriate music and studied it carefully, will often find their choirs falling short of musical success unless they possess knowledge of the age group with which they work and have the necessary skills and techniques to manage their behavior in rehearsal. Knowing about your students and learning these skills and techniques is as important in the preparation of choral directors as is the acquisition of musical knowledge and the development of musical skills. Unfortunately, behavior management is an area that is often neglected, leaving choral directors only partially equipped to perform their jobs well.

Whom Are You Teaching?

Knowledge and understanding of the unique characteristics of the age group with whom you work can enhance your effectiveness as a teacher, resulting in improved student behavior and learning. Your knowledge (or lack thereof) will be reflected in your rehearsal plans and techniques as well as in your one-to-one relationships with the singers. Students can sense if their teachers really understand who they are, and will often respond accordingly.

First of all, students of any age are human beings who deserve to be treated fairly with the care, concern, and courtesy you would normally use in any relationship. More often than not, this care, concern, and courtesy will be returned to you as you and your students build a mutual respect for one another. This mutual respect can go a long way in building positive behavior patterns.

Adolescence

At the middle school/junior high and high school levels, you will have a preponderance of students who are classified as adolescents, so an understanding of this stage of human growth and development is critical to your success as a teacher of this age group. Webster's *Ninth New Collegiate Dictionary* defines adolescence as "the process of growing up," or "the period of life from puberty to maturity," and "a state of development . . . prior to maturity." The words *process*, *period of life*, and *state of development* indicate a transitional time between childhood and adulthood, and adolescent students can be either or both on any given day! They are eager to be treated as adults with certain important responsibilities and can often perform delegated duties with maturity. Then, without any warning, they will slip back into the more comfortable and familiar behavior patterns of childhood, frustrating themselves as much as their parents or any adults with whom they are associated.

During this transitional period, change rather than stability is the norm. Vivian Center Seltzer (1989, p. 1) states that "adolescence is more than an extended period of change. It is an interval of continuous changing." Emotional, physical, psychological, and social changes occur, often quite rapidly, as the young person moves from childhood to adulthood. Mentally and physically, adolescents are at their peak, but "paradoxically, the quality of inner experience is often at its lowest point" (Csikszentmihalyi, 1987, p. 103).

The onset of puberty, which usually occurs between the ages of twelve to fourteen and one-half (and sometimes earlier), is the simplest way to pinpoint the beginning of adolescence. Puberty can be defined as "the process of becoming physically and sexually mature and developing the adult characteristics of one's own sex" (Kimmel and Weiner, 1985, p. 592). Physical signs of puberty include rapid growth spurts, the appearance of pubic hair, growth of the testes and penis in males, and development of breasts and the first menstruation period in females. These physical changes can sometimes cause self-consciousness, especially in those students who begin to develop sooner or later than everyone else.

Due to rapid growth spurts, students of this age will often become gangly and clumsy, as if they don't know what to do with their arms and legs. Because of hormonal changes, students of this age will experience an increased interest in the opposite sex, and will have emotional reactions that are often out of proportion—either completely ecstatic or totally devastated—to their cause. There is almost an obsession with how they look at all times, and they often experience excessive fatigue or excessive energy. Girls usually mature earlier and at a faster rate than boys, so it is not unusual to find some girls towering in height over boys, especially in middle school/junior high.

Because adolescents are neither children nor adults, their peer group becomes extremely important to them. In fact, the peer group may become more important than their relationships with parents and other adults. It is comforting for them to associate with people who are going through the same transitional process, and often, very close friendships develop during this time. They will stick close together, are intensely loyal to one another, and often wear similar clothing, talk a certain way, and have their own kind of music. Because adolescents are searching for their own identity, belonging to groups becomes very important for supportive reasons, and because they are unsure of just who they are at this point in their lives, they are often extremely sensitive to criticism.

Applying the Knowledge

How can this knowledge of adolescence affect your teaching and your students' behavior and learning? Simply, by accepting their characteristics and taking them into consideration in your relationships with your students as well as when you plan rehearsals and activities for them, you will be using this knowledge to everyone's advantage rather than working against it. Adolescence is a powerful force, and teachers who acknowledge this fact and who are creative in dealing with this age group can develop choral programs that are quite successful.

For instance, consider the importance of peer approval and adolescents' need to belong to groups. A choral ensemble is a group, and if students at your school perceive choir as a popular and acceptable endeavor, they will likely be eager to join. Singing in choir can even serve as a substitute family during these transitional years.

Knowing that adolescents enjoy wearing the same type of clothing that identifies their membership in a certain group, you may consider the purchase of choir T-shirts or hats with the school insignia on them, or whatever is "in" at the time. Because they are preoccupied with their looks and it is important for them to wear (and not to wear) certain things, involve your students in the decision. This will also take into account their eagerness for adult status and responsibility.

When students have been delegated certain responsibilities, and after weeks of successful work, they suddenly fail to complete an important task, certainly show disappointment and displeasure and decide on a suitable punishment if necessary. At the same time, however, encourage them by reminding them of their successes and by letting them know that you expect them to succeed again. This approach not only acknowledges the transitional stage between child and adult and punishes their lack of responsibility, but also encourages them to move forward at the same time.

When students exhibit excessive energy levels, especially at the preadolescent and early adolescent stages, this fact must be taken into account when planning and carrying out rehearsals. Rather than wasting valuable time trying to get them to be quiet and complaining about their energy level, begin rehearsal with warm-up exercises to help with mental focus, add various physical activities to get rid of some of the energy, try to schedule their rehearsal earlier in the day when they may not be so active, or plan to rehearse small amounts of many different compositions during rehearsal to encourage a better attention span.

The excessive energy level of your students cannot be changed, but the preceding suggestions show many ways to work *with* this adolescent characteristic. Actually, many teachers of middle school/junior high students consider this excessive energy level a positive characteristic. The challenge to these directors, then, is to focus that energy in a productive and positive direction. Once their energy is channeled, this age group has been known to "move mountains." At the opposite end of the spectrum, older adolescents will often suffer from excessive fatigue. When this occurs, rather than complaining about it, accept it and plan accordingly.

Because of rapid growth, students will often trip over or drop things. When this occurs, be careful how you react. Often an understanding look followed by a smile is all that is required to help the student recover. At other times, fellow choir members will laugh and tease the person who tripped and fell. If the person laughs *with* the choir and recovers fairly easily, then carry on with the rehearsal. If you can determine the choir's response is a destructive one and the person who tripped appears emotionally hurt, you must intervene. Never allow the choir to ridicule a fellow member in a situation like this. Remember that students of this age can be extremely sensitive to criticism and are not eager to be singled out from the group. At awkward times such as these, students will appreciate your knowledge and understanding of them.

Because girls usually mature earlier and at a faster rate than boys, you may want to organize your choral program by having choirs of the same sex, especially at the middle school/junior high level when this characteristic is more obvious. By singing in choirs of all girls or all boys, young adolescents may feel freer to be themselves and, as a result, may accomplish more musically. Because boys' voices are beginning to change at this time, you will be able to work more diligently with them as they learn ways to manage their newly emerging voices, and they may not be quite so embarrassed by their lack of vocal control if girls are not in the same group with them.

To acknowledge their new interest in the opposite sex, consider combining the girls' and boys' choirs into a large mixed ensemble that meets after school several days a week. This arrangement will open up an entirely different type of choral literature for your students in addition to satisfying a social need for this age group.

The best help you can provide for your adolescent singers during this transitional time in their lives may be to serve as a strong role model for them. All aspects of their young lives are in a constant state of change, and they appreciate having someone they can count on, day after day, to be a steady influence. They also appreciate knowing the boundaries within which they will work. This means having a specific set of rules, created jointly by you and the students, to help guide their actions in choir. Adolescents may act as though they don't like the rules, but they need the security provided by specific boundaries as well as the consequences they might expect when those boundaries are crossed. This, too, is something on which they can count.

Discipline Takes Courage

All teachers want to be liked, and new teachers are especially eager for their students to hold them in high regard. Things are so much more pleasant when everyone is happy. Unfortunately, things won't always be pleasant, and everyone won't always be pleased with decisions you make, actions you take, or with the music that you choose.

In the area of behavior management, new teachers must sometimes muster up an extra amount of courage to do what must be

done, because their actions or words run the risk of making someone unhappy. Perhaps the disciplined student (and all their friends)
won't like you for a time. Perhaps parents will be displeased with the
punishment you have imposed on their child, or maybe the administration won't approve of the way you handled a situation. All of
the above can be unsettling, especially for a new teacher who wants
(and needs) to be liked.

Therefore, in a misguided effort to be liked, teachers may shy
away from doing what needs to be done to create and maintain a
classroom environment conducive to learning. Soon, they will find
themselves and their students operating in a chaotic and confusing
situation in which little or no learning is taking place. In addition,
these teachers will discover that their students are in control of the
classroom, for when students sense that their teacher is afraid of
them or hesitant about taking the appropriate action to restore
order in the classroom, they will often do whatever they please
whenever they please. They know the teacher doesn't have the
courage to discipline them. In a situation like this, students have
lost respect for their teacher, and their ability to learn has been
severely hampered.

The most desirable and pleasant situation for teaching and learning is when your students both like and respect you. If, however, you
must make a choice between the two, respect is always the wiser
choice. If students have respect for you, they are likely to cooperate
with you and learning can take place. Eventually, they may come to
like you as well, but if not, you still have their respect. If students
like you as a person, but have little or no respect for you as their
teacher, everyone loses, so you must have the *courage* to discipline
your students. They will appreciate you for it!

When disciplining a student, make sure you disapprove of the
action rather than of the student; in other words, the behavior is
undesirable, not the student. And work to correct specific actions
rather than making broad, general statements such as "Class, you
are being horrible today!" With a comment like this, the students
don't know what behaviors are inappropriate or what behaviors to
change. More specific comments such as "You are talking too much
between pieces," or "please remember to raise your hand to speak,"
are much more helpful because they inform the students of what
they can change.

On a day when everything seems to be going wrong, you may be pushed into saying something that is impossible to do. These emotional comments can function as *empty threats*. Comments such as the following can function in this way:

1. *"If you do that one more time, I will not allow you to sing at contest next week."* What if the student is the section leader of the tenor section which has only four singers? Are you prepared to carry out this threat if he continues to misbehave?
2. *"If the class doesn't quiet down, we won't go to lunch today."* Can you legally omit lunch from your students' schedules?
3. *"You cannot move to your next class until the entire choir has been completely quiet for one minute."* What would be the consequences of this action should you carry through with it? Are you prepared to write late passes for each student or to explain to the principal why sixty students were tardy for fifth period?

With an empty threat, the prospect of punishment is removed for the students, because they strongly suspect you cannot or will not carry it out. In such cases, you can count on the undesirable behavior to continue. To be effective, make sure that you can carry out the punishment before you speak in anger or out of frustration.

Preventive Discipline

Obviously, the primary goal of behavior management is not to control students but to create an environment for optimal learning. The easiest and often the most effective way to manage student behavior is through *preventive discipline*; that is, to structure the rehearsal environment so that positive behavioral patterns (and therefore, better learning) are encouraged. This suggests a front-end approach for prevention rather than the frequent hand-wringing, after-the-fact approach of "what should I do *to stop* my students' undesirable behavior?"

Listed below are suggestions for structuring the learning environment for optimal musical success. Hopefully, you will observe that while many of the suggestions are nonmusical in content, all suggestions have the potential to influence behavior, which, in turn, influences musical success.

1. *Create pleasant and neat surroundings for your choirs.* Physical surroundings send a message (perhaps subconsciously) to the singers and can affect the success of a rehearsal. When singers enter a choral room in which chairs are neatly arranged with enough space for each student to sit comfortably, the floor is free of trash, the lighting is good, the room temperature is comfortable, and the bulletin boards have been changed recently, they will come into rehearsal with a different impression than if the room is in complete disarray. If students sense order, planning, and a reasonable concern for their physical comfort, they are more likely to respond in positive and pleasant ways. If they sense confusion and disorganization due to lack of planning or lack of concern, their response may not be quite so positive and pleasant. Valuable time and energy is then lost in getting their attention so that the rehearsal can begin.

2. *Have a brief set of rules, state them in a positive way, and be consistent in enforcing them.* As stated earlier, knowing the boundaries within which they are to work and learn fosters a sense of security among students. They appreciate knowing what is expected of them, even if they complain and create ways to test you and the rules.

Involving students in the establishment of the rules is often a good idea. This process gives them an opportunity to contemplate the reasons behind the rules rather than viewing the rules simply as a list of forbidden behaviors. When you write the rules, remember to state them in a positive way. For example, rather than "Do not be late for class," use "Be on time to class."

In addition to stating the rules, include the consequences for breaking the rules, and be consistent in enforcing them. If you punish an infraction one day and not the next, students will become frustrated and confused as to what the rules really are. If you discipline one singer and not another, not only is the unwanted behavior likely to continue, but also, students may begin to think of you as an unfair teacher. If Julia, your best soprano and choral librarian talks out during rehearsal, she must be punished in the same way as you would punish François, who is a known trouble-maker. Even if you feel that enforcing the rules one particular day will interrupt the flow of the rehearsal and you want to ignore the misbehavior, you must not! You have to be consistent in every way for the rules and consequences to work.

Choral directors (and teachers in general) frequently report that talking is one of the biggest concerns in the classroom. Tardiness, chewing gum, eating and drinking in class, and not having their music and a pencil are also mentioned as ways that singers can fall short of their directors' expectations. Like the example here, a brief set of rules, stated positively, and a corresponding set of consequences may help solve these problems.

RULES

1. Leave all gum, food, and drinks outside the choral hall.
2. Be on time to rehearsal.
3. Have all necessary music and a pencil at every rehearsal.
4. Remain quiet when not singing so that you can hear what the director has to say.

CONSEQUENCES

First offense: Verbal warning
Second offense: Stay after school
Third offense: Parents are called
Fourth offense: Student sent to principal

3. *Always begin the rehearsal on time, even if all singers are not present.* By waiting to begin until everyone is there, you give the choir the power to decide when to begin rehearsal. To train your choir members to arrive on time, have a system in place to take care of tardies, communicate this system to your singers so that they know what will happen if they are late, and enforce this system consistently. For example, because good attendance is critical for everyone in a choral ensemble, you may want to link tardiness to students' grades. Establish a rule that, after three unexcused tardies, your grade (or portion thereof) will be lowered by a certain number of points. Students will need to be informed of this rule at the first rehearsal, and you must enforce it consistently for all choir members.

4. *Before class begins, list on the board the order of music to be rehearsed.* Sharing the order of rehearsal with your singers suggests an organized director who places importance on optimal use of time allotted for rehearsal. In addition, by having an opportunity to arrange their music in order at the beginning of rehearsal, singers will

make the transition between selections more quickly. The faster rehearsal pace which results will eliminate idle time, which often encourages talking and other unwanted behaviors among the singers.

5. *Have an efficient system for handling music.* If time is spent giving out and taking up music, opportunities will exist for students to begin disruptive behavior. Time and energy is then spent disciplining the offenders as well as refocusing the choir on the musical activities ahead. This begins the rehearsal in a negative way.

If possible, store music and folders in a cabinet with numbered slots and assign each student a folder with a number corresponding to a slot in the cabinet. Store all folders in the cabinet and place all appropriate music in each student's folder before rehearsal begins. Position the cabinet so that when the singers come into the choir room, they can pick up their music or return it to its appropriate place when the rehearsal is over.

6. *Study music carefully before rehearsal.* Nothing can substitute for preparation—even with the simplest music. If you wait to learn the music along with your choir, your skill as a leader will be severely hampered, and everything is likely to suffer.

Careful study of the music before rehearsal yields several benefits. Rather than struggling with an unfamiliar score, you can focus almost entirely on the singers and their performance. Preparation gives you the freedom to use eye contact more frequently, which, in addition to preparedness, suggests confidence in what you are doing as well as sincerity. You will be free to move out from behind the conducting stand more often, and your listening ability for detecting errors is likely to improve as well. All these benefits will improve rehearsal efficiency, and because the majority of your attention will be focused on the singers and their performance, their attention is likely to be more focused as well.

7. *Have a rehearsal plan.* Equally important to the careful preparation of music, a good rehearsal plan will give focus and purpose to the day's activities. Since choirs will sing in performance the way they have sung in rehearsals, every rehearsal should be crafted as artfully as any concert.

Begin each rehearsal with two or three warm-up exercises that build technique and focus attention in addition to warming up the voice. Vary the exercises from day to day to challenge singers' minds as well as their voices. If the same set of vocalises are selected for every rehearsal, choir members will soon be able to perform them without thinking. Remember, the more actively involved students are, the less likely they are to misbehave.

The number of pieces selected can impact the success of your rehearsal. Generally, the younger the students, the more frequently you need to change activities or selections. A college choir may be able to rehearse two pieces in an hour's time, but that practice would prove deadly for a middle school choir whose attention span is much shorter.

In addition to the number of pieces chosen, the order in which you decide to rehearse your selections is a critical issue and relates directly to behavior management. For example, planning to rehearse a piece that is demanding, both vocally and mentally, at the end of rehearsal just doesn't make good sense. The potential for frustration is high in a situation like this, and frustration often leads to behavior problems.

Rather than simply singing through the music and fixing whatever goes wrong, have something specific on which to work in every selection. A systematic approach to learning music can often result in better retention over time, thus avoiding the frustration of having to fix the same problem over and over again. That frustration can lead to boredom, and boredom often results in behavior problems.

Rehearse pieces with varying keys, tempi, and moods to extend the attention span of your choir members. Working on a long series of slow pieces can drag the pace down (and everything else with it, including the pitch), while working on a long series of fast pieces can wear out a choir very quickly and make the rehearsal pace seem harried. Variety is the key.

8. *Create a positive and supportive atmosphere.* In the learning process, students should be allowed to make mistakes without fear of ridicule or embarrassment. Mistakes are not failures but rather necessary steps on the road of learning. Dale Topp (1987) suggests that we should think of our singers' efforts in rehearsal as an offering to us. If singers' efforts are viewed in this way, our reaction to their attempts will be tempered by this viewpoint.

As students make genuine efforts toward success, encourage them along the way with such comments as "Much better that time!" This informs the singers that they are improving nicely toward the goal but haven't arrived yet. Stating a positive comment before giving constructive criticism is always a good idea. Comments such as "The German diction was much better that time; now, let's go back and see if we can keep a steadier tempo" will not defeat a choir, yet gives them an accurate and honest appraisal of their progress. Even if nearly everything goes badly (and you can determine singers are doing their best), a director can honestly say "Good effort!"

When you and the singers have been working on a particular problem and it is finally corrected, react vigorously with comments such as "That's it!" or "That's what we want!" rather than with comments (delivered without even looking up from the score) such as "Okay, now let's turn to page 7." Granted, the latter statement is not a negative comment, but honest, enthusiastic, and positive reactions can be so much more effective.

9. *Maintain eye contact.* Eye contact suggests confidence, preparedness, sincerity, and an eagerness to share ideas and information. When directors approach their choirs in such a manner, a certain atmosphere is set which may encourage students to participate in positive ways rather than to behave poorly. Perhaps less lofty, but just as effective: when teachers are consistently looking at their students, their students may be less likely to misbehave.

10. *Minimize teacher talk.* When students are not actively involved in a task or activity, they will often find other things to do. Unfortunately, many of these things will be disruptive. Students who are singing, however, are engaged in a more active role and are likely to remain on task longer than those students who are listening to their directors talk. Obviously, some verbal instruction is necessary during a rehearsal. The key to avoiding discipline problems is simply to minimize the amount of talking you do. This suggests that you have given some thought to the information beforehand so that the instructions will be stated as clearly and succinctly as possible.

When a large amount of talking is necessary (giving breaths to each section of the choir, or learning correct pronunciation of a foreign language, for example), the "talk and do" system is a helpful approach. This approach suggests that the director selects small parameters and gives instructions for this segment of the music only. The choir then sings the section to illustrate that they understand the information. Then the director moves to the next segment of the music, gives more instructions, and the choir sings.

This way, the choir's attention to the information will be better, and, because the singers will be more actively involved, their behavior is likely to be better as well. In addition, you will really know whether they understand what you have asked them to do because they will have had to sing it. This provides tangible evidence of their degree of understanding.

Charlene Archibeque (1992, p. 18) suggests using "the rule of seven," which means telling the choir what you want them to do in seven words or fewer (for example, "twice the energy, half the volume," or "this time, much more facial involvement"). Another way to minimize time spent in talking is to think of sending a telegram on a very limited budget. In a situation such as this, you would choose carefully not only the number of words, but also the quality of the words for maximum communication at little cost.

Announcements should be brief and to the point. To avoid potential discipline problems, write the announcements on the board, or find other alternative methods to get the information out. If you want an accurate list of the phone numbers for all your singers, for example, calling each person's name during rehearsal and asking for his or her phone number leaves most of the choir idle and thus creates the potential for discipline problems. A more efficient way to gather the same information is to send around a list of their names with instructions to write their phone number beside their name. This alternative causes only a slight disturbance as the list goes around the class and allows more rehearsal time to be spent on musical concerns rather than on nonmusical ones. Additional alternatives include a weekly newsletter or a special area on the bulletin board that is reserved for announcements. Of course, for the bulletin board idea to be effective, you must train your choir members to look at it regularly.

11. *Work with the entire choir as much as possible.* As we have discussed previously, students who are actively involved in an activity are less likely to engage in undesirable behavior. Therefore, plan your rehearsal so that you are working with the entire group rather than with one or two sections for long periods of time.

If you need to work for an extended time with one or two sections of the choir, hold a sectional rehearsal before or after school, or during lunch if your schedule allows. If you have the facilities and personnel to do so, you may want to use the choral rehearsal time as

an opportunity for sectional rehearsals of the entire choir. In this situation, assistant directors or the section leaders can take one or
more of the various sections of the choir to a nearby room to work
alone for a portion of the rehearsal. After a specified amount of
time, the sections will reconvene in the choir room for a rehearsal
of the entire choir.

When working with one section of the group for brief periods of
time during rehearsal, involve the other singers in some way.
Because student involvement may be low, the least effective
approach may be "follow your own part while the altos sing."
Because student involvement is more active, a better technique
may be to "sing your part on 'oo' while the altos sing on the text,"
or, if the ranges are moderate, have the altos sing with the sopranos
as they learn their part. If you are working with the tenors and basses, have the sopranos sing with the tenors and the altos sing with
the basses. This way everyone is participating. In addition to promoting better rehearsal discipline, the singers' overall knowledge
and understanding of the music increases because members of one
section learn firsthand what is happening in other sections' parts.
This can have a positive effect on performance due to an increased
level of involvement and understanding by the singers.

Photograph by Thom Ewing.

12. *Be sensitive to students' fatigue and frustration levels and accommodate students' attention spans.* Often, singers will have more difficulty than you expect with a musical problem, and, in an effort to sing the music successfully, choral directors will remain too long on the problem area. Students become frustrated or tired, and will begin to misbehave. This is a definite signal to move to something else and you would be wise to heed it. In a situation such as this, leave the problem unresolved, and tell the singers that you will return to it at the next rehearsal when they are fresh and you have had opportunity to study additional causes and solutions.

13. *Stop.* Often, the level of excitement or the amount of talking during a rehearsal will escalate to such proportions that something must be done to regain control of the choir's attention. Sometimes unconsciously, directors will begin to raise their voices in an effort to be heard, and the louder the choir talks, the louder the director will talk. In a situation like this, nothing productive can be accomplished, and the rehearsal suddenly becomes a shouting match. When this occurs, the most effective way to handle the situation is simply to stop. The singers will not notice for a time, but eventually, they will be aware that the rehearsal is not proceeding. At this time, the director can point out what has happened, and then the rehearsal can continue at a more manageable level.

14. *Be flexible on special day rehearsals.* During the year, various activities such as the homecoming dance, class elections, and football playoffs are going to occur and have the potential to affect the success of choir rehearsals. Rather than fighting against the realities of life in junior high/middle school and high school, be flexible in planning your rehearsal on such days. This is not the time to plan tedious work, because students' minds will not be focused as usual. They will appreciate your acknowledgment of their other interests, and are more likely to cooperate with your plans for the day.

15. *Show care and concern for your students as people and make an effort to know their names.* When choral directors teach large numbers of students every day, knowing the names of all their singers can be a real challenge. This challenge, however, is definitely worth the effort involved. Students will feel important to you and to the

choral program and may behave better in the long run. In addition, calling a student by name is much more humanizing than "Hey, you!," or "you in the red sweater!"

No matter how busy things get, always remember the human factor. Choir directors work with human beings who, in addition to vocal cords and diaphragms, have feelings unique to the human condition. Unfortunately, some directors often find themselves so involved with the music and its preparation for a demanding concert schedule that they may forget their students' needs from time to time.

Opportunities must be provided to nurture human relations between director and choir, and among the choir members themselves, because when singers and director genuinely care about one another, mutual love and respect is created. In addition, a oneness of heart and mind will form that can make a real difference in any musical endeavors.

16. *Establish a reasonable concert schedule.* If directors plan a concert schedule that is too demanding for their singers, genuine musical understanding will often have to take a backseat to learning the music as fast as possible for performance. This is not to suggest that performance hinders learning; quite the contrary, if kept in proper perspective, performance can serve as a showcase for student learning and musical understanding. Kept in balance, performance can also serve as a powerful motivator. When too much stress is placed on performance, however, students and director can find themselves racing from one concert to the next with no time for real learning to take place or for new ideas to be digested. This often causes frustration that can result in behavior problems among the students. They may feel that they are being used to further the reputation of the choir director or the school, and this is not a pleasant or desirable feeling.

Plan a reasonable concert schedule for your choir based on the age and ability of the students, and always consider such things as the length of time available for preparation, and whether any of the selections on the preceding concert can be programmed on any future concerts for different audiences. Often, directors will have to decline an invitation to perform and will be called on to defend their action. Stand firm, and remember, you are the one in charge of the singers' music education. They must not be exploited.

17. *Involve students in leadership roles.* So often, peer pressure is associated with negative influences, but this does not have to be the case. By serving as choir officers or section leaders, students assume partial responsibility for the choir's success, and in this way, can have a positive influence on the musical and social behavior of their fellow singers. This system can be so effective that, often, little or no intervention by the director is necessary. In the process, student leaders have the opportunity to learn valuable life skills such as responsibility, organization, teamwork, and dependability.

18. *Plan for the aesthetic in every rehearsal.* All choirs need to learn and perform correct notes and rhythms, use good breath support, strive for good diction, and use correct vocal technique to produce a beautiful sound. However, the choir director must not stop here. Emphasis on perfecting the technical aspects of the music is simply not enough. To be truly successful, choral ensembles must be led beyond the technical aspects to experience the aesthetic qualities, for this is when music can make the most lasting and pervasive impact. Making beautiful music, even in small portions, will yield satisfaction along the way and provide motivation to persevere. If students are motivated and the musical rewards they are experiencing are deeply felt, their behavior will be focused on maximizing the likelihood of musical success. So plan for the aesthetic (even for a few measures) in every rehearsal, and watch how the power of music can make a positive impact on student behavior.

Summary

Lack of skill and knowledge in the area of behavior management can negate the efforts of even the most talented musicians. Until these partially prepared choral directors acquire the skills necessary to manage their students' behavior in rehearsal, they are likely to experience frustration and their choirs may fall short of musical success.

Understanding the age group with which you work is the first step necessary for building positive behavior patterns in your students. Working successfully with middle school/junior high and high school students requires a knowledge of adolescence, and this knowledge will be reflected in everything you do, including your selection of music, rehearsal plans, teaching strategies, and in your one-to-one relationships with the singers. Adolescence is a powerful force. Teachers who acknowledge this fact and who work *with* their students' characteristics at this age, rather than complain about them, can develop choral programs that are quite successful.

So that their students will like them, new choral directors may be reluctant to do those things that can create and maintain an environment conducive to learning. In situations such as this, students usually misbehave, or they lose respect for the teacher, and eventually, everyone loses. Remember that *discipline takes courage*. Be careful to disapprove of the action and not of the student, work to correct specific misbehavior rather than making broad, general statements, and avoid making empty threats.

The easiest and often most effective way to manage student behavior is through preventive discipline. By structuring the learning environment so that positive behavior patterns are encouraged, this approach attempts to prevent discipline problems from occurring in the first place. Having a clean and pleasant rehearsal hall, involving students in the creation of classroom rules, having an efficient method for handling music, being positive and supportive, maintaining eye contact, and knowing your students' names are just a few of the nonmusical suggestions that have the potential to affect the musical efforts of the choir. Musical suggestions that can impact student behavior (and therefore, their musical success) include studying the music and planning rehearsals, working with the entire choir as much as possible, establishing a reasonable concert schedule, and planning for the aesthetic in every rehearsal.

Mini-Projects

1. Susan, the Choral Librarian, tripped and fell as she walked into her high school choir rehearsal with a large stack of music. The music flew everywhere and, although physically unhurt, Susan was embarrassed and began to cry. How would you handle this situation? Discuss this issue with your classmates.

2. Occasionally doing activities together as a group can nurture human relations between the director and the choir, and among the choir members themselves. Name three inexpensive group activities that junior high/middle school choir students would enjoy. Name three inexpensive group activities that high school choir students would enjoy.

3. Newberry High School is holding its Homecoming Dance this Friday night, and during sixth period, the principal will be announcing the Homecoming Queen. You have a choir rehearsal during sixth period, but you know that any tedious work on the choir's music will be difficult to achieve on this particular day. Taking into account the students' level of excitement and short attention spans, list several activities that *could* be successful. Be creative.

4. Read and study the rehearsal observance form (Figure 9.1). Then make appointments to observe several choral rehearsals directed by different conductors of different age groups. Use the questions on the form to guide your observations, and fill out the form for each visit. Discuss how your answers to the questions are related to the musical success and general behavior of the choirs.

YOUR NAME:_____

DIRECTOR'S NAME:_____

SCHOOL: _____

CHOIR OBSERVED: _____

DATE OF OBSERVATION:_____

1. Was the choir room visually attractive (bulletin boards, posters, free of trash, etc.)?
2. Was the choir room set up neatly for the students before they came in? If not, how did this affect student behavior?
3. How was music handed out? How much time was used?
4. Were announcements given? If so, when? Approximately how much rehearsal time was used?

Figure 9.1 Rehearsal Observance Form. Reprinted by permission of TMEC *Connection*, published by the Texas Music Educators Conference.

5. Generally, was the rehearsal a positive experience? If negative comments were necessary, did the director praise the choir when the problem (social or academic) was corrected?
6. Did the students come to the rehearsal ready to work or did the director have to "pull them together" and focus their attention? If so, how was this done?
7. Did the students' attention/efforts remain fairly consistent throughout the rehearsal or did it sag at any point? If it sagged, *where*, and (in your opinion) *why?*
8. Did the rehearsal end in a positive way? Do you think the choir will look forward to the next rehearsal? Why or why not?
9. How would you describe the rehearsal pacing?
   ___too slow   ___appropriate   ___too fast
10. What percentage of time was used for:
    talking by the director_____
    singing by the choir_____
11. Were warm-ups used? If so, were they strictly used to warm up the voice or did they deal with vocal technique as well? Were they connected to the music that was rehearsed?
12. Was sightreading incorporated into the rehearsal in any way? If so, when and how?
13. How many pieces were rehearsed? Approximately how much time was spent on each piece?
14. Was the order of pieces rehearsed conducive to a good rehearsal? If so, why? If not, why not?
15. Did the director seem to be thoroughly familiar with the music? Did he/she seem to have a rehearsal plan?
16. What percentage of time was used for:
    rehearsing sections of the choir? _____
    rehearsing the entire choir? _____
17. What did the director have the idle sections doing while he or she rehearsed one or two sections of the choir?
18. When repetition was necessary, was it "repetition with a reason"?
19. What was the seating arrangement of the choir?
20. How would you describe the director's overall communication skills (clear, concise directions, well-modulated voice, efficiency, etc.)?
    ___poor   ___fair   ___good   ___excellent
21. Based on your answers to the questions above, give the rehearsal a general score (1 to 10, with 10 being the highest score). This score should reflect your opinion of student and teacher behavior as well as the musical success and effectiveness of the rehearsal.
                  1 2 3 4 5 6 7 8 9 10
Briefly explain your score.

Figure 9.1   Continued

References

ARCHIBEQUE, CHARLENE. (1992). Making rehearsal time count. *Choral Journal, 33*(2), 18–19.

CSIKSZENTMIHALYI, MIHALY. (1987). The pressured world of adolescence. *Educational Horizons, 65*(3), 103–105.

KIMMEL, DOUGLAS C., and IRVING B. WEINER. (1989). *Adolescence: A developmental transition.* Hillsdale, NJ: Laurence Erlbaum Associates.

SELTZER, VIVIAN CENTER. (1989). *The psychosocial worlds of the adolescent: Public and private.* New York: John Wiley & Sons.

TOPP, DALE. (1987). Climbing the ladder: Rehearsing for public performance. *Choral Journal, 28*(2), 25–31.

Additional Reading

CANTER, LEE, and MARLENE CANTER. (1992). *Assertive discipline: Positive behavior management for today's classroom.* Santa Monica, CA: Lee Canter and Associates.

COLLINS, DON L. (1993). *Teaching choral music.* Englewood Cliffs, NJ: Prentice-Hall, Inc.

MADSEN, CHARLES H., and CLIFFORD K. MADSEN. (1983). *Teaching/discipline: A positive approach for educational development.* Raleigh, NC: Contemporary Publishing.

MERRION, MARGARET. (1990). How master teachers handle discipline. *Music Educators Journal, 77*(2), 26–29.

ROGERS, DOROTHY. (1972). *The Psychology of Adolescence,* 2nd ed. New York: Appleton-Century-Crofts.

ROSSMAN, R. LOUIS (compiled by). (1989). *Tips: Discipline in the music classroom.* Reston, VA: Music Educators National Conference.

VANDERVEER, ELIZABETH. (1989). Stopping discipline problems before they start. *Music Educators Journal, 75*(9), 23–25.

10

Vocal Techniques and Musicianship Skills

Mr. Rucker noticed that the sopranos in his middle school mixed chorus were having intonation difficulties in a very high passage from one of their selections. The sound was thin and strained as well as out of tune. However, he had chosen six pieces to perform at a local festival next week, and time was running out. He believed he had to continue pounding the notes so the choir could at least get from beginning to end without having to stop. Why should he have to spend time teaching the basics of good vocal technique anyway? He wasn't a voice teacher, he was the choir director!

Vocal Techniques

In some school districts, private vocal instruction is offered for interested and talented students during the school day. Voice teachers work with choral students on an individual basis to teach and refine good vocal technique as well as to sing quality literature for the solo voice. This fortunate situation can provide a good support system for the choral program by enhancing the overall achievement level of singers. In addition, because students have been introduced to basic vocal technique in their voice lessons, a simple reminder from the choir director during rehearsal to breathe correctly or to use more head voice or to drop the jaw will suffice. This can save valuable rehearsal time.

For most students, however, the choral director will be their voice teacher, and the only vocal instruction they will receive will occur during the choir rehearsal itself. In addition to the preparation of music for performance, therefore, choral directors such as Mr. Rucker need to provide regular and systematic opportunities within the context of the daily rehearsal for young singers to develop their emerging voices. Sufficient time must be devoted to teach them the basic tools of correct vocal production—even if it means a less strenuous performance schedule for the year.

Occasionally, entire rehearsals may be needed to introduce new concepts or to secure a particularly troublesome technique, especially for beginning or intermediate level choirs. During these rehearsals, choral directors will often need a rather creative approach to maintain their students' attention. The most effective approach may be to blend the teaching of vocal technique with the act of music-making. Eight to fifteen minutes, spread out across each rehearsal, can be devoted to development of skills and techniques, followed by their direct application to the music currently in preparation. This way, students can see the connection between the development of technique and its use in singing music rather than viewing the two as separate and distinct entities. In addition, by using a portion of each rehearsal for exercises followed by the rehearsal of music, students will experience a variety of activities, thus promoting opportunity for an increased attention span.

The Voice

Most musical instruments possess a vibrator, a generator, and a resonator. The vibrator sets the air in motion, the generator is the force that sets the vibrator into motion, and the resonator reinforces or multiplies the vibrations. In vocal production, the vocal cords serve as the vibrator, the exhaled breath as the generator, and the resonators include the mouth, pharynx, and nasal cavities.

The voice is perhaps the most personal of all instruments because it is housed within the body. Because each person's physical characteristics are different, no two voices will sound alike, but the fundamentals of good vocal production are the same for everyone.

Correct Posture and Physical Preparation for Singing

Good posture is the most basic tool for correct singing. Because the body serves as the musical instrument for singers, students must be taught that the manner in which they hold their bodies will affect the sound they can produce.

If singers are seated during rehearsal, they must sit with their weight shifted forward such that they could move easily to a standing position (see photo). Feet are flat on the floor, shoulders are back, and the head and chest are up. When using music during rehearsal or performance, students must be encouraged to hold their music up and out so that the head is in alignment, freeing the vocal mechanism to work properly. The back is leaning slightly forward and away from the back of the chair. (Some chairs promote good posture for singing while others do not. If you are fortunate to have chairs specifically designed to promote good posture, your singers can simply sit up straight with their backs against the back of their chairs.)

When singing from a standing position, students must distribute their body weight evenly on both feet, perhaps placing one foot slightly in front of the other for better balance. Knees are never locked or stiff, but are slightly flexed, and the chest is comfortably up. Ask students to imagine their upper torsos being held up by an invisible thread connected to their breast bones. (A reminder during rehearsal to pull up on that thread can improve posture immediately.) The head should never jut forward but rather should be up and in line with the spine, and the ears should be in line with the shoulders. As shown in the photo, the resulting stance is one of reaching out to the listeners with alertness and confidence.

In addition to teaching your students the correct posture for singing, you must encourage the concept that singing is a physical activity. An alertness and intensity (never tension) must be present to be most effective, but the body must be relaxed at the same time! In fact, Gary Mabry (1992, p. 31) states that "the best sound you make is the one you produce when you are most

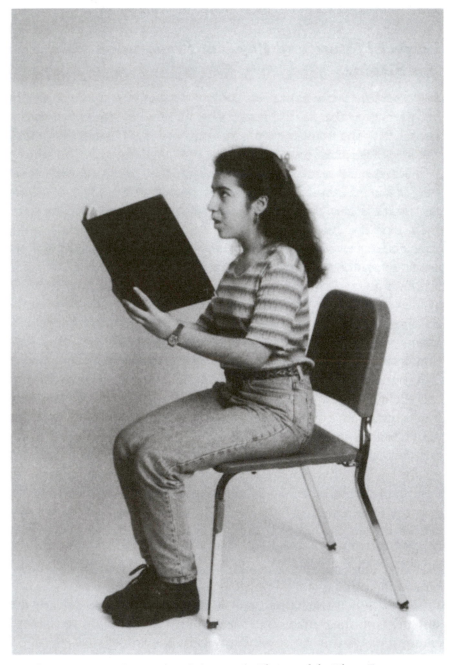

Correct posture for singing while seated. *Photograph by Thom Ewing.*

relaxed." He advocates letting yourself sing rather than making yourself sing.

Used both at the beginning of rehearsal and at any time during

Correct posture for singing while standing. *Photograph by Thom Ewing.*

rehearsal in which tension has become a problem, the exercises shown below can be helpful for relaxation as well as for promoting physical involvement in the singing process:

1. Stretching (with arms extended) upward, downward and to either side
2. Shoulder rolls
3. Lifting both shoulders, trying to touch your ears, and then relaxing
4. Neck rolls (careful not to stretch the head too far backward)
5. Stretching upward on tiptoe, trying to touch the ceiling, and then bend over, going limp like a rag doll
6. Massaging your neighbor's shoulders and neck
7. Bending over at the waist and slowly standing up by straightening the spine one vertebra at a time

Use of Mental Imagery

Evoking everyday sensations and experiences during rehearsal can be helpful when working on vocal techniques. While this chapter contains many exercises to aid in the vocal development of singers at any level, at first glance some of the exercises may not seem appropriate for use with older students. Asking a sophomore in high school to bark like a dog or to laugh like a witch may prove problematic unless your *presentation* of these visual images reflects their maturity. In working with older students, for example, don't actually ask them to bark or laugh; just ask the choir to echo your sounds and then speak with them intelligently about the sensations they felt. If you have developed a good rapport with your singers, they may be more receptive to the idea. If you believe, however, that your choir members would not accept this type of activity, choose a more "mature" exercise from the same list, and save barking like a dog and laughing like a witch for use with younger singers.

Breathing

To produce a good tone, students must be taught to breathe correctly and to manage their breath. Even when singing correctly, however, young singers will have a certain amount of breathiness to their voices. This is normal and should be acceptable. The same amount of audible air in a more mature singer, however, may be indicative of a myriad of problems.

Until taught the correct way, some students may actually breathe backwards. When asked to inhale a deep breath, their chests and shoulders will rise and their abdominal area will pull in. To teach the correct concept of breathing, mention the idea of a balloon and the fact that it gets larger when air is blown into it. The same should be true when a singer inhales correctly. The abdominal area as well as the back should expand as the air is taken in, the chest should not rise but remain comfortably up, and the shoulders should remain stationary.

To experience the activity of the diaphragm, ask several students to lie down on the floor. Being in this position forces the students to use their breathing muscles in the correct way. Now, place a book in the area immediately below their rib cage and ask them to inhale and exhale. Those students who are watching can actually see the breathing muscles in action as the book moves up and down, while those lying on the floor can feel it. After experiencing this correct sensation, they can recall it as they are singing.

The exercises shown below will assist the development of correct breathing technique:

1. Panting like a dog (Haasemann and Jordan, 1991, p. 51)
2. Sniffing
3. Exercises that employ a short rhythmic pattern to be echoed by the singers using consonants such as "f," "s," "ch," and "sh" (Haasemann and Jordan, 1989).
4. Use the rhythm of a familiar song like "Happy Birthday" and have singers perform it on consonants such as "f," "s," "ch," or "sh." For variety, divide the choir into two or three parts and try it as a round (Haasemann and Jordan, 1989).
5. Take in a big breath as though you were sipping the air in through a straw. (Remind students that a balloon gets larger as air is blown into it.) Using a hiss, let the air out slowly. Have a contest to see who can last the longest.

As they are experiencing the activity of their diaphragms, students must be taught that the breath is the only power that should propel the voice. Help from the jaw, the eyebrows, the tongue, the neck, or the shoulders is not only unnecessary but can be detrimental to a pleasant, well-produced tone. This is difficult for young singers to achieve, but, with persistence and patience, it can be accomplished over time.

Exercises that enable singers to feel the breath support propelling the tone include the following:

6. Barking like a dog. Have students make barking sounds like a small dog, then like a big dog. Have them begin at one pitch level (low or high) and while barking, move gradually to the opposite pitch level (Haasemann and Jordan, 1991, p. 86).
7. Bubble exercise. While singing a musical line, students feed an even flow of air through closed lips, causing the lips to vibrate (and the nose and face to itch!). If the lips do not vibrate consistently, the column of air is not consistent. For those who have difficulty relaxing their lips for this exercise, placing the thumb and index finger at the corners of the mouth to press the lips together will help.
8. Tongue trill. Singers sing a musical line while trilling the tongue. Again, a consistent flow of air is necessary for success.
9. Students sing syllables such as "ha," "ho," or "he" in a staccato articulation, making quick pushes from their diaphragms on each note of the exercise.*

Ha   ha   ha   ha   ha

Placement and Resonance

To assist students in making the most beautiful sounds possible, the concepts of placement and resonance must be introduced and rein-

---

* All vocal exercises in this chapter are written in the key of C, and, in most cases, do not contain any repetitions of the exercise at higher or lower pitches. This should in no way suggest that the key of C is the pitch level on which you should begin; rather, it is a presentation of the exercises in a simple format. Each director should decide the starting pitches for each exercise and also determine whether the repetitions of the exercises should ascend or descend (or both).

forced consistently during choir rehearsals. Because each student's physical characteristics are different, however, the end results will vary from singer to singer. Students must learn to utilize their own physical characteristics to full advantage by activating the possibilities for resonance in their voices.

The exercises below will help students understand and experience the resonance potential in their voices:

1. Ask singers to hold the back of one hand over their mouths while humming a pitch. Make sure the lips are closed and the teeth are apart. Slowly move the hand away as they change to "ah" or "oh." Try to keep the humming quality in the sound.

2. Sing a familiar song on "zing," "ming," or "mom"; elongate consonants

3.

8.

zing-a zing-a zoo zing-a zing-a zoo zing-a zing-a-zoo zing-a zing-a-zoo

zing - a   zing - a   zing - a   zing - a   zoo

9.

See _____ ah _____

10.

ng   ee - eh - ah - oh - oo

Register Consistency and Range Extension

Because they are imitating singers heard on the radio and on recordings, many untrained singers will unknowingly exhibit bad vocal habits. The problem encountered most frequently is an almost exclusive use of their chest voices. Consequently, students are often fearful of singing anything "high" because they lack the skills necessary to sing in this range. Good vocal training, using exercises like those listed below, will assist students in discovering the head voice and then in blending it with the chest voice so the two registers can function as a single unit.

These exercises will help beginners to find and use their head voice:

1. With the lips in an "oo" position, sigh from high to low; begin on increasingly higher pitches (Caution: Be certain that breath support is low and the throat is relaxed to avoid closing off the vocal tract.) (Haasemann and Jordan, 1991, p. 87).

2. Laugh like a tiny, thin witch on "hee hee hee," and gradually

move down to the "ha ha ha" of a 300-pound man (Haasemann and Jordan, 1991, p. 51).

3. Make "hooting" sounds like an owl (Haasemann and Jordan, 1991, p. 85).

After they have discovered and experienced this upper register, singers will need to blend it with their chest voice by using exercises that descend from their middle or upper-middle range, moving down by half steps until they have crossed over their break. Using this type of exercise will assist in carrying the head voice down, rather than allowing the chest voice to be brought up. Generally, as the pitch goes down, the singing should become softer and lighter. In addition, having students slowly lift their hands beside their bodies as the vocal line descends may help them make a smoother transition between registers.

These exercises will help students to travel smoothly throughout their entire range:

1. Make a siren noise with the lips in an "oo" position; move up and down in pitch within a gradually expanding range (Haasemann and Jordan, 1991, p. 85).

2. (Note: As the pitch gets lower and lower, change to "bloo" to avoid breaking into chest voice).

blah   blah   blah   blah   blah

3. (Note: Sing at a very fast tempo).

blah blah blah blah blah blah blah blah blah blah blah blah blah blah blah

blah   blah   blah   blah   blah

When working to extend range, create exercises to be sung staccato and fast so that singers won't have time to close off the vocal mechanism in a panic. Several helpful examples are shown here:

4.

doo - bie   do - bie   doo - bie   doo - bie   doo - bie   doo

5. (Note: Vary vowels.)

yah   hah   hah   hah   hah

6. (Note: Vary vowels and, on the top note, have students bend over at their waists. This physical movement will take their minds off the fact that the notes are "high" and will also force them to use their diaphragms correctly.)

yah   hah   hah   hah   hah   hah   hah

7. (Note: Divide the choir in half and have one group sing (a) and one group sing (b). Be careful to tune the octaves!)

(a)

ah _____

(b)

ah _____

8.

mee   ah _____

Flexibility

After students begin to use and blend their head and chest voices with some ease, you will want to devise exercises that continue to encourage flexibility. Flexibility is a skill that enables singers to exe-cute fast runs and leaps as well as to maneuver easily between registers. To avoid tension creeping into the voice during the exercises shown below, suggest that the singers roll their heads slowly and gently in a circular motion. Vocal flexibility and agility depend on a freely produced tone generated by an even flow of breath.

1. (Note: Without stopping the breath, restate a new vowel on every pitch.)

2. (Note: Without stopping the breath, restate a new vowel on every pitch.)

3.

4.

5.

Dynamics

Beginners often have misconceptions about dynamics in music. When asked to sing loudly, their responses will frequently border on yelling, and their soft singing will often be supported by little or no breath. While they need to experience the outermost boundaries of their dynamic range, beginners need to understand that there is a difference between "yelling" and singing a well-supported *forte* tone. In addition, proper support for *piano* passages must be encouraged.

To help singers experience the possibilities within their own dynamic range, you must teach them that dynamics are relative. On the board, write the terms *forte* (f), *mezzo forte* (mf), *mezzo piano* (mp), and *piano* (p). After briefly explaining what each term means, and that the list is in order from loud to soft, have them sing an exercise to discover just how loudly their choir can sing while still producing a pleasant sound with correct breath support. To reinforce the sound and feel of a good *forte*, use several different exercises and revisit them frequently.

To teach the concept of supporting a soft sound, have the choir sing any exercise with a *forte* dynamic. Immediately following, have them sing the same exercise, preparing to sing *forte*, but actually singing with a *piano* dynamic. Rapid alternation between *forte* and *piano* within one exercise will help reinforce the idea that, for both dynamic levels, the amount of support should be the same.

After establishing a good *forte* and *piano* with the choir, use these outer boundaries to work toward producing the other dynamic levels as well as the concept of *crescendo* and *decrescendo*. Insist on good breath support at all times, and always remember that, the younger the choir, the smaller their dynamic range will be. Junior high choirs cannot (and should not be asked to) sing the same *forte* that an adult choir can achieve with ease.

Intonation

Choral directors are known to say "You are flat, basses!," "Sopranos, your notes are sharp!," or "Choir, you are a half step lower now than you were at the beginning of the piece. Why can't you sing in tune?" Choirs need feedback during rehearsal, but the feedback must be more informative than these comments. Why are the basses flat? Why are the sopranos sharp? Why is the choir slipping in pitch? What can be done to fix the problems? Not only must the choir be taught to hear when they are out of tune, but they must also understand what can be done to correct intonation problems—or, even better, to prevent them from ever happening.

Difficulties in intonation can arise from a wide variety of problems, one of which is the environment in which the choir sings. The temperature of the room can affect pitch; usually, the hotter the room becomes, the more the pitch will sag. Make sure the temperature of the rehearsal room and the concert area is regulated for comfort.

The acoustics of the rehearsal or concert hall can affect a choir's intonation. Often, simply moving from the rehearsal hall to the performance area or from one performance area to another can cause problems, especially when the acoustics are radically different from those to which the choir is accustomed. Whenever possible, schedule a rehearsal in the performance area so that the singers can become adjusted to their new acoustical environment. In situations such as these, urge your singers to listen even more carefully than usual.

Students will have difficulty singing in tune whenever they are unable to hear themselves accurately as they sing. Often, a change of standing or seating positions may provide a better arrangement for individuals to hear their own parts in relation to others. Try placing the outer voice parts next to one another to provide more stability, or try singing in a mixed position of quartets or trios. Sometimes just asking a few singers to move to a different position within their own section will improve or alleviate intonation difficulties.

Whether it is from an unusually strenuous rehearsal or because students did not get enough rest the night before, fatigue is known to cause intonation problems. First, the singers' level of concentration will be lower, and, if their minds aren't engaged, they are likely to sing out of tune. Second, because they are tired, students may not possess the energy necessary to sing with proper breath support. In this case, the pitch will sag. On the other hand, because the director continues to ask for better breath support, students may try too hard and begin to overuse their breathing muscles. This will cause tension, and tension often results in sharping. Always plan your rehearsal so that vocal fatigue will not be a problem, but on days when fatigue is an issue, alter your rehearsal plan to accommodate the singers. Remind them that, because their instrument is housed within their bodies, they must take care of their bodies, and this includes getting enough rest.

The wrong choice of literature for your choir can cause intonation problems. Demanding tessituras, extreme dynamic levels, or excessive length are all aspects of a musical selection that may cause a choir to sing out of tune. Simply because they are too young or too inexperienced to be successful with such demands, faulty intonation may occur. Therefore, always consider the age and maturity level of your singers as well as their musical abilities when selecting music for your choir.

When choirs do not sing with unified vowels, their intonation will suffer. The problem is related to the placement of the voice that results in a brighter or darker vowel. Discrepancies can occur among individual singers as well as among the sections of the choir. To provide consistent opportunities for singers to unify their vowels, create warm-up exercises using the five primary vowel sounds. Encourage your singers to really listen, both to themselves and to the singers around them. The exercises shown below will help intonation.

Choirs must be encouraged to tune vertically as well as horizontally, and opportunities for fine tuning and listening must be provided in rehearsal. Vertical tuning refers to the harmonic aspect of the music, while horizontal tuning refers to the melodic character of each individual part. Whether vertical or horizontal, however, singers need to listen very carefully and continually adjust their own voices to the voices of their fellow singers.

To sing in tune horizontally, singers first need to know what each interval sounds like. Repeated practice to sing accurate intervals can make a big difference in a choir's intonation. Taking more generous steps as the melody ascends, and taking smaller steps on the way down is always a helpful rule to follow. The following exercises will assist in horizontal tuning:

Steven Powell (1991, pp. 40–41) states that for choirs to sing in tune harmonically, they should first learn to tune the fundamental harmonic interval, the octave. Once the octaves are in tune, Powell advocates working on fifths, followed by major and minor thirds, sixths, fourths, inversions of the preceding intervals, and finally seconds and sevenths. Create your own harmonic exercises to assist students in vertical listening and tuning. Also helpful is rehearsing out of rhythm any troublesome harmonic sequence in music currently in preparation, allowing the singers enough time to listen carefully and to adjust their own notes for better intonation.

A choir's intonation is likely to suffer when, after weeks and weeks of rehearsal with the piano doubling their parts, they are suddenly asked to sing a piece *a cappella*. The singers may feel like "the rug has been pulled out from under them." Overuse of the piano during rehearsal can promote a real dependency on it. Choir directors must avoid this potential problem by encouraging their singers to discover for themselves the intervals or harmony necessary to perform a piece accurately, with good intonation. This route is definitely the longer, slower route to take, but it is the only route to choose if you want your students to become independent singers.

Intonation problems can also be caused by poor vocal production. Not enough intensity or too much tension can cause flatting or sharping, so the wise choral director is constantly encouraging good vocal habits. Proper posture and breathing technique, correct alignment of the head and body, a relaxed jaw, and a healthy blending of the head and chest voices are just a few aspects that contribute to accurate intonation. No matter what the exercise, always insist on good vocal production.*

Diction

Because the parameters of this text prevent an in-depth study of diction, a few general comments will be made, and a list of books on English, French, Latin, German, and Italian diction will be provided for more thorough reference. A working knowledge of the International Phonetic Alphabet (IPA) is necessary for success in this endeavor.

Because the various sections of the United States have their own

---

*   Several of the exercises listed in this chapter come from Frauke Haasemann and James Jordan (see References). These valuable materials for the choral conductor can be obtained from Hinshaw Music.
Books written for students that include information to help them understand the vocal mechanism and how it works include: *World of Choral Music*, Silver Burdett and Ginn, 1988, pp. 9–27; *Something to Sing About for Young Voices*, G. Schirmer, 1984, pp. 24–28; and *Something to Sing About*, G. Schirmer, 1982, pp. 25–33.

peculiarities in the pronunciation of the English language, different choirs will have certain words that are troublesome to them. Because most beginning singers will want to sing the same way they speak, choral directors need to assist the singers in achieving non-regional diction. First, the director must make students aware of their "accent," and then must demonstrate the correct way to pronounce various words when singing.

For each language, including English, the director must be aware of the correct sounds needed, which articulators are involved, and how they are used to produce each sound. Some modification may be needed at various times because of the differences between solo and choral singing. For example, in a choral setting, the singers may need to exaggerate the open or closed position of a vowel to provide greater unification as well as a clearer understanding, while a soloist has more freedom because he or she does not have to blend with anyone else. For the words "great time," in solo singing you are likely to pronounce both the "t" of "great" and the "t" of "time." However, because the "t" is an explosive consonant, a choir may need to elide the two "t"s to avoid undue attention on the two words that are sung.

No matter what the difficulty, diction can always be at least part of the problem. For example, if the choir is having trouble with intonation, the problem may be that their vowels are not unified. If the tempo is slowing down, the choir may not be singing consonants on time and in a rhythmic fashion. If the tone quality seems harsh, the placement of the voice (resulting in brighter or darker vowels) may be causing the difficulty.

SINGING IN THE ORIGINAL LANGUAGE. Each foreign language text, with its unique sounds, flavor, and word stress, is set to music by the composer, and when the original language is translated into another language, the overall effect of the composition can be changed, sometimes dramatically. For this reason, music should be sung in its original language whenever possible. If, however, you choose to sing a piece that has been translated into English, look carefully to determine that the original meaning of the text is still intact, that the word stress of the English language fits the musical stress, and that the choice of words used does not sound forced or trite.

Deciding whether or not to sing a piece in its original language is often difficult, especially for directors of young choirs. Young singers spend hours to achieve the correct notes and rhythms while working on good vocal production at the same time. To add a foreign language to this task may prove overwhelming to the singers and director alike. However, if the music is carefully chosen to fit the ability level of the choir, and a systematic approach is used to teach the foreign language, young choirs can be successful. In fact, they will often be pleased by the challenge presented to them, and will work hard to meet it.

When choosing a piece to introduce a foreign language to young singers, look for brevity, refrains that have repeated text, or pieces with only a few verses. This will hopefully avoid student frustration during their initial experience with new sounds. Because Latin is a fairly straightforward language to learn, and a large amount of choral music is written in Latin, this may be the place to begin.

A good example of a piece well-suited for introducing young singers to foreign languages is *Psallite* by Michael Praetorius. The composition is brief, containing only twenty-four measures. It begins with eight measures of Latin, which are repeated at the end, and the middle section consists of two short German phrases sung first by the women, then by the men, and then by the entire choir.

BEYOND THE DICTION. Careful and clear delivery of the text is an important part of any vocal or choral performance. Even when the diction is impeccable, however, if the singers do not have an understanding of the text, the performance will be less than it could be. Unfortunately, this is an area that is often neglected. Assuming the singers will relate to the words and their meaning without help or guidance, conductors will sometimes fail to mention the text except for pronunciation purposes.

Early in the rehearsal process, spend time with the text, reading it and discussing it for understanding. Guide students as they discover the connection between the words and the composer's choice of mood, tone color, texture, harmony, melody, form, tempo, and number of voice parts. This study will help the singers build a sensitivity to the words and their meaning, and can provide a real opportunity for them to involve themselves on a deeper level. This involvement can make a big difference in the overall performance of the piece.

Books on Diction

Colorni, Evelina. (1970). *Singers' Italian: A manual of diction and phonetics.* New York: G. Schirmer.

Cox, Richard G. (1970). *The singer's manual of German and French diction.* New York: G. Schirmer.

Grubb, Thomas. (1979). *Singing in French: A manual of French diction and French vocal repertoire.* New York: G. Schirmer.

Hall, William D., ed. (1971). *Latin pronunciation according to Roman usage.* Tustin, CA: National Music Publishers.

Hines, Robert S. (1975). *The singer's manual of Latin diction and phonetics.* New York: Schirmer Books.

Marshall, Madeleine. (1953). *The singer's manual of English diction.* New York: Schirmer Books.

May, William V., and Craig Tolin. (1987). *Pronunciation guide for choral literature (French, German, Hebrew, Italian, Latin, Spanish).* Reston, VA: Music Educators National Conference.

Moriarity, John. (1975). *Diction: Italian, Latin, French, German; the sounds and 81 exercises for singing them.* Boston: E. C. Schirmer.

Pfautsch, Lloyd. (1971). *English diction for the singer.* New York: Lawson-Gould Music Publishers.

Stapp, Marie. *The singer's guide to languages (English, Italian, French, and German).* Published by the author and available from The Music Rack at the San Francisco Conservatory of Music, 1201 Ortega Street, San Francisco, CA 94122.

Uris, Dorothy. (1971). *To sing in English; A guide to improved diction.* New York: Boosey and Hawkes.

Musicianship Skills

Sightreading

Some choral directors believe strongly in the use of hand signals and solfège syllables to teach their students to sightsing. Other directors use the number system, and still others have their singers sing the letter names of the notes. Unfortunately, some choral directors use no system at all, or worse, they completely ignore this vital aspect of music education. If students are not taught how to sightsing, the learning process for every piece of music will be laborious at best, and will likely become frustrating for all concerned. In addition, your students will be only partially prepared for any future musical experiences. Choral directors must meet the challenge of giving every singer a complete music education, including sightsinging!

No matter which method you use, opportunities for students to improve their sightsinging skills must be provided at every rehearsal. Many directors place sightsinging instruction and exercises at the beginning of the rehearsal, after the warm-ups. Unlike the warm-ups that need to be at the beginning, sightsinging exercises are more flexible and can occur at any point during the class period. Especially if you create your own exercises related to music in rehearsal, the logical place to do them is directly before you rehearse the music containing the potential problem. This will also help to vary the routine of a daily rehearsal.

To practice their skills, your students will always need music to sing. A good source of music is a church hymnal that contains hundreds of four-part hymns. Homophonic in texture, most are fairly straightforward, but several can present a challenge, especially harmonically. Before using the hymnals, however, be sure to speak with your principal about your ideas and explain how the hymnbooks will be used. In addition, you would be wise to state a disclaimer before your students' first experience with singing hymns to inform them that you are not advocating any particular religious beliefs, but rather consider these books a collection of music for them to use strictly for sightsinging practice. Because some students may find the hymn texts to be objectionable, you may want to consider always singing on neutral syllables, numbers, or solfège syllables.

Intermediate and advanced choirs will often profit from sightsinging new pieces that they will actually rehearse and perform. If these pieces are beyond their sightsinging abilities, however, asking them to sightread them may cause frustration, risking a negative first impression of the music. A better plan may be to pass out music that is below their performance abilities but that will present an appropriate challenge to their sightsinging abilities. Beginning sightsingers may not be skilled enough to achieve even moderate success in this type of activity, so you will want to carefully select their sightsinging materials. You will want to plan a sequence to ensure success so that student attitudes will remain positive as they work to improve their skills.

Consider this list of activities that can help promote music literacy. Notice that there is an element of fun and competition in most of them.

1. Have a "Melody for the Day" notated on the board for each rehearsal. Occasionally, use a portion from a familiar song and award a "prize" to the student who identifies the song first. The students must do their singing silently, in their heads. If a piece that is currently in rehearsal contains a particularly troublesome interval pattern, include the problem intervals when you compose a melody to sightsing. This activity will provide additional practice for the students as well as show them a connection between sightsinging and the performance of music.

2. Notate one or two measures of rhythm on the board for each rehearsal and have the choir study and then perform them. Sometimes use a troublesome rhythm from a piece that is currently in rehearsal, and have a contest to guess from which composition it comes.

3. Purchase a large-sized deck of cards that are large enough for all singers to see when they are held up in front of the choir. These are sold frequently at party stores. Remove all 9s, 10s, jacks, queens, and kings from the deck, and shuffle the remaining cards well. (The ace will serve as the tonic and the 8 as the octave above). Establish a tonic and instruct the choir to sing first the tonic and then the scale degree of the card that you are holding up. For example, if you turned up a 6 for the first card, the choir would sing the tonic and then the sixth scale degree. Vary the exercise and make it more challenging by asking them to sing the intervals down from high "do."

4. Buy several packs of regular-sized playing cards and remove all 9s, 10s, jacks, queens, and kings. Divide the remaining cards from each deck into four groups of eight cards each. After you have divided the choir into small groups of three to four students each, give each group one set (ace through 8) of the cards. Then have one person in each group shuffle their eight cards and then lay them out, face up, in a straight line on the floor. The resulting arrangement of cards will be the pitches, in order, of their melody. Tell them that their melody is to be four measures of 4/4 time, and they can

use whole, half, quarter, and eighth notes. Each group must decide on a rhythmic scheme that would create four measures of 4/4 time. Allow time for practice, and then have each group sing their melodic creation for the remainder of the choir.

5. Another activity using regular-sized playing cards is to have the small groups lay down two cards at a time. They must sing the resulting interval and then name it. For example, if the leader laid out a 3 and a 5, the group would sing "mi to sol, minor third," or "3 to 5, minor third."

6. Give rhythmic and/or melodic dictation. Compose short examples of approximately four measures each, and sometimes include rhythmic and melodic patterns from music currently in rehearsal. By manipulating the rhythmic and melodic figures, the students are likely to understand the notation better, and their increased understanding will enhance the performance of the music.

7. Hold sightsinging contests between the various sections of the choir. Section leaders can serve as teachers as their group studies their part from the assigned exercise. Have each group sightsing their exercise for the class, and, after listening to each section, choose the group that did the best job. Keep score over a period of time and reward the winning section with some special means of recognition or a special activity.

Many books are available for use in the teaching of sightsinging. Here is a partial list:

1. *The Folk-Song Sight Singing Series* compiled and edited by Edgar Crowe, Annie Lawton, and W. Gillies Whittaker, published by Oxford University Press, 1969. This series consists of ten books of folk tunes from many countries and are carefully graded for use in schools.
2. *Patterns of Sound* by Joyce Eilers Bacak and Emily Crocker (in two volumes) published by Hal Leonard, 1988.
3. *Successful Sight Singing* by Nancy Telfer, published by Neil A. Kjos Music Company, 1992, 1993. This series consists of Books 1 and 2 with a Teacher's Edition available.
4. *Sing Choral Music at Sight* by Tom Anderson, published by the Music Educators National Conference, 1992. This book has accompanying reproducible master sheets for almost 200 exercises for students to study, sing, and master.

5. *Vocal Connections* by Ruth Whitlock, published by Southern Music Company, San Antonio, TX 78292, 1990. These materials consist of a Teacher's Kit with permission to make transparencies of grids and exercises for classroom use only; optional hard copies for each student are available as well as two audio lessons on tape.

6. *Essential Musicianship* by Emily Crocker and John Leavitt, published by Hal Leonard, 1995, 1996. Available are student texts and a teacher's edition in four levels designed to teach vocal technique, theory, and sightreading skills. They can be used separately or in conjunction with the Essential Repertoire books from the same series; objectives based on the National Standards for Arts Education.

Ear Training

Developing your singers' aural skills is a critical and important part of their choral and vocal training. Good aural skills will help in such areas as intonation, blend, balance, and sightreading, and can do much to develop confident and independent singing in your choir members. Unfortunately, this part of their training is often hindered by a dependence on the piano due to its overuse during rehearsal. Rehearsing without the aid of a piano is definitely more difficult, and initially, may be the longer route to take, but over time, and especially after certain basic skills have been mastered, you and your students will notice that music is learned much faster and with less tedious rehearsal time than before. In addition, your choir's intonation and blend are likely to improve because students have been challenged to listen and to think more carefully.

Whenever possible, therefore, rehearse *a cappella*, and when singers ask you to play their part for them, respond "No, but I will play it with you," or, better still, "No, but I will help you to work it out." Help them to isolate problem intervals or point out important patterns of notes for them, or guide them to discover why a particular passage is troublesome by looking at the other vocal parts or accompaniment that surround it.

During warm-up exercises, ask the accompanist not to play the exercise itself with the choir, but to use the piano only to establish the new key as the exercise ascends or descends by half steps. Not only will the singers have to listen more carefully, but you will be able to hear their problems or successes more readily. Rather than always ascending or descending by half steps, occasionally move the exercise by whole steps, or randomly choose a new key for each repetition of the exercise. This practice will encourage choir members to remain alert—both mentally and aurally.

Additional ideas for developing aural skills in your singers are shown below:

1. Often, just by saying the word "listen," the choir will be reminded to use their ears, and their tone quality, blend, and balance will improve immediately.
2. Experiment with various seating arrangements so that choir members will hear other parts or different voices singing the same part around them.
3. While the choir is sustaining a three- or four-part chord, ask them to listen carefully to all voices around them as they turn slowly in a full circle.
4. While sustaining a three- or four-part chord, ask one section at a time to move either up or down by half or whole steps. Repeat this practice as the choir experiences singing many unusual chords in many different keys.
5. Choose a pitch that can be sung in octaves by both men and women, and that lies in a comfortable place in the middle of the range. Do the following exercise, varying the intervals sung, both up and down:

5a.   Minor Second

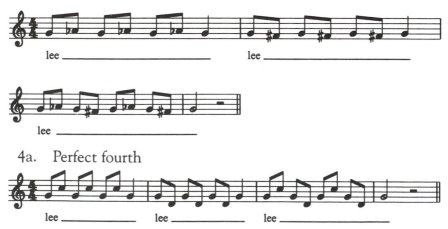

4a.   Perfect fourth

6. Before singing a piece of music, have the choir sing an arpeggio in the key and then have them sing their first pitch. This will not only establish tonality for the singers, but also will show the relationship to the tonic of each section's initial pitch.

Movement

Using physical activities in rehearsal can extend students' attention spans, wake up a lethargic choir, deepen your singers' level of involvement in the music, and provide opportunities for pent-up energy to be spent in constructive rather than destructive ways. In addition, using movement brings another dimension to learning by making tangible that which the singers cannot see as they sing. Through physical sensation, choir members may be able to understand better any musical concepts that are confusing to them.

For example, if your choir is having difficulty achieving a legato line, ask them to stomp the beat as they walk in a circle while singing the piece. This experience will illustrate what they are doing incorrectly. Then ask them to walk the beat while concentrating on the time and space *between* beats as they sing the piece again. They will likely begin a gliding motion. Their physical movement will produce musical results, and the singers are likely to understand what it is that they are to do to achieve a legato line. So that they will ultimately produce the desired musical results without movement, repeat this experience often until they can remember what it feels and sounds like.

If the singers are having difficulty reaching an unusually high note, have them throw an imaginary baseball as they sing the high note. This physical movement will enhance the amount of energy they use. Another way to help students reach high notes with ease is to ask them to bend over from the waist as they sing the top note. Rather than causing them to close off the vocal mechanism by thinking how high the note is, this contrary movement will help them concentrate on singing properly, and the bent-over position will force them to use their diaphragms in the correct manner.

Additional ideas for using movement in rehearsal include:

1. If phrasing is a problem, ask the singers to move their arms in an arc to illustrate the phrasing for their part. Another helpful

Using the arms to show the shape of a musical phrase. *Photograph by Thom Ewing.*

activity for phrasing is to have them pull an imaginary rubber band or piece of taffy.

2. To deepen the choir's involvement in and understanding of a selection, have half the choir (if space permits) move creatively as the remainder sings the piece. Reverse the process so all will have the opportunity to move.

3. To enhance your singers' emotional portrayal of their music, divide the choir into pairs and ask them, as they sing, to use facial expressions and arm gestures to portray the mood of the piece. Insist that they look each other in the eye as they sing.

4. To feel the two strong beats in 6/8 meter, ask the choir to sway from side to side to the beat as they sing.

5. If flatting on descending passages is a problem, have the singers raise their arms slowly as they sing the notes that descend.

The preceding suggestions regarding the use of movement in rehearsal are only the beginning. Ideas are limitless, so use your creativity to enhance the musical learning and understanding of your choir members.

Summary

Within the confines of the choir rehearsal, sufficient time must be devoted to teach correct vocal production and good musicianship skills. This instruction should be provided daily and in a systematic fashion, especially for beginning singers, even if it means a less strenuous performance schedule for the year. Designing exercises and activities that are related to the music in rehearsal will be an efficient use of time, and will teach students that a connection exists between development of technique and its use in performance.

Correct posture and good breathing technique and management are the most basic tools to be taught for correct singing. Helping students further in the areas of placement, resonance, register consistency, range extension, and flexibility will ensure that they are producing the best sounds possible. Dynamic possibilities must be explored and experienced, and, so that the choir will sing with good intonation, the reasons for out-of-tune singing must be discovered and corrected.

When singing in English, students must be assisted in achieving nonregional diction. Because the unique sounds, flavor, and word stress of a foreign language are an integral part of the entire composition, music should be sung in its original language whenever possible. For young singers, Latin may be the place to begin because the sounds are fairly straightforward, and the rules are few.

Students must be challenged to go beyond the clear and careful delivery of the text to a complete understanding of the words they are singing. In addition, helping them to discover the connection between the text and the composer's choice of mood, tone color, texture, harmony, melody, form, tempo, and number of voice parts will provide a real opportunity for involvement on a deeper level.

A deeper involvement can also be encouraged through the use of movement in rehearsal. Engaging the physical side of learning may help choir members understand musical concepts that are confusing to them by making tangible that which the singers cannot see as they sing. In addition, the use of movement can extend students' attention spans, wake up a lethargic choir, and provide opportunities for pent-up energy to be spent in constructive rather than destructive ways.

Sightsinging and ear training cannot be ignored in the total education of singers. Perhaps more important than the method chosen is the opportunity, provided daily and in a systematic fashion, for these skills to develop within the choir rehearsal. Learning to sightsing will help your students learn their music faster and with less frustration, and good aural skills will help in such areas as intonation, balance, blend, and sightsinging. This broadened instructional process will develop musicians who are knowledgeable, confident, and independent singers.

Mini-Projects

1. Visit several local choir rehearsals and observe the amount of time devoted to vocal technique. How did the directors improve their choir's sound within a group setting?

2. Write at least four exercises to help in each of the areas of placement and resonance, register consistency and range extension, flexibility, and dynamics. In each area, make two of the exercises suitable for middle school/junior high singers, and two of the exercises appropriate for high school singers.

3. Make a list of four exercises and/or activities to be used in a choir rehearsal to improve intonation problems.

4. Select two contrasting pieces of music that are unfamiliar to you. Read aloud the text for each piece and decide on the meaning. What mood(s) are portrayed by the words that may suggest ideas for musical interpretation?

5. Choose one of the pieces from Mini-Project No. 4, and, using the International Phonetic Alphabet, write out the pronunciation of each word of the text.

6. List several ideas for using movement to solve musical problems in the rehearsal.

References

HAASEMANN, FRAUKE, and JAMES JORDAN. (1991). Group vocal technique. Chapel Hill, NC: Hinshaw Music.

————. (1989). Group vocal technique: A video tape. Chapel Hill, NC: Hinshaw Music.

————. (1992). Group vocal technique: The vocalise cards. Chapel Hill, NC: Hinshaw Music.

Mabry, Gary. (1992). Head position and vocal production. *Choral Journal*, 33(2), 31.

Powell, Steven. (1991). Choral intonation: More than meets the ear. *Music Educators Journal*, 77(9), 40–43.

Additional Reading

ALT, DAVID. (1990). Misunderstanding breath support for singers. *Choral Journal*, 30(8), 33–35.

ANDERSON, TOM. (1992). *Sing choral music at sight*. Reston, VA: Music Educators National Conference.

CALDWELL, J. TIMOTHY. (1995). *Expressive singing: Dalcroze eurhythmics for voice*. Englewood Cliffs, NJ: Prentice-Hall.

CARLSON, STANLEY A. (1993). Want the boys in your middle-school choir? *Choral Journal*, 33(9), 27–29.

CHERNIN, MALLORIE. (1993). Vowel modification made easy. *Choral Journal*, 34(2), 31–32.

COMBS, RONALD, and ROBERT BOWKER. (1995). *Learning to sing non-classical music*. Englewood Cliffs, NJ: Prentice-Hall.

DOSCHER, BARBARA M. (1991). Exploring the whys of intonation problems. *Choral Journal*, 32 (4), 25–30.

FEDER, ROBERT J. (1990). Vocal health: A view from the medical profession. *Choral Journal*, 30(7), 23–25.

GARRETSON, ROBERT L. (1990). The singer's posture and the circulatory system. *Choral Journal*, 30(9), 19–22.

GILES, MARTHA MEAD. (1991). Choral reading built on the basics. *Music Educators Journal*, 77(6), 26–29.

MARVIN, JAMESON. (1991). Choral singing, in tune. *Choral Journal*, 32 (5), 27–33.

Movement in the middle school choral rehearsal (video). (1992). Reston, VA: Music Educators National Conference.

PFAUTSCH, LLOYD. (1994). *Choral therapy: Techniques and exercises for the church choir*. Nashville: Abingdon Press.

TELFER, NANCY. (1993). Sight-singing in the choral rehearsal. *Choral Journal, 34*(1), 39–40.

WOLVERTON, VANCE D. (1989). The high school choral director as voice teacher. *Choral Journal, 29*(9), 23–26.

CHAPTER 11

The Changing Voice

As Ms. Nichols' fifth period middle school choir hurried into the choir room, several boys raced to the piano to check whether their voices had dropped in pitch since the last time they had checked. Ms. Nichols found that Ken, an eighth grader, had gained a few lower notes and would probably be moving to the baritone section. Juan, a seventh grader, was extremely excited to discover that he would finally be moving into the cambiata section. Because the high notes of the soprano part had become difficult to sing comfortably, Ann asked if she could try singing alto for a while.

After making the appropriate changes, Ms. Nichols wondered what she was going to do about the music the choir was preparing for the spring contest, now only one week away. Ann, Ken, and Juan had served as strong leaders in their former choir sections, and there was very little time for these singers to learn the notes for their new voice parts. Oh, she thought, the joys of teaching at the middle school level!

No issue in choral music education can be quite so exciting and unsettling at the same time as the phenomenon of the changing voice. Because it is an important rite of passage, most boys eagerly anticipate their voice change, yet the process of changing can be filled with many frustrating and embarrassing moments for them.

Girls' voices change, too, and the process they experience can fill young female singers with confusion and self-doubt.

Choral directors and voice teachers who work with singers whose voices are changing encounter many challenges and learn quickly that the only thing on which they can count with any confidence is *change*! Singers at this stage of development have been jokingly called vocal chameleons; therefore, teachers of this age group must be very flexible, and must possess an incredible amount of knowledge concerning what is happening to their singers during the transition from childhood to adulthood. This knowledge and flexibility can make a real difference in the musical success of the individual singers and their choral ensembles, as well as in the young singers' continued interest in singing and their attitude toward music in general for the remainder of their lives.

The middle school/junior high school level can serve as a pivotal point where students, based on their experiences, will decide whether or not to continue in choral music for the future. If the singers encounter a successful and fulfilling experience led by a knowledgeable and understanding director, they are likely to anticipate with great eagerness their choral participation in high school and beyond. On the other hand, if they are met with a well-meaning director who has limited knowledge about adolescent vocal development, they are likely to experience frustration, limited musical success, and may decide that continued participation in choir is not what they want to do. Irvin Cooper, a well-known researcher in this area, stated quite strongly that the problem in junior high school choral music is not the child's but rather, is due to the teacher's lack of understanding or misunderstanding of early adolescent voices (Cooper and Kuersteiner, 1970, p. 16). Therefore, teachers of adolescent singers have a real responsibility to inform themselves regarding the care and development of changing voices so that musical success can occur, and so that their students will want to continue singing in the future.

Signs of a Change

Vocal mutation, or voice change, is directly related to the many changes that occur during the period of adolescence called puberty.

Occurring most often during the middle school/junior high school years but sometimes earlier or later, adolescents experience many physical changes, including rapid growth spurts in both height and weight, and their primary sex organs begin their maturation process. This process triggers the appearance of such secondary sexual characteristics as growth of facial and pubic hair in males, and a broadening of the hips and breast development in females. The boy's larynx grows both in length and in the antero-posterior direction (front to back), resulting in the appearance of the "Adam's apple." Their vocal cords lengthen by one centimeter and become much thicker than the female's, allowing for a lower, fuller sound. The girl's larynx grows in length as well, but not so much in width, and their vocal cords grow in length by 3–4 millimeters (Barresi, 1986).

To determine whether their singers are experiencing vocal mutation, choral directors need to look for signs of physical maturity, listen for changes in range and tessitura, and look *and* listen for any evidence of vocal strain in their students. In his research, John Paul Johnson (1981) found that an exclusively aural determination of tessitura range may not be as effective as a visual and aural determination, because the eye can detect signs of tension and strain that may not be so apparent in the sound. Tightening the muscles in the neck, raising the chin and jutting the jaw forward to reach higher notes, and dropping the head down in an attempt to sing lower notes just outside their singing range are all indications that vocal strain is present. These singers need immediate attention so that they might be evaluated and possibly reassigned to another section of the choir. In addition, they will need to be reminded and encouraged to practice healthy vocal habits.

Female Voice Change

Lynn Gackle (1991), a researcher in the area of changing voices, has focused her research on the adolescent *female* voice. She cites a dearth of information and research in this area, possibly because the changing process for girls is not nearly so noticeable as it is for boys. Although it may be less dramatic, a voice change does occur.

Gackle (1991, p. 21) describes the female voice change as "shades of change," suggesting that the overall sound of a treble voice remains intact, but the richness, depth, and warmth will change. She cautions choral directors and voice teachers against classifying girls' voices at this age as sopranos or altos but rather as "light soprano" or "rich soprano." Equal-voiced music, or music in which the ranges for all voice parts are very similar, is a wise choice for changing female voices. In addition, she suggests that the girls be encouraged to switch parts as long as the ranges are comfortable. This practice may also result in increased musical independence.

Characteristics that may indicate the female voice change during adolescence include voice cracking, hoarseness, increased breathiness and huskiness to the sound, uncomfortable singing or difficulty in phonation, a lowering of the speaking fundamental frequency, the development of noticeable registers, and a fluctuating tessitura that may cause the adolescent girl to become uncomfortable when singing the voice part she has sung with ease and pleasure in the past (Gackle, 1991, p. 18). Because the fluctuations are sporadic and unpredictable, Gackle suggests that a change in voice part can be helpful, but may be necessary only for a short time. In addition, she advocates that vocalization continue throughout the vocal range, avoiding strain in both the upper and lower portions.

Figure 11.1 shows adolescent female voice ranges and tessituras, and Figure 11.2 shows the lift points found at various stages of the female voice during adolescence reported by Gackle (1991, pp. 23–24).

According to Anthony Barresi's research and experience, the voice change for females occurs in two stages. In Stage 1, "the vocal range narrows slightly and the tone quality becomes rather thin,

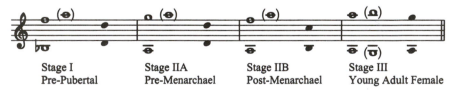

Stage I	Stage IIA	Stage IIB	Stage III
Pre-Pubertal	Pre-Menarchael	Post-Menarchael	Young Adult Female

Figure 11.1   Adolescent female vocal ranges and tessituras (Gackle)

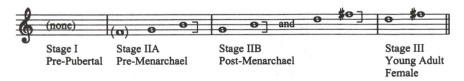

Stage I	Stage IIA	Stage IIB	Stage III
Pre-Pubertal	Pre-Menarchael	Post-Menarchael	Young Adult Female

Figure 11.2   Adolescent female lift points (Gackle)

somewhat colorless, and husky or breathy" (Barresi, 1986). In Stage 2, the chest voice emerges due to the growth and strengthening of the laryngeal muscles and cartilage. As the process continues for females, the huskiness gradually disappears and vocal agility improves, and by the eleventh grade, lift points appear. For sopranos, the lift point occurs at approximately e^2, while for altos, the lift point is approximately b^1.

Barresi agrees with Gackle that the change for females is mainly a change in quality; therefore, referring to these young singers as Treble 1 and Treble 2 rather than as soprano and alto makes more sense. For all females, regardless of voice classification, vocalization throughout their entire range should continue. Refer to Figure 11.3 for the ranges and tessituras reported by Barresi (1986) for female voices during vocal mutation.

| Stage 1 | Stage 2 |

Figure 11.3   Adolescent female vocal ranges and tessituras (Barresi)

Male Voice Change

Boys have a much more dramatic experience when their voices change, and, possibly for this reason, research in the area of the male changing voice is quite extensive. The knowledge is varied, however, and experts often disagree. In fact, in the latter part of the nineteenth century, a major controversy ensued over whether boys' voices, throughout their voice change, should be exercised at all (Cooksey, 1977a, p. 5). After much discussion over the years, this theory was gradually abandoned in favor of singing through puberty under the guidance of competent teachers who encourage healthy vocal production and who are knowledgeable about the changing voice. Furthering discussion among music educators in the early 1950s and 1960s in America, three men and their theories of the changing voice emerged. These three pedagogues were Irvin Cooper, Duncan McKenzie, and Frederick Swanson, and the results of their research and vast experience are summarized here.

Irvin Cooper's approach to the changing voice refers to a boy's

Photograph by Thom Ewing.

voice in the first stage of change as a *cambiata* (plural: *cambiate*) voice; thus, his approach is frequently called the cambiata plan or concept. According to Cooper's research and through many years of practical experience with adolescent male voices, the majority of boys will enter the process of the first change in grade seven, although the process can begin earlier or later for some. The cambiata voice has a distinctive quality and must be controlled in volume to avoid a strident sound. This first stage of change can last from a few months to several years, and Figure 11.4 shows the range and tessitura that can be expected (Cooper, 1970, pp. 18–19):

Figure 11.4   Cambiata range and tessitura (Cooper)

Cooper (1970, p. 22) found that voices in the cambiata stage can often give the aural illusion of sounding an octave lower than is actually the case, and, therefore, voice classification is frequently incorrect. He suggested that the cambiata voice be heard in comparison to a known bass or baritone singer so that an accurate assessment can be made.

Frequently, after an active summer when strenuous demands are often made on the boy's voice, the cambiata voice changes to baritone. The new baritone has very little agility, and these singers will have difficulty executing rapidly moving notes and wide intervallic leaps. Cooper was quick to point out that these new baritones must not be considered as an adult tenor or bass voice. Figure 11.5 shows the baritone range and tessitura of adolescent voices (Cooper, 1970, p. 18–19):

Figure 11.5   Baritone range and tessitura (Cooper)

Cooper believed that range and tessitura are the most important aspects to be considered when selecting repertoire for choirs with changing voices. He warned that the changing voices should not be made to fit the music selected, but rather, the music should be selected to fit the boys. Additional concerns are (Cooper, 1970, pp. 58–63):

1. Choose music with interesting parts for all voices. Nothing is as boring to a middle school/junior high singer as a part that only provides harmony for a melodic line.
2. Pay close attention to difficult intervallic leaps. Boys lose agility as their voices change, and wide leaps, especially those that require a register change, will be difficult for them to execute.
3. Check the articulation speed required to sing the music. Sopranos are fairly flexible, but cambiate move slower, and baritones move the slowest of all.
4. Choose quality music with texts that will appeal to young singers.*

Duncan McKenzie's approach to the male changing voice is often called the alto-tenor plan. The alto-tenor voice is still an alto, but the voice has lowered sufficiently so that the young singer can sing in the tenor range. In his book, *Training the Boy's Changing Voice* (1956), McKenzie stated that the voice change is a gradual process, and that all boys, whether destined to be adult basses or tenors, will pass through each stage of vocal mutation. The stages and their ranges advocated by McKenzie (1956, p. 30, 32) are shown in Figure 11.6.

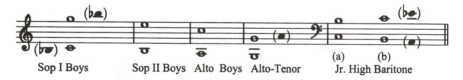

Sop I Boys   Sop II Boys   Alto Boys Alto-Tenor   (a)   (b)
                                                          Jr. High Baritone

Figure 11.6   Vocal ranges and tessituras (McKenzie)

* Don L. Collins (1993, pp. 151–52), a choral educator and former student of Irvin Cooper, established the Cambiata Vocal Institute of America in 1979, which has as its purpose to disseminate widely the philosophy and methodology of the cambiata concept to those who teach vocal music to adolescents as well as to university personnel in charge of music education. The address for this organization is 1806 Bruce Street, Conway, AR 72032. The Cambiata Press publishes music written specifically for choirs with changing voices. The address for this specialty publishing company is P. O. Box 1151, Conway, AR 72032, or contact them by using this toll-free number: 1-800-643-9967.

When a boy's voice changes rather quickly, McKenzie's plan suggests that this voice will become a bass. If the voice change is slower, this usually indicates a tenor. He also stated that some voices will actually move upward in pitch once they have attained their lowest notes (McKenzie, 1956, p. 28).

McKenzie (1956, p. 34) believed that using vocal exercises to move the voice downward helps develop the lower notes and causes the higher notes to disappear. He warned, however, against forcing the low notes, and advocated that boys always sing in their most comfortable ranges throughout their voice change, avoiding both the top and bottom extremes of their ranges. To help develop the emerging lower voice, vocal exercises that descend are helpful.

In his book, *Music Teaching in the Junior High and Middle School* (1973, p. 188), Dr. Frederick J. Swanson reported on his study of 82 boys, where, in a sizeable number of cases, he found that their voice change was rapid rather than gradual. For a significant number of boys, "areas of silence" developed between the bass tones and the treble tones where the young singers had blank spots or notes that they will not be able to produce. To aid in smoothing out the shift between the intact treble notes and the emerging lower notes, Swanson, like McKenzie, suggested descending exercises to help merge these two registers. Descending exercises allow for the head voice to be carried downward rather than for the chest voice to be carried upward.

Swanson (1973, pp. 194–99) stressed the importance of choosing appropriate literature for boys whose voices are changing. The range and especially the tessitura must be suitable for the singers, allowing them to sing only that which is comfortable for them without any strain whatsoever. The text must be one that they will find masculine and appealing. He suggested that teachers develop their arranging skills when teaching this age so that they can craft music specifically for their own choir members and their requirements. He strongly advocated that separate choirs be offered for boys so that their individual needs might be met more easily. Figure 11.7 shows the ranges advocated by Swanson (1961, pp. 63-66).

Although their views do not always agree, Swanson, McKenzie, and Cooper have provided music educators with a wealth of infor-

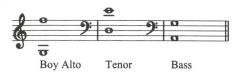

Figure 11.7   Vocal ranges (Swanson)

mation. Drawn from their own research and years of experience, these pioneers created a necessary awareness regarding the changing voice. Their valuable research has been continued more recently in the work of John Cooksey, Anthony Barresi, Terry Barham and Darolyne Nelson, and Lynn Gackle.

In the *Choral Journal* (October 1977 through January 1978), the American Choral Directors Association published a series of four articles on the changing voice by John Cooksey. In Part I, Cooksey presents a brief history of the male changing voice, focusing on the work of Irvin Cooper, Frederick Swanson, and Duncan McKenzie. In Parts II–IV, the author reviews additional research, and then presents and explores his own contemporary, eclectic theory for the training and cultivation of the junior high school male changing voice. Highlights from these articles as well as from his more recent book, *Working with the Adolescent Voice*, are presented here.

From his research and experience, Cooksey found that vocal mutation is directly related to the physiological and psychological changes that occur in the adolescent male. He believes that the boys should be fully informed about these changes so that their voice change can become an adventure rather than a nightmare for them.

He believes that vocal mutation occurs most dramatically in the eighth grade for a majority of boys and tapers off considerably by the middle of the ninth grade. Less noticeable are the beginning signs of voice change, usually occurring in the seventh grade. The male voice changes in specific developmental stages, but the *rate* of change for each boy will vary. For example, in any one grade level, you can find boys in any of the first four stages of vocal mutation. Regardless of which stage of change the singers are in, however, work with changing voices should always begin with each boy's comfortable, middle singing range.

Cooksey (1992, p. 10) divides the process of vocal mutation into

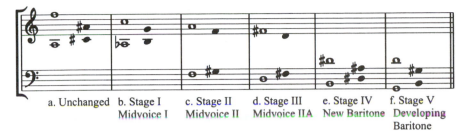

| a. Unchanged | b. Stage I Midvoice I | c. Stage II Midvoice II | d. Stage III Midvoice IIA | e. Stage IV New Baritone | f. Stage V Developing Baritone |

Figure 11.8   Vocal ranges and tessituras (Cooksey)

six different stages, the ranges and tessituras of which are shown in Figure 11.8.

Cooksey (1992, p. 13) found that the boy's speaking voice pitch averages about two to three half steps above the lowest pitch of his singing voice range, then gradually changes to four to six half steps above in the postmutational stage. This information can be helpful in classifying voices correctly. Individual voice testing should be done at least every six to eight weeks so that the choir director will be aware of each boy's range and tessitura as well as other factors including posture, breath control, dynamic capabilities, and pitch agility.

Cooksey believes that voice types are not produced by increased training but, rather, voice types are predetermined genetically, so he warns against trying to "create" a tenor, baritone, or bass voice. He also believes that boys should not have intensive private voice training until their voices have "settled." This view is supported by laryngologists and speech pathologists (Cooksey, 1977b, p. 8).

Cooksey urges the choral music profession to demand that quality music be written with the challenges of the changing voice in mind. This literature must accommodate the boy's voice at every stage of change, especially in the demands of range/tessitura, frequent and sudden register changes, rhythmic agility, dynamics, and breath control (Cooksey, 1977b, p. 16).

In their brief but informative book, *The Boy's Changing Voice: New Solutions for Today's Choral Teacher,* Terry J. Barham and Darolyne L. Nelson state that they have based many of their ideas on Cooksey's research. From their own extensive testing and experience with changing voices, however, the authors have reduced Cooksey's six categories of the changing voice to four categories

Treble Cambiata I Cambiata II Baritone

Figure 11.9   Vocal ranges (Barham and Nelson)

with slightly different ranges (Barham and Nelson, 1991, p. 7); these categories are shown in Figure 11.9.

Barham and Nelson advocate the testing of all boys' voices individually at least every six to eight weeks during the school year, and suggest the following method of testing:

1. Test the boys in a room that is separate from the girls.
2. Have each boy say "Hello" and notate their spoken pitches on a chalkboard. Make sure that these pitches are labeled with the boys' names. (Their spoken pitches will lie near the bottom of their singing range and will help in deciding their voice category.)
3. Give each boy a copy of the four categories of the changing voice so they will know where they fit into the process of vocal mutation.
4. Ask each boy to sing the following exercise (Figure 11.10) to determine the upper limits of his vocal range. Using the boy's speaking pitch as the tonic, move up by half-steps until signs of vocal strain indicate that the highest notes have been reached. For each boy, notate this pitch above his speaking pitch on the chalkboard.

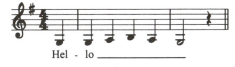

Hel - lo _____

Figure 11.10

5. Beginning with each boy's speaking pitch and then descending by half-steps, use the following exercises (Figure 11.11) to locate the lower limits of each boy's voice. For each boy, notate this pitch. Praise him on some aspect of his singing

Hel - lo _____

Figure 11.11

that you heard during the testing procedure (Barham and Nelson, 1991, pp. 9–10).

Barham and Nelson (1991, p. 11) advocate creating a safe environment for boys with changing voices. To aid in the development of a positive self-image, the boys should be informed about the process of vocal mutation. Girls can provide moral support for their male peers if they, too, are informed. Keeping a wall chart so that each boy's progress is visible may encourage male camaraderie and support. In a mixed choir, be sensitive to what terminology you use for the unchanged male voices. "Treble I" and "Treble II" may be more easily received than "Soprano I" and "Soprano II," because the boys know that the soprano part is sung by girls! Where you physically place your unchanged male voices can make a big difference in their morale as well. Boys who are still singing treble parts should never be placed within a section of girls, but rather at the edge of their section right next to a boys' section. This way, they are likely to feel more comfortable.

Anthony Barresi (1986) defines the process of vocal mutation as the transformation of a child's voice into a voice that *approximates* that of an adult. He agrees with other experts that the stages of change for both males and females are predictable, but the age at which the change begins and the rate of change vary for each student.

Vocal mutation happens most often during the ages of 11 to 13 as pubertal changes become visually apparent. Evidence that a boy's voice is beginning to change first appears in his speaking voice; sometimes, the lowering of the speaking voice can precede a change in the singing voice by three months.

Figure 11.12 shows the various stages of male vocal mutation as well as the range and tessitura for each stage (Barresi, 1986). Stage 1 is often called "boy alto," and Stage 2 is comparable to the cambiata category or the alto–tenor voice. Stage 2A is a brief stopping place between Stages 2 and 3, and Stage 3 is the post-

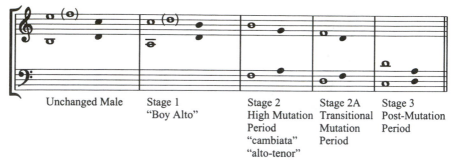

Unchanged Male	Stage 1	Stage 2	Stage 2A	Stage 3
	"Boy Alto"	High Mutation Period "cambiata" "alto-tenor"	Transitional Mutation Period	Post-Mutation Period

Figure 11.12 Vocal ranges and tessituras (Barresi)

mutational period from which adult tenors and basses will eventually emerge.

In 1986, Barresi created an informative videotape entitled *Barresi on Adolescent Voice*. Included in this presentation is an overview of the process of vocal mutation, vocal changes associated with puberty, Barresi's stages of voice change, and tips on vocal training for voices in the process of change. A real highlight of the video is when seven young singers (two female and five male) illustrate the various characteristics and difficulties encountered during each stage of vocal mutation. To hear the vocal problems that occur when the singers were asked to sing outside their comfortable singing range is especially enlightening. Choral directors of singers with changing voices can certainly benefit from viewing these demonstrations.*

Choosing Music for Changing Voices

Remembering all the vocal characteristics presented in this chapter, choral directors must choose carefully the literature their singers will rehearse and perform. By choosing appropriate literature, a myriad of problems will be solved before the first rehearsal even begins, and successful singing can be achieved. Conversely, if music is chosen carelessly for adolescent choirs, no amount of hard work and dedication on the part of the singers or the director can create musical success. The choice of music is just that critical.

* *Barresi on Adolescent Voice* is available from: The University of Wisconsin-Madison, 726 Lowell Hall, 610 Langdon St., Madison, WI 53703; (608) 263-6322

Photograph by Thom Ewing.

A very high degree of musical success can be achieved at the middle school/junior high school level if the music chosen falls within range parameters that accommodate the potential of boys' and girls' changing voices. First and foremost, examine closely the range and especially the tessitura of the music. Check carefully when considering music written for adult voices (SATB). The range for the tenors and basses may be appropriate but the tessitura may be too high or, more likely, too low. And if the music you are considering falls under the broad umbrella of music written for adolescent choirs, don't stop there. Look more closely to see if the selections meet the requirements of *your* adolescent choir *at that particular time* (Collins, 1993, p. 486). Remember that frequent change is something on which you can count when you teach this age group!

Singers whose voices are changing lose flexibility and control, so music with frequent and sudden register changes as well as melismatic passages at very fast tempi must be avoided. Music that requires either very soft or very loud singing over long periods of time must be avoided as well, especially if the dynamic demands occur during passages where the singers are in the outermost limits of their range.

Phrasing with regard to breath support and control should be examined closely. Young singers whose voices are changing have a tendency to expend too much breath too soon, thus making extremely long phrases difficult to complete successfully. This is unfortunate, because so much music from the Renaissance period has appropriate ranges and tessituras for young singers (especially adolescent boys), but the long lines requiring intense breath support make some selections questionable choices for this age group. Not all Renaissance music will be problematic for choirs with changing voices; just remember to consider breath-support requirements in addition to range and tessitura when choosing music from this period.

Because singers at this age are not only struggling with a voice change, but are also learning to sing in parts with more security, choosing music with interesting vocal lines for all voice parts will be appreciated and helpful. A part that only supplies harmony to support the melody in the soprano part can sometimes be less interesting and more difficult to execute than a harmony part that is more melodic in nature.

A quality text that will appeal to adolescent singers is a must. Remember these singers are no longer children, so avoid music with words that might sound childish. Adolescent singers are interested in and capable of understanding more sophisticated texts. Music with foreign language texts are certainly suitable for this age if approached carefully, and, while they may initially balk at the idea, the singers will ultimately be proud of their accomplishments.

After reading what to avoid, you may be asking yourself if any music exists that is appropriate for junior high/middle school students to sing! The answer is: "Yes!" During the past twenty years in particular, contemporary composers have begun to write music specifically for this age group with all of its challenges, and the joy of finding these pieces is worth the effort required. In addition, music-series books for grades seven and eight (published by Silver Burdett and Ginn, and Macmillan publishing companies) are showing increased sensitivity to the musical needs of this age.

Figure 11.13 G. Schirmer, Octavo No. 12396, *Boatmen Stomp* (1979) from the First Set of "New Songs to Old Words" for three-part chorus of young voices with piano accompaniment. *The Boatmen Dance* by D. D. Emmett, words by Michael A. Gray. Copyright © 1980 G. Schirmer, Inc. All rights reserved. International Copyright Secured. Reprinted by Permission of G. Schirmer, Inc. (ASCAP).

Figure 11.13 Continued

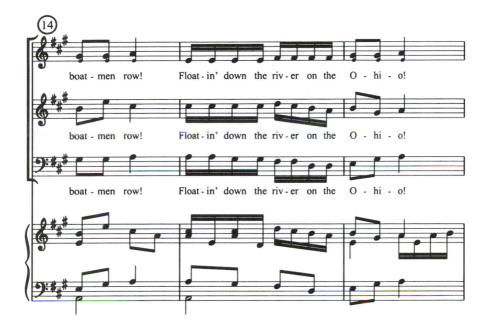

Figure 11.13 Continued

Figure 11.13 Continued

Figure 11.13 Continued

Figure 11.13 Continued

Figure 11.13　Continued

Sample Music

Figures 11.13 and 11.14 were selected to illustrate music that would work well with middle school/junior high school choirs with boys whose voices are changing. The first piece, *Boatmen Stomp* by Michael A. Gray is written for three-part young male voices and was tested successfully on several choirs to determine its suitability for changing voices. To provide versatility without any stigma attached, the voice parts are labeled High Voice, Middle Voice, and Low Voice. Refer to Figure 11.13 for a good example of music written for three-part boys.

The range and tessitura requirements for *Boatmen Stomp* are certainly appropriate. For the Low Voice, the range is A to b. The tessitura for the verses is B to e, and for the choruses, the tessitura is d to a. For the Medium Voice, which is sung an octave lower than it is written, the range is g-sharp to f-sharp[1]. The tessitura for the verses is b to e[1], and for the choruses, the tessitura is a to d. The High Voice, which sings only during the choruses, has a range and tessitura of e[1] to a[1].

For all parts, the melodic movement is predominately diatonic within a moderate tempo, so the flexibility demands are appropriate. The text and sea chantey style would certainly appeal to boys, and the dynamic demands are moderate.

Shown in figure 11.14, *Good Timber Grows* by Roger Emerson is written for a four-part chorus of mixed voices. The range for the tenor part is f to d[1], and the tessitura is f to b-flat[1], or a perfect fourth. The baritone range is c to c[1] (with an optional G at the end), and the tessitura is the same as for the tenor (f to b-flat[1]). The dynamic demands are not excessive, and because of the slow tempo and predominantly diatonic motion, the flexibility demands are appropriate for voices which are changing. A portion of the piece features the tenor and baritone parts singing in unison.

The range for the sopranos is c[1] to b[1] with a tessitura of d[1] to a[1]. For the altos, the range is B to a[1], and the tessitura is d[1] to g[1]. For a portion of the piece, these two parts sing in unison.

Because this piece is moderately easy, this selection is not only an appropriate choice for changing voices, but it is also an excellent piece for a beginning-level choir which is learning to sing in

Figure 11.14 *Good Timber Grows* (1989), music by Roger Emerson, SATB, *a cappella.* Text: anonymous. Copyright 1989 EMERSONGS. All rights reserved. Used by permission. International copyright secured.

Figure 11.14 Continued

parts. The text is suitable and young people find it very appealing.

Repertoire Lists

Several repertoire lists are available to assist you in choosing literature for your middle school/junior high choirs. In the Selected Choral Repertoire list for this book (Appendix), some of the music for Grades 1 and 2 under the tenor–bass choir is appropriate for changing voices. Several other extensive and helpful lists are found in (1) *Teaching Choral Music* by Don Collins, Prentice-Hall, 1993, pp. 486–95; (2) *The Boy's Changing Voice: New Solutions for Today's Choral Teacher* by Terry J. Barham and Darolyne L. Nelson, Belwin Mills, 1991, pp. 27–55; and (3) *Working with the Adolescent Voice* by John Cooksey, Concordia, 1992, pp. 66–68. All lists offer a wide variety of music and give publishing information.

The Collins list categorizes the musical selections by voicing such as two-, three-, and four-part mixed, two-, three-, and four-part male, two- and three-part female, and collections. The majority of music listed under the four-part voicing was written specifically for early adolescent voices. Also included is selected music written for adult SATB voices with ranges and tessituras that are appropriate for young singers.

The Barham and Nelson list is especially helpful because each work is graded by difficulty, and the range for each voice part is given. Musical selections are identified in the following voicings: unison; two-part/SA/TB; three-part/SSA/SSAA; SAT/SAC/SSC; SCB; three-part mixed/SAB; SATB/SACB/SSAB/SSCB; three-part/CCB boys; four-part/CCBB/TTBB boys; and collections and larger works.

The Cooksey list is more limited than the other two lists and categorizes the musical selections into music for male ensembles and selections for mixed choir. A variety of voicings is found within each category.

To stay informed on the adolescent changing voice, you must read current literature, attend summer workshops and various convention sessions, and, perhaps most important, pay close attention to your own singers and their experiences. In addition, seek guidance from colleagues in your area who have experienced success with this age group, and learn from their work. And always remember the importance of selecting the right music for your singers.

Summary

A great deal of information on the changing voice has been presented in this chapter, and, as you have noticed, not all of it is in agreement. There are, however, several important points on which most or all the experts agree.

Although the rate of change between voices will vary, and experts disagree on the number of stages as well as the actual range and tessitura designations, adolescents' voices will pass through fairly predictable stages of change on their way to adult voices. At each stage, the voice has definite characteristics due to the physiological changes that occur during puberty. While the onset of puberty cannot be predicted with any degree of accuracy, most experts agree that the majority of voices begin to change during the seventh grade (ages 12 to 13) with some singers beginning as early as grade six (ages 11 to 12) or as late as grade eight (ages 13 to 14). The high mutation period usually occurs during the eighth grade for most adolescents, and then the voice-changing process begins to taper off during the next few years. Remember, however, that age and grade level are not totally reliable indicators of voice change, but serve only as guides.

Choral directors must listen carefully and frequently (at least every six to eight weeks) to their young singers. By listening, they can become aware of unhealthy vocal habits, and can more accurately assign voice parts so that their singers will be singing in their most comfortable range at all times. In addition to listening, choral directors must look for signs of physical maturity and vocal strain. These aural and visual cues should be recognized and dealt with on a consistent basis to prevent poor habits from forming. At all times, insist on good vocal technique and its development.

Several experts suggest that, at the middle school/junior high level, directors may want to offer separate choirs for the boys and the girls. This way, the boys can receive the added vocal attention that they may require as their voices change. In addition, the absence of girls may make this sometimes embarrassing time somewhat less difficult. Because all the boys are going through similar experiences and may work more slowly as their voices change, the girls will be free to move more quickly if they are in a separate ensemble. Combining the boys and girls choirs occasionally, or even on a regular basis, may be a good idea, because at this age, they have suddenly discovered the opposite sex and will enjoy singing together. This system will expose all singers to a greater variety of music literature as well.

Be sensitive to those boys whose voices may be changing at a slower rate than the others. Choosing neutral designations such as "high," "middle," and "low" voice may help ease their embarrassment while they are still singing the soprano or alto part. Physical placement within the choir is critical as well for these boys. Seating them in a position close to the boys' sections will help them feel more comfortable.

While at times approximating an adult range and/or tessitura, the adolescent voice is not an adult voice and should never be treated as such. In the area of dynamics, directors should always remember that a young singer's *forte* is not the *forte* that can be achieved by an adult. Asking for a bigger sound than your singers are capable of producing will not only produce an unpleasant tone quality, but will also encourage poor vocal techniques and habits. A certain amount of breathiness in adolescent voices is normal and should be acceptable, but the amount of breath support required to achieve very long vocal lines is often difficult for young singers to produce. Due to the thickness and rapid growth of vocal cords, a lack of flexibility and control is a prominent characteristic, especially during the high-mutation stages of the voice change.

If the music selection is appropriate, a very high degree of musical success can be realized with choirs of adolescent singers. Range and tessitura are the first aspects to consider, and should be appropriate for your choir at that particular time. Because of the loss of flexibility and control, music with frequent and sudden register changes as well as melismatic passages at very fast tempi should be avoided. Dynamic requirements should be moderate, and music with extremely long phrases may be a questionable choice because singers whose voices are changing tend to expend too much air too soon. Interesting, though not extremely difficult, part writing will help young singers learn to sing in parts. A quality text that appeals to adolescent choir members is very important.

Mini-Projects

1. Observe choral rehearsals at local middle schools and junior high schools. Listen carefully to the sound produced by this age group as well as the musical problems encountered with both boys' and girls' changing voices. Notice techniques employed by the director in solving these challenges and write down any vocalises that seem especially helpful.

2. While observing at these schools, ask to see copies of the music that the students are rehearsing. Are the selections appropriate for the choir?

3. Observe choral rehearsals at local middle schools and junior high schools. Notice the social behavior of these adolescent singers. Pay close attention to techniques employed by the director to manage the students' behavior and to channel their high energy level in positive directions.

4. Contact a local voice teacher who teaches middle school/junior high students and ask if you might observe a voice lesson for one girl and one boy. Notice the characteristics of these voices that are discussed in this chapter.

References

BARHAM, TERRY J., and DAROLYNE L. NELSON. (1991). *The boy's changing voice: New solutions for today's choral teacher*. Miami: Belwin Mills.

BARRESI, ANTHONY. L. (1986). *Barressi on adolescent voice*. Videotape. Madison, WI: University of Wisconsin, UW Videotapes, Room 726, 610 Langdon Street, Madison, WI 53703.

COOKSEY, JOHN M. (1977a). The development of a contemporary, eclectic theory for the training and cultivation of the junior high school male changing voice (Part I: Existing theories). *Choral Journal*, 18(2), pp. 5–14.

COOKSEY, JOHN M. (1977b). The development of a contemporary, eclectic theory for the training and cultivation of the junior high school male changing voice (Part II: Scientific and empirical rindings; some tentative solutions). *Choral Journal*, 18(3), pp. 5–16.

COOKSEY, JOHN M. (1977c). The development of a contemporary, eclectic theory for the training and cultivation of the junior high school male changing voice (Part III: Developing an integrated approach to the care and training of the junior high school male changing voice). *Choral Journal*, 18(4), pp. 5–15.

COOKSEY, JOHN M. (1978). The development of a contemporary, eclectic theory for the training and cultivation of the junior high school male changing voice (Part IV: Selecting music for the junior high school male changing voice). *Choral Journal*, 18(5), pp. 5–18.

COOKSEY, JOHN M. (1992). *Working with the adolescent voice*. St. Louis: Concordia Publishing House.

COOPER, IRVIN, and KARL O. KUERSTEINER. (1970). *Teaching junior high school music*, 2nd ed. Boston: Allyn and Bacon.

GACKLE, LYNNE. (1991). The adolescent female voice: Characteristics of change and stages of development. *Choral Journal*, 31(8), pp. 17–25.

JOHNSON, JOHN PAUL (1981). *An aural/visual examination of selected characteristics associated with the male voice mutation*. Unpublished master's thesis, University of Wisconsin-Madison.

MCKENZIE, DUNCAN. (1956). *Training the boy's changing voice*. New Brunswick, NJ: Rutgers University Press.

SWANSON, FREDERICK. (1961). The proper care and feeding of changing voices. *Music Educators Journal*, 48, pp. 63–66.

SWANSON, FREDERICK. (1973). *Music teaching in the jr. high and middle school*. Englewood Cliffs, NJ: Prentice-Hall.

Additional Reading

Adcock, Eva. (1987). The changing voice: The middle/junior high challenge. *Choral Journal, 28*(3), 9–11.

Andrews, Frances. (1971). *Junior high school general music.* Englewood Cliffs: Prentice-Hall.

Coffman, Wesley. (1987). The changing voice—The elementary challenge. *Choral Journal, 28*(3), pp. 5–7.

Collins, Don L. (1987). The changing voice—The high school challenge. *Choral Journal, 28*(3), pp. 13–17.

Collins, Don L. (1993). *Teaching choral music.* Englewood Cliffs: Prentice-Hall.

Collins, Don L. (1987). The changing voice—A future challenge. *Choral Journal, 28*(3), pp. 19–20.

Fowells, Robert M. (1983). The changing voice: A vocal chameleon. *Choral Journal, 24*(1), pp. 11–17.

Garretson, Robert L. (1993). *Conducting choral music,* 7th ed. Englewood Cliffs, NJ: Prentice-Hall.

Harrison, Lois. (1978). It's more than just a changing voice. *Choral Journal, 19*(1), pp. 14–18.

Harrison, Lois. (1983). *Getting started in elementary music education.* Englewood Cliffs, NJ: Prentice-Hall.

Johnson, John Paul. (1988). Stages of a boy's changing voice. *TMEC Connection, 3*(1), pp. 4–5.

Phillips, Kenneth H. (1992). *Teaching kids to sing.* New York: Schirmer Books.

Phillips, Kenneth H. (1995). The changing voice: An albatross? *Choral Journal, 35*(10), 25–27.

Phillips, Kenneth H. and Steven W. Emge. (1994). Vocal registration as it affects vocal range for seventh- and eighth-grade boys. *Journal of Research in Singing and Applied Vocal Pedagogy 18*(1), pp. 1–19.

ROE, PAUL F. (1983). *Choral music education*, 2nd ed. Englewood Cliffs, NJ: Prentice-Hall.

RUTKOWSKI, JOANNE. (1981). The junior high school male changing voice: Testing and grouping voices for successful singing experiences. *Choral Journal, 22*(4), 11–15.

SIPLEY, KENNETH. (1994). Improving vocal self-image and tone quality in adolescent girls: A study. *Choral Journal, 35*(3), pp. 35–38.

CHAPTER **12**

Pop Ensembles and
Musical Productions

Mr. Cortez, a first-year choral director, went to a show choir confer-
ence during the summer to learn about choreography and to find new
repertoire for his group. He met yesterday with students and parents
from the outfit committee to choose this year's performing attire, and,
today, he is shopping at the local music store for sound equipment.
Because he has not had experience with this type of group, Mr. Cortez
is having to learn everything from the very beginning, and his head is
spinning! Although he is excited about having a show choir at his high
school, he hopes that he can keep it in perspective. He had no idea that
there were so many things to consider!

Pop Ensembles

Choirs that perform popular music are quickly becoming an integral
part of the entire choral experience for today's students. The per-
vasiveness of popular music throughout our culture, the fact that
most adolescents consider it "their music" and enjoy listening to it,
and the influence of performing groups seen on television have all
contributed to an increased interest in groups that focus on music
composed in a popular style.

A great variety exists in the pop ensembles of today. Some groups have a total concentration on vocal jazz, while others may focus on popular music, Broadway tunes, country music, or rhythm and blues. Still others feature a combination of all these styles. The choice of focus may depend on the director's own interest and expertise, students' abilities and interests, the area of the country in which they live, or all of the above. The size of pop ensembles can vary as well. Generally, groups range in size from twelve to twenty-four singers.

When you take your first job, you may inherit a choral program with a pop ensemble already in place, and you will need to evaluate whether you want to have such a group as part of the choral program at your school. You may decide to leave the group the way it has been in years past, to disband it altogether, or you may want to keep it, but change its musical focus or how the members are selected. Whatever you decide, your decision should be based on your philosophy of music education, student interest and ability, scheduling concerns, and parental as well as administrative support.

On the positive side, an ensemble that sings popular music can provide several benefits for all who are involved in performing and for those who listen. First of all, students can learn a wide variety of music as well as different styles of singing, especially if the singers are also in a traditional choir. Second, student recruitment and retention can be enhanced. In many schools, to be a member of the pop group is the most coveted membership of all for some young people; therefore, the mere existence of the group may boost enrollment in the choral program, and can provide motivation for those singers whose goal it is to be selected. Third, relationships between the school and the community can be strengthened through performances at local civic clubs, churches, and nursing homes.

On the other side of the coin, however, there are some potential pitfalls of which you should be aware before you begin working with a pop ensemble. Because of its very nature, such a group requires a tremendous amount of time and attention. Various other duties are required in addition to rehearsing with the choir (often after school or in the evening): the instrumentalists need rehearsing; parental permission slips for various off-campus performances need to be given out, signed, and collected; transportation of people and equipment to these performances needs to be arranged; choreography needs to be planned or a choreographer needs to be contacted; the equipment needs to be kept in good repair; and, the outfits need to be chosen. The list could go on and on. To allow yourself the time and energy necessary to run the entire choral department, you will need to delegate some of the responsibilities related to the pop group to students and parents. If you don't, things can get out of balance very quickly, and you run the risk of providing only a very small portion of a well-balanced choral music education for your students. Keeping things in proper perspective is the key.

Students who participate in a pop ensemble will benefit greatly from concurrent membership in a traditional choral ensemble. In fact, this dual participation is often required by directors, not only to provide the students with a well-rounded music education, but also to ensure that the students in the pop ensemble know about and use healthy vocal technique. With increased requirements for high school graduation, however, students may not be able to schedule more than one choir during the regular school day. In situations such as this, you may want to consider rehearsing the pop ensemble several afternoons or evenings a week.

For smaller choral programs, or ones in which it is not economically feasible to offer a separate group for popular music, several options exist. Some choral programs have a madrigal group, or similar small ensemble, that is the school's most advanced choir. This smaller, advanced choir can "become" the pop ensemble in the spring after the annual choral festival or contest. Another possibility is for the traditional choir to include a number of popular arrangements, perhaps with choreography, in their repertoire throughout the year. This flexibility of sound and style can enhance the breadth of the students' music education as well as provide a versatile program for a variety of audiences with a minimum amount of time and effort.

The Audition

Aspects to be considered during an audition for a pop ensemble include:

1. *Vocal abilities.* Singers should come prepared to sing a solo in the style of their choice. Since most pop ensembles perform with

microphones, you may want to have students use one as part of their audition. Be sure to provide an accompanist, or communicate to the students that they will need to bring their own. Taped accompaniment may be allowed, but will obviously require a tape player.

2. *Movement abilities.* Pop ensembles need students who can learn movement sequences quickly and perform them with ease while they are singing. So that the judges can observe these abilities, have someone (perhaps a student) teach the singers a short movement routine during their audition.

3. *Musicianship skills.* Because students in a pop ensemble perform frequently and they need to learn their music very quickly, a test of their sightsinging abilities and aural skills may be included in the audition. However, if the director has the requirement that students must be in a traditional ensemble concurrently with the pop ensemble, this information will already be known and can be deleted from the audition for this choir.

4. *Choral blend.* In addition to individual voice quality, you will want to experiment with different vocal combinations to determine the members of the pop ensemble. Sometimes singers with beautiful soloistic qualities will be very difficult to blend with the entire ensemble, or one grouping of singers will give a better overall sound than another grouping will. This experimentation should probably take place during the call-back audition.

5. *The singer's overall presentation.* Because the focus of a pop ensemble is almost entirely on entertainment, the way a singer presents himself or herself is a very important factor to observe during the audition. Poise under pressure, facial expressions and eye contact, posture, grooming, and movement abilities all contribute to an overall image. Endurance can be an issue when singing and moving to one piece right after another, so the physical fitness of each singer should be considered as well.

Membership in a pop ensemble usually requires a rather demanding time commitment, and often requires a financial commitment as well. This information needs to be communicated to students and parents alike *before* the audition process begins. Having both the students and their parents sign a paper that lists these commitments may be a good idea.

Programming

The programming techniques discussed in Chapter 6 also apply to ensembles that focus on the performance of popular music. Choosing a variety of music and giving thought to its order will usually result in a smoother flow and a more pleasing program. Varying the styles, keys, and tempi of the music will help achieve these goals. An additional consideration for pop ensembles should be the physical endurance required to perform choreography for each piece. Programming a soft, slow number after an extremely fast and loud piece with demanding physical movements will allow the singers to catch their breath and rest their voices. The judicious placement of solos, duets, trios, and quartets can achieve the same effect as well as add length to a program.

Choreography

Choreography adds a visual component to the overall performance and is a large part of the appeal of pop ensembles. Care should be taken, however, to choose movement that will enhance, not detract from the musical presentation. Remember that the choir is a choir, and not a dancing group that also sings, or worse: a dancing group that *cannot* sing!

Some directors prefer to do their own choreography, while others rely on students who are interested and qualified in this area. Additional possibilities include involving a fellow faculty member who has a background and interest in dance, or, if funds are available, hiring a local dance teacher, or a student majoring in dance at a nearby college or university.

To create a natural connection between the musical portion of the performance and the physical movements, have the choreographer study and listen to the music first. Focusing on such aspects as the tempo, text, form, phrasing, and overall mood of the piece will often suggest the choreography. For example, if the piece is a slow love song with soft dynamics, a minimum of movement is suggested. A selection in ABA form may suggest that the choir repeat the opening movement sequence when the A section returns. The musical phrases and sections will guide the number of repetitions of the various movements chosen.

Sometimes, the most common mistake is too much movement, causing the choir to be in a perpetual state of breathlessness in addition to giving a hurried and "busy" visual image that can detract from the singing. When the music is fast and extremely complex, a moderate amount of movement may be desired to enable the singers to concentrate more completely on the musical aspects of the performance. More active choreography can be reserved for fast tunes with fewer voice parts or less challenging harmony, for example.

Because the most important component of the performance is the music, teach it first. When the choir can perform the piece with confidence (or even has it memorized), spend time on the choreography, perhaps using textual cues to signify a new gesture or a change in direction. Revisit the music periodically as the choreography is learned, and, when everything is finally put together, be aware that everything is likely to be rather shaky at first until the singers are comfortable with all components of the performance.

Tone Quality

Generally, singers of popular music will use more breath in their sound than when singing in other styles, particularly if the sound is amplified. In vocal jazz, or in any popular style with very close harmonies, the use of vibrato will be minimal. Otherwise, tone quality is a very subjective issue, and therefore, will vary from director to director.

The use of amplification can make a difference in the choir's overall tone quality. Some directors use the sound board to make many adjustments for blend and balance, allowing more freedom in their singers' vocal production, and therefore, more individuality in their sound. Other directors strive for a more homogeneous tone quality, and all singers must compromise their individuality somewhat to achieve that tone quality. The resulting sound is pleasant, well-blended, and balanced, but this practice may cause vocal problems if continued over a long period of time because of the vocal adjustments required of the singers. Some directors don't use amplication at all (except for the instrumentalists), and allow their students to sing in full voice. This practice may also result in unhealthy vocal production if the students continually oversing, either to be heard over the instrumentalists, or to compensate for a small choir with no amplification, or when singing in a large performing area with no amplification.

Performing Outfits

Several issues should be considered when selecting the outfit that a pop ensemble wears:

1. The outfit should allow for freedom of movement because choreography is likely to be a component of the performance.
2. Because of the energy expended in each performance, the outfit will probably need frequent cleaning. Clothing that needs to be dry cleaned will obviously be more expensive than an outfit that is machine washable.
3. The outfit must be tasteful and appropriate for a group of young people to wear. The singers will be representing their school when performing for community groups, and they need to make a positive impression.
4. Include the students in the decision. Asking a few parents to be on the selection committee may be a good idea as well.
5. Shoes can sometimes present a problem. Whatever you choose, they must allow the singers to move easily. For girls, consider character shoes in black or neutral colors, and, for boys, suggest a thin-soled lace-up shoe (called a jazz shoe).

High schoool pop ensemble.

6. Because of the expense involved in outfitting a pop ensemble (or any ensemble, for that matter), longevity should be considered. Is the outfit in a style that will remain current for a number of years? Can minor adjustments such as a different vest or bow tie create a new look without having to purchase a completely new outfit? Parents will appreciate your consideration of their financial investment.

Mobility of the Group

Because of the instruments and equipment involved in a pop ensemble, moving the group from place to place will be difficult and can be expensive. A pick-up truck can be used for groups that use a minimum amount of equipment. A covered trailer may be the best choice for larger amounts of equipment, but you must have a vehicle to pull the trailer. This problem may be solved through a fund-raising effort sponsored by the Choral Parent Organization.

In addition to moving the instruments and equipment, you must obviously transport the singers. Release forms and/or permission slips will be required, especially if several of the singers are driving. Choral parents can be utilized in this endeavor as well, although most parents work and are not free during the day.

Another consideration in the mobility of a pop ensemble is the fact that many of your shows will likely occur off-campus on an unfamiliar stage or performing area. This can affect the choreography. If the stage at your school is an unusual shape, for example, and you design movements to use this configuration for school performances, will the group be able to adapt easily to an area of a different shape and size? Choosing movements that are flexible and easily adaptable is usually a good idea.

Finally, teach the singers and instrumentalists how to set up and strike the sound equipment. To save time and to alleviate anxiety, the equipment may be color-coded for ease in the correct attachment of cables. A thirty-minute show can require up to three or four hours when adding together the time to get to the performance area, set up the equipment, rehearse, perform, take down the equipment, and travel back to school, so be sure to communicate to parents and students the total time required for each performance.

Accompaniment

Various options exist regarding the accompaniment for a pop ensemble. Taped accompaniment removes the need for instrumentalists, but requires a good sound system, and singers may find it difficult to stay with the tape. When utilizing instrumentalists, a keyboard and drumset can provide a basic accompaniment, and when the keyboard is an electronic piano, an electronic piano with synthesizing capabilities, or a synthesizer, all types of clever sounds are possible. When students are available, an instrumental ensemble comprised of bass and rhythm guitars, a drum set, and one or more electronic keyboards can provide exciting, full accompaniments for the group.

Directors will need to audition the instrumentalists before accepting them as part of the pop ensemble. Sightreading abilities, improvisatory skills, cooperation, and reliability are a few things to be checked. If a player has unusually good soloistic abilities, you may want to consider using an instrumental solo as part of the program. Often, you will have singers in the group who are also capable of playing various instruments. In this case, they may want to rotate out of the choir occasionally to play an accompanimental part.

Sound Equipment

MICROPHONES. When using amplification, microphones will obviously be needed. Wireless (or cordless) microphones allow for freedom of movement, but their expense can prohibit their use by many schools. Microphones requiring cables for their power are generally less expensive, but can restrict the choreography. When amplifying a small group of singers or when using only three or four microphones to amplify the entire choir, omni-directional microphones usually work best because they pick up sound from all directions. Uni-directional microphones work best when each performer holds a microphone in his or her hand.

AMPLIFIER. An amplifier provides the power for the entire system, including the microphones, sound board, speakers, and any electronic instruments.

SOUND BOARD. The sound board allows a person to control the sound from a central location. Each part of the system that is plugged into the sound board is assigned its own channel, allowing adjustments in balance to be made. Sound boards range in size from as few as four channels to as many as sixty-four channels. (A pop ensemble can work without the use of a sound board, but no adjustments can be made to the sound and an alternative power source will be necessary.)

SNAKE. A snake is basically a long extension cord. Performers plug their microphones into the body of the snake and the snake is then connected to the sound board which is often a great distance away from the stage area.

MAIN SPEAKERS. The main speakers project the ensemble's sound toward the audience.

MONITOR SPEAKERS. Monitor speakers project the ensemble's sound into the performing area, allowing the singers and instrumentalists to hear themselves without the delay of sound experienced from the main speakers. The choir will begin to sing slower because of this delay when monitor speakers are not used.

Musical Productions

The production of a Broadway musical is often part of a high school choral program and offers many potential benefits. First of all, the *esprit de corps* of the entire school can be enhanced as everyone works toward a common goal. When all students have an opportunity to audition for a musical part in the production, and when other students, faculty, and staff are involved in various nonmusical responsibilities such as building the set, designing the costumes, planning the make-up, selling ads for the program, taking publicity photographs, and selling tickets, lots of positive energy can be generated. This broader base of involvement also prevents one person from having to do all the work.

Secondly, involving the entire school in producing a musical can serve as a recruitment tool for the choral program. As they participate on a short-term basis, more students will get to know you and the current choral students, and as a result, may decide to join choir. As faculty and staff become familiar with you and your activities, they may advise interested students to join the choral program.

A third benefit of producing a musical can be a financial one. When the publicity is well-done, and the quality of the performance is consistently high, people will look forward to each production, and ticket sales will be strong, but expenses must be kept to a bare minimum to see a good profit. When the musical is financially successful, a portion of the proceeds may be channeled toward the choral department and can enhance a sometimes meager budget.

Finally, when businesses are involved with the production in various ways, ties with the community can be built or strengthened. This outside interest in and support for school activities can benefit the activities as well as the students involved in them.

When deciding whether to produce a musical at your school, you should be aware of several potential pitfalls. Of primary concern should be the tremendous time commitment required of all participants. The time involved is in addition to the responsibilities necessary for you to direct, and for your students to participate successfully in the overall choral program at your school. If not planned efficiently and kept in proper perspective, after-school and evening rehearsals may place the students' schoolwork in jeopardy.* On the other hand, the enthusiasm and excitement produced by successful rehearsals and performances can boost the energy levels of both faculty and students, and, in this way, can have a positive effect.

An additional concern often raised by critics of producing a musical at the high school level is the type of vocal production often required of the cast. In an attempt to sound like the Broadway stars that they all admire, or to be heard in a large auditorium or over an instrumental ensemble, high school students will tend to overuse their chest voice and "belt" the sound. Obviously, this can be detrimental to the overall vocal health of young singers and should not

---

* Check with your school district to determine whether there is a limit to the number of hours per week that students may rehearse.

be encouraged. To reduce the potential strain on the singers, consider using lapel microphones or omni-directional microphones to amplify their voices.

Choosing the Right Show

Once you have decided to produce a musical at your school, you will need to select the show. To help in this endeavor, contact the four primary agents who handle musicals,* and they will provide you with a catalog, on-approval scores, and sometimes, an audio tape. Several things must be taken into consideration when choosing the show.

You must determine the musical requirements necessary for the production and match these requirements with the musical resources available at your school. These resources include potential singers for principal parts, instrumentalists for accompaniment, and the number of singers who are qualified and available for the chorus. The perceived difficulty level of the show as well as the suitability of the musical requirements for young voices must also be taken into account.

Just as important is the determination of potential production difficulties. The size of the stage, the scenery, the costumes, the make-up, the lighting, and any special effects are all factors that could prohibit the choice of some musicals (Roe, 1983, p. 319). If the financial resources and personnel necessary to realize these production requirements are not available to you, consider a less elaborate show. Keep your expectations realistic, and remember, sometimes less is more!

Scheduling

All the rehearsals and, of course, the performance dates must be scheduled and entered into the master calendar. This should occur as early as one year before, but no later than four to five months before the production. In addition to the dates, you must

---

*   (1) Tams-Witmark Music Library, Inc., 560 Lexington Ave., New York, NY 10022; (2) The Rodgers and Hammerstein Repertory, 120 East 56th St., New York, NY 10022; (3) Music Theatre International, 545 Eighth Ave., New York, NY 10018; (4) Samuel French, Inc., 45 West 25th St., New York, NY 10010.

reserve rehearsal space. The choral room, the gymnasium, and various large classrooms can serve as alternatives when the stage is not available.

Auditions

The audition committee should include the choral director, the drama instructor, and several other faculty members. Hold the auditions on several successive days and make sure that the dates are well publicized in advance. Include in the requirements a solo, a dance sequence, and a short dramatic segment, and, during the audition, consider each student's speaking voice, personality, and overall suitability for the part. Availability for after-school and evening rehearsals must be determined at this time.

If there is an unusually good turnout and the level of talent is high, you may be able to double-cast the principal parts. At the very least, choose several understudies in case of illness or other unforeseen emergency involving the principal cast. Post the results of the auditions promptly.

Delegation of Responsibilities

It is wise to have an overall director of the show, and the logical choices for this position are the drama instructor, the choral director, or a faculty member who has had experience in community theatre or dramatic training and experience in college. However, so that the production of the musical can truly be an all-school event, and so that all the responsibilities will not fall to one person, the director should delegate various duties among fellow faculty members, students, and parents. For instance, the publicity committee can handle all the details involved in publicizing the event. The industrial arts teacher can be responsible for the sets, the art teacher can head the backdrop committee, and the home economics teacher can organize the selection and creation of costumes. All financial matters can be delegated to the treasurer of the Choral Parent Organization, and the drama coach can be responsible for the acting. Of course, the choral director will prepare the musical portion of the show with the help of the band or orchestra director (if an instrumental ensemble is used for the accompaniment).

Publicity

The publicity committee needs to have a detailed plan for getting the word out to the community as well as to the school population. In addition to newspaper articles, radio and television announcements, and announcements over the public address system at school, hanging attractive posters in various businesses throughout the community can be an effective way to advertise the musical. Provide the usual "who, what, when, and where," and, if tickets are being sold, be sure to include the price, as well as where and when they can be purchased.

Summary

Pop ensembles are a pervasive force in choral music education today, and can offer benefits to all concerned if kept in proper perspective. You will need to decide whether to start or continue such a group when you begin your first job, and the decision should be based on your philosophy of music education, student interest and ability, scheduling concerns, and parental as well as administrative support. Students can benefit greatly from concurrent membership in a traditional choral ensemble.

Groups can vary in their musical focus, tone quality, and size. Depending on the director's concept of the group and the financial resources available, the style of choreography, type of accompaniment, and sophistication of the sound equipment can vary as well. Aspects of an audition to be considered include the student's vocal abilities, movement abilities, musicianship skills, and overall presentation. You may also want to experiment with various combinations of singers as you make your final decisions.

Traditional programming techniques also apply to pop ensembles. In addition, the physical endurance required to do choreography for each piece should be considered when planning the order of the program. Choreography adds a visual component to the overall performance, and should enhance the music, not detract from it. The movements can be suggested by the musical characteristics discovered in the piece.

The performing outfits selected for the choir should allow for freedom of movement, ease in cleaning, and be appropriate for young people to wear. Involve students and their parents in the decision.

Off-campus performances can present extra responsibilities, including the transportation of instruments, equipment, and students; permission slips; and, having a different area in which to perform the choreography. Because they need to share the responsibility for the group, and because the time required for these shows can be so extensive, the students should be taught how to set up and take down the sound equipment.

Accompaniments for a pop ensemble can vary from tapes to a full instrumental group. Sound equipment includes an amplifier, sound board, snake, microphones, main speakers, and monitor speakers.

The production of a Broadway musical can foster a real spirit of working together toward a common goal when the entire school is involved in various ways. Recruitment for the choral department may be enhanced, and, if planned carefully, the musical can be a money-maker as well. The time commitment to produce a show is challenging, so rehearsals must be planned efficiently to protect both the students and the adults who are involved. The use of good vocal technique must be encouraged at all times.

Choosing the right show involves matching the musical requirements with the musical resources available at your school. Consider just as carefully any potential production difficulties such as the size of the stage, costumes, and special effects that are necessary. Remember to have realistic expectations!

All the rehearsals and, of course, the performances, must be scheduled on the master calendar in a timely fashion. Rehearsal space must also be reserved.

The audition committee should include the choral director, the drama instructor, and several other faculty members. Include in the audition a solo, a short dramatic segment, and a dance sequence (for shows that involve dancing). Consider each student's speaking voice, personality, overall suitability for the part, and the availability for after-school and evening rehearsals. Choose several understudies, and perhaps, even double-cast the principal parts. Post the results of the auditions promptly.

One person must serve as the director of the show, but this person does not need to do all the work! Responsibilities should be delegated to students, parents, and other faculty members. This larger base of involvement will not only help to distribute duties, but also will make the musical truly an all-school event. Publicize it well.

SELECTED REPERTOIRE FOR POP ENSEMBLES

Title/Category	Voicing	Arranger	Publisher
Theme and Show Openers			
Get on Your Feet	SATB	Alan Billingsley	CPP/Belwin 1503GC1X
Rhythm of the Night	SATB	Teena Chinn	Columbia Pictures 2408RC1X
Riders to the Stars	SATB	Alan Billingsley	Kamakazi Music 432-18014
Rockin' the Paradise	SATB	Mark Brymer	Hal Leonard 08638961
Be There	SATB	Mark Brymer	Hal Leonard 08637181
One Voice	SATB	Jerry Nowak	Jenson 480-30454
Real Good Time Tonight	SATB	Kirby Shaw	Hal Leonard 08662100
The Best Is Yet to Come!	SATB	Don Besig	Shawnee Press A-1805
Let It Shine!	SATB	Kirby Shaw	Hal Leonard 08665975
I've Got the Music in Me	SATB	Alan Billingsley	Jenson 432-09024
Broadway/Entertainment			
They Call the Wind Maria	TTB	Kirby Shaw	Hal Leonard 08665998
I Hope That Somethin' Better Comes Along	TTB	Gary Fry	Welbeck Music Corp. 2405
Vamps!	SSA	Kirby Shaw	CPP/Belwin CO153C2X
Let's Hear It for the Boy	SSA	Alan Billingsley	CPP/Belwin 1588LC2X
Once Upon a Dream	SATB	John Leavitt	Cherry Lane Music CL 1021
Waitin' for the Light to Shine	SATB	Mark Brymer	Hal Leonard 08639481
Light at the End of the Tunnel	SATB	Mark Brymer	Hal Leonard 08638291
Hold On	SATB	Ed Lojeski	Warner Bros. 08200062

Favorite Son	SATB	Jay Althouse	CPP/Belwin 0180FC1X
Natural High	SATB	Alan Billingsley	Fiddleback Music 432-14014
Ease on Down the Road	SATB	Mac Huff	Warner Bros. 08720969
Highlights from *The Wiz*	SATB	Mark Brymer	Hal Leonard 445-23014
Disney Spectacular	SATB	Mac Huff	Hal Leonard 08426511
Steppin' Out on Broadway (Medley)	SATB	Jay Althouse	CPP/Belwin CO145C1X
Don't Touch That Dial	SATB	Mark Brymer	Hal Leonard 08637501
After-Beeps	SATB	George Strid	Shawnee Press A-1909
All the Things You Are	SATB	Kirby Shaw	Hal Leonard 08720244

The Twenties, Thirties, and Forties

Cry Me a River	SSA	Kirby Shaw	Hal Leonard 8666071
Chattanooga Choo Choo	SSA	Mac Huff	CPP/Belwin T3200CC1
For Me and My Gal (Medley)	SATB	Lon Madsen	Columbia Pictures CO105C1X
Charleston, Flappers, and Razz-a-Ma-Tazz	SATB	Joyce Eilers	Hal Leonard 08541600
The Best of Big Band (Medley)	SATB	Anita Kerr	Hal Leonard 08565631
Mack the Knife	SATB	Kirby Shaw	Weill-Brecht-Harms 441-12064
You Made Me Love You	SATB	Kirby Shaw	Hal Leonard 08720037
Over the Rainbow	SATB	Roger Emerson	Jenson 403-15104
Moonglow	SATB	Ralph Hunter	Belwin Mills 60662
Rock-a-Bye Your Baby with a Dixie Melody	SATB	Ed Lojeski	Hal Leonard 08254521
Puttin' on the Ritz	SATB	Kirby Shaw	Hal Leonard 08661900

Vincent	SATB	Roger Emerson	MCA 08200238
Satin Doll	SATB	Kirby Shaw	Hal Leonard 08745839
A Nightingale Sang in Berkley Square	SATB	Puerling/Mattson	Hal Leonard 07357775

The Fifties and Sixties

Blue Velvet	TTB	Mark Brymer	Hal Leonard 08637015
Calendar Girls	TTB	Jeff Funk	Acuff-Rose C0314C4X
Earth Angel	TTB	Roger Emerson	Jenson 403-05190
The Great Pretender	TTB	Kirby Shaw	CPP/Belwin 5745GC4X
The Best of Doo-Wop (Medley)	TTBB	Ed Lojeski	Hal Leonard 08212956
My Special Angel	SSA	Ed Lojeski	Hal Leonard 08721255
Simply Supreme: A Medley	SSA	Mark Hanson	CPP/Belwin CO256C2X
Baby, I'm Yours	SSA	Roger Emerson	Hal Leonard 40326197
Judy's Turn to Cry	SSA	Jerry Nowak	Shawnee Press B-536
Lollipop	SSA	Roger Emerson	Jenson 40326033
50s Rock and Roll Medley	SATB	Kirby Shaw	Hal Leonard 08662500
Love Potion No. 9	SATB	John Higgins	Warner Bros. 408-12194
Steam Heat	SATB	Kirby Shaw	Hal Leonard 08664134
Happy Together	SATB	Ed Lojeski	Hal Leonard 08222401
Best of the Beach Boys (Medley)	SATB	Ed Lojeski	Hal Leonard 08200669
Come Go with Me	SATB	Ed Lojeski	Hal Leonard 08209830
The Boy from New York City	SATB	Kirby Shaw	Warner Bros. 44125050
Bandstand Boogie from American Bandstand	SATB	Kirby Shaw	Hal Leonard 08655661

Seventies

Free Ride	SATB	Mac Huff	Hal Leonard 08730156
Daniel	SSA	Roger Emerson	Hal Leonard 40326249
Takin' Care of Business	SATB	Mac Huff	Sony Music Corporation

Patriotic

America the Beautiful	SATB	Kirby Shaw	Hal Leonard 08637319
God Bless the U.S.A.	SATB	Don McAfee	MCA Music
Celebrate America!	SATB	Mark Brymer	Hal Leonard 08637361
An American Trilogy	SATB	Ed Lojeski	Hal Leonard 08200555
America … The Dream Goes On	SATB	Higgins/Lavender	Warner Bros. 408-01014
Sing for You America	SATB	Kirby Shaw	Hal Leonard 08663471

Country

That Good Old Country Music (Medley)	SATB	Jay Althouse	Shawnee Press A-1619
If the Good Lord Only Lets You Love Me	SATB	Roy Straigis	Belwin Mills MC 4620

Gospel

Peace in the Valley	SSA	Ed Lojeski	Hal Leonard 08360101
Too Hot Down There!	3-Part	Joyce Bacak	Jenson 402-20290
Ride On!	SATB	Kirby Shaw	Hal Leonard 08716371
Operator	SAB	Kirby Shaw	Hal Leonard 08661002
Home on That Rock	SATB	Kirby Shaw	Hal Leonard 08657750
I Saw the Light	SATB	Anita Kerr	Hal Leonard 08565601
Take My Hand, Precious Lord	SATB	Ed Lojeski	Hal Leonard 08374375
Revival (Medley)	SATB	Richard Derwingson	Jenson 420-18014

Amazing Grace	SATB	Ed Lojeski	Hal Leonard 08300531
Joyful, Joyful (Sister Act II)	SATB	Warren/Emerson	Buena Vista Music Co.

Others

Can't Stop Dancin'	SATB	Mark Brymer	Jenson 445-03014
When You Were Lovin' Me	SATB	Buck Buchholz	Jenson 429-23014
The Dream Never Dies	SATB	Ed Lojeski	Hal Leonard 08212950
In the Arms of Freedom	SATB	Steve Bach	Alfred Publishing 7353
What Would I Do Without My Music	SATB	Ed Lojeski	Hal Leonard 08276950
River of Dreams	SATB	Mark Brymer	Hal Leonard 08200155
Respect	SATB	Greg Gilpin	Irving Music 1497RC1X

Mini-Projects

1. Locate two directors in your area who have pop ensembles at their schools but who have differing concepts of this type of group. Observe a rehearsal at each of the schools and compare what you see and hear.

2. With a fellow music student, attend a performance of a pop ensemble. Discuss the choice of music, program order, choreography, outfits, balance between singers and accompaniment, and overall performance of the group. What changes would you make, if any, and why?

3. Visit a music store and familiarize yourself with the sound equipment currently available.

4. Visit with local directors and ask to see the performing attire worn by the pop ensemble. Discuss various pattern designs they may have used in the past, and if they have current catalogs of performing attire, ask if you may borrow them. Look through the catalogs

to see what is available for pop ensembles and what you might choose for your own group if you had one.

5. Observe a rehearsal of a pop ensemble on a day when the students are working with the choreographer and notice how he or she teaches the movements to the choir.

6. Write one of the four primary agents who handle Broadway musicals and request a catalog. After studying the catalog, order a score on approval and become familiar with the musical resources, properties, and costumes required for the show that you ordered.

7. Attend several rehearsals at a high school as they prepare for a musical production. Observe the delegation of responsibilities and the organization of rehearsal time.

Reference

ROE, PAUL F. (1983). *Choral music education*, 2nd ed. Englewood Cliffs, NJ: Prentice-Hall.

Additional Reading

COLLINS, DON L. (1993). *Teaching choral music.* Englewood Cliffs, NJ: Prentice-Hall.

COMBS, RONALD, and ROBERT BOWKER. (1995). *Learning to sing non-classical music.* Englewood Cliffs, NJ: Prentice-Hall.

GARRETSON, ROBERT L. (1988). *Conducting choral music*, sixth ed. Englewood Cliffs, NJ: Prentice-Hall.

GRIER, GENE. (1991). Choral resources: A heritage of popular styles. *Music Educators Journal, 77*(8), 35–39.

OSTRANDER, ARTHUR E., and DANA WILSON. (1986). *Contemporary choral arranging.* Englewood Cliffs, NJ: Prentice-Hall.

ROBINSON, RUSSELL L. (1994). *Getting started with jazz/show choir.* Reston, VA: Music Educators National Conference.

CHAPTER 13

Management of a Choral Program

Ms. Chin is feeling frantic and frustrated. The music she ordered two weeks ago has not arrived; the choir brought their uniforms for a photograph on Thursday, but the photographer came on Friday; and the front office is demanding the progress reports, due yesterday, for three students with borderline grades. In addition, the student who serves as choral librarian has been sick with the flu all week, and music is all over the choir office and in the workroom as well. Because of the Spring Festival and Solo and Ensemble Competition, Ms. Chin hasn't had a free weekend in several weeks, and her stress level is rising. How can she possibly rehearse five choirs with all these demands and worries?

Often, musicians have little patience for keeping up with correspondence, getting grades in on time, or organizing a fund-raising campaign. These nonmusical details take precious time away from what they are best qualified for and most eager to do: make beautiful music! Unfortunately, these nonmusical details of running a choral program will not go away, and, if not managed properly, can overwhelm the director and have a very negative impact on the musical portion of the job. Choral directors must first acknowledge that management is an important and necessary component of directing choirs; then a systematic way of handling these details must be created. Then, and only then, can a choral program be all that it can be.

Because they may not fully understand the teaching of music, some administrators may often base their judgment of your teaching effectiveness not on the musical successes, but on how efficiently you manage the choral program under your direction. Because music programs are in jeopardy all over the country, don't give the administration any reason whatsoever to question whether the choral program is an important part of their total offerings. Make sure you discharge your responsibilities—both musical and nonmusical—so that they will be evaluated as successful.

Teacher Burnout

Choosing and preparing appropriate music for up to six choirs, planning exciting rehearsals and executing them with enthusiasm and diligence, conducting after-school rehearsals, and making preparations for solo and ensemble participation are just a few of the *musical* responsibilities with which a choir director is charged. When the myriad of duties involved in managing the choral department are added, the job can quickly become overwhelming.

Youthful enthusiasm and a high level of energy often cause new directors to think that they can "do it all" by themselves, and for awhile, this may be possible. After a few years, however, the fact that you are working (and working *hard*) during every waking hour in the week and often over the weekends will make the normal stress level of the job very difficult to handle in a healthy manner. To avoid suffering teacher burnout as well as to be the most effective teacher possible, take care of yourself by eating properly and by getting enough rest and exercise, and by planning recreational time for yourself with friends and family. In addition, and perhaps most important, learn early in your career how to delegate responsibilities to others. Parents are often eager to get involved with their child's educational experiences, and students can benefit greatly by discharging responsibilities themselves.

Parent Organization

A Choral Parent Organization can be extremely helpful in the area of managing a choral program. Delegating duties to willing and eager parents can ease the burden of nonmusical responsibilities, allowing the director to focus almost entirely on the musical portion of the job.

When you begin your first job, a parent organization may already be in place. If none exists, and you feel the need to organize one yourself, discuss your proposal with the principal in case there are school policies of which you need to be aware. Then, as close to the beginning of the year as possible, mail invitations to all parents for a mini-concert where each choir performs one to two pieces. Having all students involved will promote better parental attendance and will begin to build an *esprit de corps* among the choral students as well. Inform the parents that a brief business meeting will be held after the concert.

Begin the business portion of the evening by providing a brief overview of the entire choral program and your goals for each choir for the year. Then, explain your vision of and need for a choral parent organization and give a brief description of the various duties for which you hope they can provide assistance. A handout containing a list of proposed officers and committees and their responsibilities may be helpful to the parents at this first meeting.

When parents understand what is desired and expected, elect officers. After officers are elected, have the new president ask for volunteers to serve as heads of the various committees. (You may want to elect the committee heads in addition to the officers.) Before electing them or asking for volunteers, point out that parents who don't work outside the home may be able to discharge their duties more easily. Unfortunately, however, finding parents who aren't employed is rare.

Officers

The following list of officers and their duties is rather basic for any organization. The list of suggested committees can be modified according to your situation and your particular needs.

President. The president presides at all meetings, and is involved in any major decision-making, especially if it involves policy or the organization's money.

Vice President. The vice president can preside whenever the president is absent, but can also serve as the chairperson of all committee heads. When the officers make a decision on a project, for instance, the vice president can then call the committee heads to explain their committee's contribution to the current project. Each committee head then disseminates the information out to committee members, and the work begins.

Secretary. The secretary keeps accurate minutes of each meeting, and is responsible for all the organization's correspondence.

Treasurer. The treasurer keeps accurate records of all monies, and should have had at least a small amount of experience in the financial area.

Possible Committees

Projects and Activities. This committee is an extremely important one because its members will organize and supervise the fund-raising activities each year. Because of shrinking school budgets, the majority of your choral budget may have to be raised through garage sales, or selling candy, grapefruit, candles, and the like. Before embarking on your first project, find out about your school district's policy regarding fund-raising. Some districts forbid their teachers to be involved in any way. In cases such as these, the entire responsibility of raising money will fall on the shoulders of the Choral Parent Organization.

Chaperones. This committee is responsible for providing chaperones for all choir trips and activities during the year. They may also be asked to secure any buses or vans needed for transporting choral students.

Telephones. This committee is responsible for "getting the word out" as quickly as possible. Each committee member should be provided with an accurate list of all choral students' names, parents' names, addresses, and phone numbers.

Publicity. This committee is responsible for the public-relations portion of the choral program. Duties may include writing and delivering articles to the local newspaper regarding the choir's activities and achievements, and the organization of annual pictures for the entire choral department.

Performing Attire. This committee can be extremely helpful at the beginning of each school year when new outfits may be purchased or made by parents. A good amount of time is required to search for available sizes, costs, colors, and vendors, and parents can help locate this information. In addition, if parents are involved in deciding what the young people will wear, they may be less likely to complain about the decision.

Historian. This committee (or person) keeps a record of the activities of the year, including mementos and photographs to be placed in a scrapbook. This responsibility may well be accomplished by one of the choral students.

Constitution

The balance between your authority as the choral director and the authority given the Choral Parent Organization is often a difficult one to maintain. If you constantly try to run things yourself, or attempt to preside at meetings, the parents are going to wonder why you created their organization. On the other hand, if officers begin making decisions without consulting you, *you* may wonder why you created their organization! A good way to avoid this potential power struggle is to create a constitution for the group. This document should be drawn up by the officers and the Choral Director, and then proposed to and voted on by the entire membership. The constitution should state specifically the duties and responsibilities of each participant and the organization's relationship to the Choral Director and choral students. Then, when a problem arises, all you need to do is to refer to the constitution to resolve the potentially difficult situation.

Student Leadership

Involving students in leadership positions can be beneficial to all concerned. By delegating to students some of the nonmusical aspects of running a choral program, choral directors will have more time and energy to focus on the musical portion of their jobs, and the students can benefit by learning firsthand about important life skills such as responsibility, teamwork, organization, and dependability. Because they are investing more of themselves, students will likely feel more a part of the group and will sense that the director trusts them and places importance on them as individuals.

In addition to participation in the management duties of the choral program, student officers should also be involved in some of the decision-making. Representation in the Choral Parent Organization can provide student leaders an opportunity to voice student concerns and opinions.

Student Officers

Officers may be elected or appointed for each choir or for the entire choral program. A word of caution, however: do not place people in offices that have no real purpose or responsibilities. If you don't need officers in each choir, don't have them! However, electing or appointing section leaders within each choir is usually a good idea to promote team spirit, motivation, and positive behavior patterns.

Possible officers and their responsibilities include:

President. The president of the choral department can serve as the student representative to the Choral Parent Organization and in this way, will be involved in the decision-making process. The President is the spokesperson for the choir at performances and recruitment ventures.

Vice President. The vice president assists the president and will step in whenever the president is unavailable. In addition, assigning this office with a specific function such as management of fund-raising activities or being in charge of keeping accurate attendance records can help make this person feel important and necessary in his or her own right.

Secretary. The secretary is responsible for correspondence, and can work closely with the secretary of the Choral Parent Organization to perform the duties of this office. In addition, the secretary should keep the choral bulletin board both current and attractive. If these demands are light enough to allow for additional responsibilities, ask the secretary to maintain the scrapbook and to take pictures at various choral activities.

Treasurer. The treasurer, of course, deals with the financial aspects of the choral program and should work closely with the treasurer of the Choral Parent Organization. While the student vice president may be in charge of the management of a fund-raising event, the student treasurer may be charged with collecting the money as it comes in during the school day.

Librarian. The librarian is in charge of the choral library. Cataloging new music, entering it into the card file or computer, placing music back into the file when no longer in use, and keeping track of music that needs to be repaired are just a few of the very important duties of this office.

Wardrobe Manager. The wardrobe manager is in charge of the concert attire for the choral groups. If the school owns robes or tuxedos and formals, this apparel will need to be assigned to each student at the beginning of the year, cleaned at the end of the year, and stored properly over the summer.

Budget

Each school district will have a slightly different method of budgeting funds to the various departments within the schools, and you must become knowledgeable about your district's procedures. The best time to ask questions regarding finances is at your job interview. Knowing how much money is allotted for the choral department may suggest not only the economic condition of the school system, but also its level of support for music education.

If the amount of money budgeted for choir is insufficient (and it often is), request a larger figure, and come prepared to justify the increased amount. If additional funds are not available, discuss with the administration the policies regarding alternatives for raising the necessary money such as fund-raising projects or charging admission to a musical program produced by the choral department.

Costs are rising and are not likely to improve, so efficient management of the funds allocated to your department is critical. Be knowledgeable about budget procedures, keep accurate records and receipts, shop around for the best prices available, and take good care of the music and equipment in the choral department. If administrators observe that your materials are well cared for, and that you are frugal and efficient in your business dealings, they may be more apt to increase your budget.

General Operation Costs

You will need provision each year for the general operation of the choral department. Money allotted to this area should allow for at least the purchase of music and hopefully, for additional music folders or music storage containers if needed. Festival and contest entry fees, transportation costs, fees for guest conductors and clinicians, piano tuning and upkeep, and any maintenance required on performance apparel should fall into this category as well. Some costs within the general operating budget of the choral department may be covered in the budget for the entire school. For example, piano tuning and upkeep may be included within the school's general maintenance budget, and any clinician's fees may fall into the category of general instruction and materials. Pursue any possible alternatives for ways to relieve the choral department's financial responsibilities as much as possible.

Unusual Purchases

Occasionally, you will need to purchase items such as concert risers, a new piano, performance attire, stereo equipment, or a computer and software. Discussing the items needed with fellow choral directors can often yield valuable information about what has been successful, and checking catalogues to compare features and prices can help you make a more informed choice. Some of these unusual purchases, like some items within the choir's general operating budget, may be covered in the budget for the entire school, thus allowing the music budget to be used for other things.

When proposing large expenditures such as these, provide written justification for the purchase. Most important, this justification should include the educational benefits to the students. The need for the items and information on available brands and prices should be provided as well so that the administration can see that you are trying to make a wise purchase.

Alternative Sources of Income

Most likely, a large, active, and successful choral department will not be able to operate easily without supplementary funds raised from alternative sources. Fund-raising projects directed by the

Choral Parent Organization can bring in additional monies, but they may also become the "tail that wags the dog," taking valuable time away from learning about and performing music. If you have a choice, plan one large fund-raiser that has the potential to yield large profits rather than three or four projects with modest profits. Always keep in mind that students are in choir to sing and learn about music rather than to earn money.

In lieu of fund-raising projects, some parents would rather just contribute a set amount of money to the choral department. In addition to parental donations, there may be several wealthy citizens in your town or city who are interested in arts education and who would be willing to donate money for a particular item that is needed, or for a special project or trip that is desired. If this fortunate event occurs, make sure that the donors are thanked publicly and properly for their thoughtfulness, and that they are invited to see the benefits that their donation made possible.

Another alternative source of income is to charge a fee for admission to an annual musical production. This production can be a variety or talent show, a Broadway musical, a madrigal dinner, or a special Christmas program. The nice thing about this alternative is that the money earned comes from students doing what they are supposed to be doing: singing and learning about music!

Choral Library

Central to any choral program is its library. Choral directors spend countless hours of thoughtful consideration choosing and ordering the music that their choirs will sing, and large sums of money are spent yearly on the purchase of music, making the choral library a sizeable financial investment. Great care, therefore, should be taken regarding its cataloging, distribution, repair, and storage.

So that directors know what they have and can find quickly what they need, a system to organize the music is vitally necessary. Computer database programs have made the organization of a choral library much easier and more efficient, and most choral departments have, or at least have access to, a computer. If your choral department does not own a computer, consider requesting the purchase of one or hold a fund-raising project to earn the money necessary to purchase one. If you have a computer but are hesitant about using it because of lack of knowledge, take the time to learn. Records will be kept more efficiently and countless hours will be saved if the choral library is computerized.

Ordering the Music

The best time to order music is during the summer. This way, the music is likely to arrive before school begins. For purchases during the school year, check with the music vendor to verify how long it will take to receive the music, and plan accordingly. One month is a good average timetable for music to be ordered and shipped, but the process can take as little as one to two weeks or as long as several months. Nothing is more troubling than to have a performance deadline facing you and the music has not even arrived. Plan ahead!

Information you will need at the time you order the music includes:

1. Title
2. Composer, arranger, and/or editor
3. Publisher
4. Edition number (some music will not have one)
5. Voicing (SATB, SSA, TTB, etc.)
6. How many copies you need (order a few extra copies to allow for damage or loss of music over the years)
7. How you want the music shipped (sometimes you will need it to be shipped in the fastest way possible; be prepared to pay an extra charge for this service)

Cataloging the Music

Let's say you ordered thirty-five copies for the Concert Choir of *Psalm 150* by Heinrich Schütz (see photo). When the music arrives, the choral librarian counts to see if thirty-five copies were sent. Then each piece of music is stamped with the choral department's stamp (example: Westwood Jr. High Choral Dept.). Next, the piece of music is assigned the next number in the sequence of music purchases for mixed voices that your school has made. For instance, the last piece of mixed choir music ordered and received was No. 55, so *Psalm 150* will be given the number 56. The next piece of music for mixed voices that is ordered and received will be assigned No. 57. For the Schütz piece, the number 56 will be stamped on the front of each copy, and the container that will hold the music in storage will be marked with No. 56 as well. (The same idea will apply for music for treble voices as well as for music for male choir. Music of each voicing will have separate numbering sequences and should be stored in separate locations within the Choral Library.)

Each copy received will be stamped with an additional number (in this case, from 1 to 35) signifying the copy number from that set of music. This number is helpful when you assign music to a particular student, because, after the music is taken up, if copy number 7 from piece No. 56 is not returned or is damaged in some way, you will know which student had the music. This helps prevent loss or damage because students know that they will be held accountable for all music given to them, and, if the music is lost, the student, rather than the choral department, will pay for its replacement.

Simplified, the sequence of events for the choral librarian is as follows:

1. Verify the number of copies received by counting them.
2. Stamp each piece with the school stamp.
3. Assign to the piece the next number in the sequence of music purchases by voicing. This file number is stamped on each copy of the piece and is also notated on the container that will hold the piece.
4. Stamp the student copy number on each copy of the piece.

The choral librarian then enters all cataloging information about the piece, including its newly assigned number, into the computer. Examples of entries that can be put into the database about each piece in the choral library include: title; composer/editor/arranger; publisher; edition number; topic or season; number of copies; difficulty level; *a cappella* or accompanied; source of text; language; and voicing. You can see the many possibilities for cross-referencing and sorting as well as for ease in locating a particular composition even if you are unable to recall its title and/or composer.

Music showing school stamp, student copy number, and file number. © 1985
Theodore Presser Company. Used by permission. *Photography by Thom Ewing.*

Distributing the Music

Some choral directors prefer to give out and take up music at each rehearsal. This system can cause confusion as well as damage to the music by excess handling. In addition, because students will have a different copy of the music at each rehearsal, they will be unable to write in the music various reminders such as where to breathe or where to watch the conductor closely.

To save rehearsal time and to avoid excess handling of music, other choral directors assign a music folder to each student. These folders, containing all music currently in rehearsal, can be stored in a folder cabinet like the one shown in the photo. The cabinet is located where students can pick up or return their folders as they enter or leave the choral room. The music, the folder, and the slot in the folder cabinet all have corresponding numbers for identification purchases. For example, Billy's folder, marked with the number 6, contains music also marked with number 6, and his folder is kept in slot number 6 in the folder cabinet.

Using this system, new music, reminders to be taken home to parents, or a long list of announcements can be placed in all slots before rehearsal, avoiding confusion and saving valuable time. Likewise, students can leave music that they are finished using on top of their folder as the folder is placed in the cabinet. The choral librarian can easily retrieve the music in numerical order and return it to the choral library.

Some directors allow their students, on a regular basis, to take their music home for additional study and practice. Fearing the music may be lost, other directors have a check-out system in place to allow students to check out their folder at the end of the school day and to return it the following morning before school begins. Other directors prefer that all music remain in the choral room at all times.

Storing the Music

After a concert, the music will be taken up and stored in the choral library, but before it is put away, the librarian will first need to do several important things. First, a check to see that all music has been returned must be made, followed by a check to see if any repairs are needed. Choral music is handled much more than band or orchestra music and, therefore, may need more frequent repairs. Archival document repair tape is good for rips and tears because it is very thin, transparent, and will not become brittle and turn yellow with age.

After all the copies are gathered and any necessary repairs are made, the music must be placed where it will remain safely until the next time it is used. Several options are available for storage.

File Cabinets. Several letter-size file cabinets can be used to store most music quite easily. A hanging file system may work best, because it may require a bit less handling than the regular manila folders or filing envelopes. Regardless of the type you choose, each file folder should have the title and composer as well as the number of the piece written on the outside of the folder. The music, of course, is placed inside the folders, and the folders are filed numerically. If you have limited space and a limited budget, storing the music in folders inside several file cabinets may be your

Folder cabinet. *Photography by Thom Ewing.*

best choice. An additional positive feature of file cabinets is that they can be locked.

Cardboard Boxes. Cardboard boxes of the same length and width but of varying thickness are available for the storage of music. The music is always protected inside the box and, because the boxes are stored numerically on shelves, the choral director and librarian can readily see them. On the negative side, many shelves are necessary to accommodate these boxes, and choral directors often complain that they must open the box to get even one copy of the music. Repeated opening and closing of the boxes may limit how long the boxes will last before replacements are needed. In addition, it is sometimes difficult to get all copies of the music to go down evenly into the box, causing one or two pieces to be folded or crushed in the storage process. If, however, you like having your music out where you can see it, and have the space required as well as the money to purchase them, you may want to consider storing music in cardboard boxes as shown in the photo.

Boxes with Separate Lids. Another option available for the storage of music in the choral library is the use of boxes with separate lids

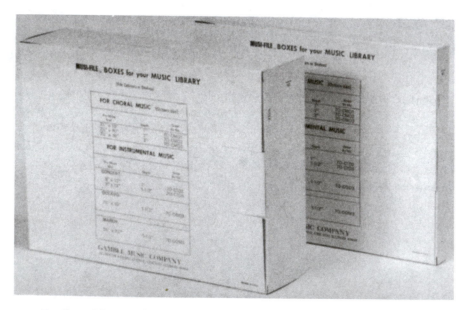

Cardboard boxes of various sizes for music storage. *Photograph by Thom Ewing.*

Cardboard boxes of varyious sizes with lids for music storage.
Photograph by Thom Ewing.

as shown in the photo. Like the cardboard boxes described earlier, shelves are required, but retrieving the music in these boxes is much easier because you simply remove and then replace the lid. These boxes are more expensive, but may last longer because they are often made out of a sturdier cardboard. The lids are an optional purchase at a small additional cost but are recommended because dust, bugs, and curious fingers will easily get into these storage containers if left uncovered.

The storage of major works, oversized music, or instrumental parts that are purchased is often a difficult task. Large boxes can be used to keep this music safe and free of dust, but the amount of space required is often a problem. Large envelopes with a brad closure take up less space but are more difficult to see at a glance. More often than not, this music is simply stacked up and placed on shelves with no covering whatsoever. This is not a good idea for obvious reasons, not the least of which is the cost of replacing just one copy of a major work.

Card File

Those choral directors who have not computerized their libraries will also need an efficient system to file music. The easiest and perhaps the most popular method is to file each piece of music by com-

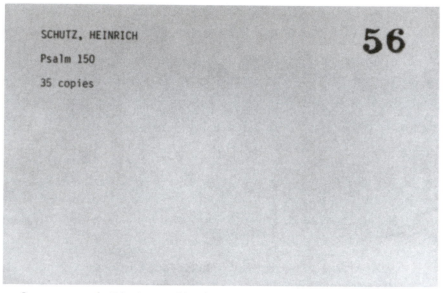

SCHUTZ, HEINRICH

Psalm 150

35 copies

56

Composer card. File this card by the composer's last name. *Photograph by Thom Ewing.*

poser as well as by title. Each piece of music for mixed choir will have a composer card and a title card that will be kept in two separate file boxes. Two separate card-file boxes must be maintained as well for treble choir music and music for male voices.

The composer card, shown in the photo, has the composer's last name listed first, followed by the first name and then the title of the composition. All composer cards (for music of similar voicing) will be alphabetized by the composer's last name. The title card, shown in the photo, has the title of the composition listed first, followed by the composer's name. All title cards (for music of similar voicing) will be alphabetized by title. Both composer and title cards will have the piece's assigned number on them. You may want to note how many copies of the piece are available as well as the date on which it was last performed.

Scheduling

A good, workable schedule is vital for a successful choral program. No matter how many students want to join choir, if choir is always in direct conflict with required classes, membership will

```
   PSALM 150                                    56

   Heinrich Schutz

   35 copies
```

Title card. File this card by the title. *Photograph by Thom Ewing.*

suffer and little growth will be realized. The time to bargain for an improved schedule is at the time you accept the new position, but before making suggestions for improvement (if any are needed), do some research. Ask for a copy of the master schedule for the entire school as well as the current schedule for the choral department.

At the very least, make sure that all choirs, with the possible exception of the pop ensemble, are scheduled to meet daily during regular school hours. The Music Educators National Conference (MENC) believes that music should be taught during the school day and that the curriculum should have sufficient time and flexibility to allow students the opportunity to elect courses in music. If students wish to participate in more than one musical organization, check when band and orchestra meet, and coordinate these groups with the choral offerings. And be sure to locate any *singletons* such as advanced trigonometry or physics (a singleton is a class that meets for one section only). If, for example, you have college-bound students in a choral ensemble that meets opposite these advanced, required classes, these students will have to be out of that choir (or out of choir entirely) for one semester or perhaps one year.

After you have taught for several years, you will begin to have a preference for certain periods during the school day. This preference varies with each choral director and his or her school as well as the age level of the students. For example, if you are not a morning person, you will want to schedule carefully the choirs you rehearse before lunch. Because middle school students' naturally high energy level may be augmented by the sugar and starch that many of them eat at lunchtime, scheduling the advanced mixed choir right after lunch may not be a good idea. On the other hand, if you are equal to the challenge and prefer having to calm students down rather than motivating them, the period after lunch may work fine.

The periods just before and after lunch are often popular for scheduling choirs. The period before lunch may work better than the period after lunch for the reasons cited above. Placing a choir in one of these spots usually gives you three 30-minute segments of time (one for lunch, and two for class), and with this flexibility, you would be able to have sectional rehearsals if you desired. For example, during segment one, let one group go to lunch while you work with the other group, reverse it for the second segment of time, and have everyone come together for the third segment. The extended amount of time can also be helpful when you schedule an off-campus performance during rehearsal time and you need a few extra minutes to get back to school for the next class period. For the majority of time, however, you will rehearse the choir for the first two time segments and then everyone will go to lunch.

Most teachers at the secondary school level have one period per day designated for planning. Many teachers prefer this period to be the first hour of the school day to allow them to get organized and to plan for their upcoming classes. Other teachers prefer their planning period to be the last period of the day so, while the day's successes and failures are fresh on their minds, they can plan for the next day's rehearsals. Some teachers use their planning periods, not for planning, but for making and returning phone calls or for running errands related to their work. If this is the case for you, you will need to request a planning period during the day when places of business are open and people will be in to receive you or your phone calls.

Often, the administration will have to be educated about the necessity of grouping by ability the students in the various choral ensembles. Don't assume that the correct students will be placed into the correct choirs unless you have specified this information. As soon as possible, therefore, make an appointment to talk with the person or persons responsible for making student schedules and provide them with the lists of students who have been selected or assigned to the various choirs for the following year. Help them to understand that choir is taught in a sequential manner much the same as English or math, and that beginning choral students would be lost in an advanced choir much the same way that ninth-grade English students would be lost in a senior-level advanced English class. This is a critical issue that is often overlooked!

Performance Attire

Wearing a specific performance outfit for concerts provides a visual uniformity, complementing the musical uniformity for which every choir strives. The choir, after all, is a group; therefore, attention should be not on various individuals but rather on the entire ensemble.

A wide variety of options, ranging from very elaborate to quite simple, is available for concert apparel. An inexpensive and age-appropriate outfit for middle school/junior high choirs consists of nice jeans (no holes, please!) and a T-shirt with the school's name on the front. Singers can purchase the style of jeans that look attractive on them and the T-shirt will provide uniformity as well as identification for each group. This idea may also work well with older choirs for casual concerts such as trips to feeder schools for recruitment programs, or for concerts with a lighter musical focus.

Another relatively inexpensive but more formal performance outfit is long black skirts and long-sleeved white blouses for the women, with black pants and long-sleeved white shirts for the men. No specific pattern is dictated except to keep the style simple. This way, students can select the style that looks best on them, and the black-and-white colors provide uniformity. Adding a colorful cummerbund or tie can add variety.

Performing in formal attire. *Photograph by Thom Ewing.*

The most formal attire is tuxedos for the men and formal gowns for the women. This route can become very expensive, but the look is quite distinctive and sophisticated. If an all-black dress is chosen, a splash of color can be added with a belt for the women and a matching bow tie for the men. Using the same dress for all choirs at your school and varying the color of the belts (and matching bow ties for the men's tuxedos) can provide identification not only for the school, but also for the various choral groups, if desired.

The wearing of choir robes is a relatively easy way to dress a choral group, and, because the cut of a robe is full, the style will look attractive on most every student. However, some students, especially boys, are reluctant to wear choir robes for various reasons. Most choral programs rarely have enough male participation, so having performance attire that may discourage boys from singing in choir is an important issue to consider. Before deciding to purchase something as expensive as choir robes, you might ask several of the boys what they think about the idea. Having one or two students model a sample robe in class so they can really see what they look like would help them (and you) to make a more informed decision.

Gathering the information necessary to make a decision on the performance attire for your choirs is a time-consuming task. Remember to delegate authority to the Choral Parent Organization and, whatever your choice, you will want to consult a student committee as well as the parents. Some aspects to be considered in the decision are given in the following paragraphs.

Expense

Choral outfits can be extremely expensive. Are your parents willing and able to purchase an outfit for their child? If a family cannot afford an outfit, what provisions will be made for that singer? Perhaps your school or school system is willing to pay for the purchase of all performance apparel or will share the expense with the choral department. The outfits are then given out to each singer at the beginning of the year. Students remain responsible for them until the outfit is returned after the final concert, and a repair or replacement fee is charged for damaged or lost clothing. You may want to require that the apparel be dry cleaned (unless it is machine washable) before it is returned for storage. Is a storage area available and secure?

Age of Choir

Try to choose apparel that is appropriate for the age of your choirs. Nothing is quite so disconcerting as seeing a middle school/junior high school choir dressed like a college group. And consider the variety of body shapes and sizes of the choir members, especially at the middle school/junior high level. Finding a dress pattern that comes in the wide variety of sizes you will need and that will also be attractive on a majority of the singers may be extremely difficult for this age group! Purchasing a ready-made uniform, wearing jeans and T-shirts, or using the black skirt/pants and white blouse/shirt idea may be the easiest way to dress young adolescents.

How Does It Look from the Stage?

Often, an outfit will look cheap or too flashy when standing face to face but will look just right from the stage. Conversely, sometimes an outfit that looks great up close will look washed out from the stage. Therefore, when making a decision on performance attire, remember that the outfit will be seen from a distance and with varying degrees of lighting. Another aspect to consider is whether the outfits will still look attractive when there are fifty of them on the stage at the same time. Sometimes the look can be overpowering or too busy, and therefore, would distract from the musical efforts of the choir.

Longevity

The quality of the material and workmanship will certainly contribute to the longevity of an outfit. Will the uniform withstand repeated wearing and washing or dry cleaning? Will the outfit wrinkle when packed in a suitcase for trips and tours? Will the style remain current long enough to get your money's worth out of the purchase before having to choose a different outfit? If the outfits are custom-made, will the same material, color, and patterns be available for new members or for returning members who grow during the summer? If the outfits or robes are purchased, for how many years will the same style be available? Will the colors match on purchases from different years? The answers to these questions are important, because parents will be unhappy with frequent changes in uniform, particularly if they are required to purchase (or make!) their child's outfit themselves, and schools will not have large amounts of money to spend on choral outfits every two to three years.

Instruments and Equipment

In *Opportunity-to-Learn: Standards for Music Instruction* (1994, p. 12), the Music Educators National Conference (MENC) gives recommendations for instruments and equipment necessary for choral music programs at the secondary level. Every room should have "a high-quality sound reproduction system capable of utilizing current recording technology" as well as access to recordings of a variety of musical styles and cultures. Each room should have convenient access to a high-quality electronic or acoustic piano that is tuned at least three times each year, and a set of portable choral risers. The recommendations also include sturdy music stands, a music folder for each choral student, conductors' stands, and chairs designed for music classes. MENC states that every school have access to computers and music software, MIDI equipment, electronic keyboards and synthesizers, and CD-ROM-compatible computers with appropriate CD-ROMs. "Also available are video cameras, color monitors, stereo VCRs, and multimedia equipment combining digitized sound and music with graphics and text."

If moving the piano from the rehearsal hall into the performing area is extremely difficult or impossible because of the building's architectural limitations, you need to consider the purchase of a piano that would remain in the performing area and be used for concerts and school assemblies that included music in some way. Even if moving the rehearsal piano is an easy task, you may want to consider the purchase of a performance piano to reduce the wear and tear, due to frequent moves, on the rehearsal piano.

Risers for choral performances are certainly desirable. Having singers on different levels not only promotes better eye contact, but also allows for every voice to be heard. A variety of styles are available today, including those with carpet to reduce noise, those with casters for ease in moving, those to which an acoustical shell can be attached, and those that have a back rail available to prevent singers from falling off the top row. Many styles even allow for various configurations in addition to the more traditional straight line or semicircular arrangements. This latter feature is certainly desirable if you have a pop ensemble that uses creative choreography.

If you have the luxury of securing a position at a brand new middle school/junior high or high school and can consult on architectural plans for the choral area, you may want to consider a flat floor with portable risers for sitting rather than a floor with permanent concrete risers built in. A flat floor offers much more versatility, especially if your program includes the teaching of nonperformance classes such as general music or music theory, or if a pop ensemble is a part of the curriculum. The nonperformance classes need a different type of space and often require desks, and the pop ensemble will need sufficient room to rehearse choreography.

The Music Industry Conference, a nonprofit organization and an auxiliary of the Music Educators National Conference, serves as a liaison between music educators and the manufacturing and publishing firms that supply materials and equipment used in music education. This group offers a guide that contains helpful suggestions for the selection, purchase, and maintenance of music education materials and equipment. Also featured are two lists, one alphabetical and the other classified, of members of the Music Industry Conference complete with their addresses and services. Helpful to the choral music educator are companies that sell computer software, choir robes, and classroom instruments, piano manufacturers, and groups that organize tours for musical organizations. This guide is published biennially as part of the January issue of the *Music Educators Journal*.

Using Technology in the Classroom

Educators can no longer afford to ignore the vast selection of technology available for use in today's classrooms and rehearsals. Because technology changes so rapidly, the task of becoming knowledgeable in this area can sometimes be overwhelming, especially for new choral directors who are already performing many responsibilities for the first time. However, an initial investment of time and effort to learn about new technology and how it can make your job more manageable and exciting will pay huge dividends in the long run. If you haven't taken a technology course as part of your college

Photograph by Thom Ewing.

curriculum, investigate a course offered by a community college, a summer workshop, or ask friends or colleagues who can help you to become familiar with the equipment and its myriad of uses.

In describing the new music curriculum to prepare students for the twenty-first century, MENC believes that current technology should be used to individualize and expand the music learning of students. In *The School Music Program: A New Vision* (1994, p. 5), MENC more specifically states that "through the use of computers, electronic keyboards, synthesizers, samplers, CDs, CD-ROMs, and various MIDI devices, every student can be actively involved in creating, performing, listening to, and analyzing music."

Management Uses

The use of a computer for management purposes alone can greatly increase efficiency as well as greatly reduce the amount of time required to perform many nonmusical tasks. Accurate and accessible records on every student can be kept in a database and updated when necessary. An inventory of the choirs' performance attire and other materials or equipment can be kept on computer. Using the computer for word-processing purposes will greatly expedite communication to parents, colleagues, and any correspondence of a general nature. Students' grades may be calculated accurately and much more quickly with the use of a grading program for the computer, and financial information can be kept accurately and updated easily. And perhaps the most valuable benefit is for the choral library to be computerized. The initial move from a card-file system to entering the information into the computer may require a great deal of time and effort, but afterward, you need only enter new pieces as they arrive, and the possibilities for cross-referencing are endless.

Instructional Uses

No matter what the program or topic, just having the opportunity to use the computer can serve as a motivator for your students, so you will likely find them eager to engage in both remediation and enrichment activities related to instruction given during the choral rehearsal. In addition, the use of MIDI (Music Instrument Digital Interface) supports a variety of devices ranging from piano-style keyboards to guitars and drums. All of these devices can produce sounds to which your students can easily relate.

Instructional programs and games designed to teach or reinforce aural skills and music theory can enhance your students' knowledge, sightsinging skills, and overall musicianship. The use of compact discs in the classroom can present to your students outstanding sound reproductions, and CD-ROMs now make it possible, along with computers, to provide simultaneous, high-quality sound, still images, and moving pictures. The opportunity to manipulate music notation and hear the results can increase student interest in music as well as foster creativity. And choral directors can use the music notation system to create such things as specialized warm-up and sightsinging exercises as well as to arrange music that is tailored for their particular choral groups.

Selecting Hardware and Software

More than likely, you will find a computer and a selection of software already in place within the choral department of your first job. If, however, you have the opportunity to purchase a new computer, many experts suggest that you look at the available software first, and then select the computer system on which the best software programs will run. Or better still, select the computer and the software simultaneously. This way, you will never find yourself in the position of purchasing inferior software simply because it will run on your computer.

In addition to software quality and availability, the functions you expect the computer to perform for the choral department must be considered when deciding on a new computer system. For example, virtually all current microcomputer systems have a built-in capability to reproduce sound, but these capabilities are very limited. If you wish to have the capability to produce high-quality sound, some sort of MIDI instrument (keyboard, guitar, drums) will be necessary, along with a MIDI interface and appropriate software. And of course, you must factor in the amount of money you have to spend. In addition to the purchase of hardware and software, you may also want to include money that will enable you to attend a computer workshop or class. This may ease the transition to a new computer and avoid much frustration in the process.

A large amount of unsuitable software is available and you must be able to distinguish between it and that which will enhance your students' musical growth. Rather than purchasing a program based on a description in a catalog, order it on approval if at all possible so you can evaluate it personally before you buy it. To guide music educators in this process, Fred Willman (1992, p. 34) suggests that teachers "choose software and supportive technology that:

1. promotes the development of higher-level cognitive skills
2. places students in roles that parallel those normally undertaken by musicians: performer, composer, improviser, consumer, and critic
3. places all musical facts and knowledge within a musical context
4. focuses on music, not symbols
5. helps students unlock the 'learning process' rather than merely attain a limited collection of musical facts
6. requires the students to make musical decisions and exercise musical judgment
7. causes students to respond to music with understanding."

As part of her master's degree at Southern Methodist University, Shari Lynn Hamann (1993, pp. 70–74) designed and tested a model to be used by classroom teachers for the evaluation of music education software. Her model poses important questions to be considered before a software purchase is made. Some practical considerations are highlighted here:

1. What computers are compatible with the software?
2. What is the minimum necessary memory (RAM) needed to run the software?
3. Does the program use sound and, if so, what additional hardware is needed to support it?
4. What is the input method and what navigation features are provided (start over, quit, help)?
5. Is the presentation of material given in a sequential manner?
6. Can you adjust the difficulty level?
7. Is adequate time allowed for the user to read the screen?
8. In aural examples, does the program establish a tonality before the question is played?

9. Is a user's manual provided that is free of technical jargon, and does it contain error message information?

Provisions for Security

As you consider the purchase of your computer system and various software programs, you must simultaneously plan for its security. The room where the equipment is located needs to be locked when not in use, and the area must be kept clean and cool. In addition, rules (and the consequences if they are broken) need to be in place to guide student behavior when using the computers (Hoffman, 1994, pp. 36–37). This will not only teach responsibility and respect for the equipment, but will also ensure that your expenditure will be available, in working order, for a long time to come.

Copyright Guidelines

Using Software: A Guide to the Ethical and Legal Use of Software for Members of the Academic Community is a brochure that has been created to foster better understanding of the implications and restrictions of the U. S. Copyright Law with regard to computer software. This helpful brochure can be obtained from either of the following organizations:

EDUCOM
1112 16th Street, NW, Suite 600
Washington DC 20036
(202) 872–4200

ITAA
1616 N. Fort Myer Drive, Suite 1300
Arlington, VA 22204
(703) 284–5355

Current Sourcebooks for Software and Hardware

William R. Higgins, Professor of Music at Messiah College in Grantham, Pennsylvania, has compiled a book entitled *A Resource Guide to Computer Applications in Music Education*, to help music educators keep current on available software for use in their classrooms. Updated annually, the book lists instructional software available for the following computers: (1) PC/MS-DOS (IBM); (2) Macintosh; and (3) Apple II. In addition, he lists MIDI sequencing software and music-printing software. References include periodicals, books, and helpful addresses for the computer user, and his book contains several appendixes dealing with topics ranging from selecting a microcomputer to repairing it.*

Offered by the Association for Technology in Music Instruction (ATMI), the *ATMI Technology Directory* is a publication that is updated annually and is available each fall. Dr. Gary S. Karpinski, Associate Professor of Music at the University of Oregon School of Music and president of ATMI, reports the directory has 400 to 500 pages listing software and hardware for teaching music. Computer-Assisted Instruction (CAI) forms the core of the list that also includes information on sequencing, notation, and multimedia programs.**

Awards

An awards banquet or ceremony can serve as a positive way to conclude the school year for students and parents alike. Everyone likes to receive a pat on the back, and an occasion such as this provides opportunity for public acknowledgment of hard work and successful endeavors.

At the very least, all choral students should hear their names called to come forward and receive a Certificate of Participation. Other awards may include Outstanding Student in each choir (voted on by each choir's membership), acknowledgment of students' selection to the All-State Choir and various other honor choirs, and ratings earned at Large Group and Solo and Ensemble Festivals. In addition, the Choral Director may want to choose an overall Outstanding Choral Student each year and engrave each

---

* This valuable resource is available either directly from William Higgins or from: Electronic Courseware Systems, Inc., 1210 Lancaster Dr., Champaign, Illinois 61821.

** For information on how to join this organization and receive this valuable publication, contact: Dr. Timothy Kloth, Treasurer, ATMI, 2336 Donnington Lane, Cincinnati, Ohio 45244.

recipient's name on a permanent plaque to be displayed in the choral room.

This is an excellent opportunity to thank publicly the members of the Choral Parent Organization for their assistance during the year. They need to feel appreciated and to know that their efforts are invaluable to the overall success of the choral program.

Don't forget to invite and publicly thank administrators such as the principal and guidance counselor, because without their support, the choral program could not be successful. If they are not as supportive as you would like them to be, their presence at the awards banquet may serve to change their attitude in a more positive direction. Hopefully, by seeing firsthand a celebration of musical success as well as the cooperation and support shown to you and the choral program by students and parents alike, they may rethink their view of the department.

An inexpensive way to hold an awards banquet is to have a covered-dish dinner in the school cafeteria. Choral students and their parents should sit together, and a head table should be provided with seating for the choral director, the president (or all officers) of the Choral Parent Organization and their children who sing in choir, the student president of the choir and his or her parents, and any invited administrators. Committees from the Choral Parent Organization can organize the food and decorations, invitations, and purchase of awards and certificates. The cost of food will be distributed among the various parents, and the decorations need not be elaborate. Paper tablecloths with handmade place cards and perhaps small vases of flowers picked from a parent's yard will help turn the cafeteria into a more festive place. Of course, if funds are available, a much more elaborate occasion can be planned, but the event *can* be held on a small budget.

Professional Organizations

As a music educator in the choral area, you should belong to two professional organizations so that you will remain current on what is happening in your field. In addition, as part of the larger body of fellow music educators, you will have opportunities to contribute your ideas and your voice on current various issues facing choral music educators. Among other benefits, both organizations publish informative journals each month and hold exciting conferences every year. These organizations are:

Music Educators National Conference (MENC)
1806 Robert Fulton Drive
Reston, VA 22091

American Choral Directors Association (ACDA)
P.O. Box 6310
Lawton, OK 73506

Summary

Because some administrators may not fully understand the teaching of music, they will often base their entire evaluation of your teaching effectiveness on how well you manage the nonmusical responsibilities of your job. In addition, if these responsibilities are ignored, or done in a haphazard manner, the musical success of the choirs under your direction can be compromised. So that the choral program can be all that it can be, an efficient and systematic way of handling these details must be in place. Delegating responsibilities to both students and parents can ease the burden, allowing you to focus more fully on the musical portion of your job. This approach may help you avoid teacher burnout, provide parents with an opportunity for involvement in their child's education, and teach valuable life skills to students, all at the same time.

The management of a choral program includes efficient handling of the financial resources allocated to your department, and may require various fund-raising campaigns to raise adequate funds. Because the choral library is central to any choral program, great care should be taken in the ordering of music, as well as in its cataloging, distribution, repair, and storage. A workable schedule is vital, and administrators must be educated regarding the placement of singers in the correct choral ensembles.

Wearing a specific performance outfit for concerts provides a visual uniformity, complementing the musical uniformity for which every choir strives. Ranging from very elaborate to quite simple, a wide variety of options is available. The expense of the outfit and how long it may be used, and how it looks from the stage are factors to consider. In addition, the outfit chosen should be an appropriate one for the age of your students.

MENC recommends that each choral program be supplied with a high-quality sound reproduction system, recordings of various musical styles and cultures, an electronic or acoustic piano, and a set of portable choral risers. The recommendations also include the purchase of music stands, music folders, conductors' stands, and chairs designed for music classes. In addition, every school should have access to computers, related equipment, and music software.

Educators can no longer afford to ignore the vast selection of technology available for use in today's classrooms and rehearsals. Computers used for management purposes can greatly increase efficiency when performing many nonmusical tasks, and instructional programs and games designed to teach or reinforce aural skills and music theory can enhance your students' knowledge, sightsinging skills, and overall musicianship. When purchasing a computer, consider software quality and availability, the functions you expect the computer to perform for the choral department, and how the equipment will be secured. Various sourcebooks for software and hardware are available to music educators.

For students and parents alike, an awards banquet can serve as a positive conclusion to the school year. At the very least, all choral students should hear their names called to come forward and receive a Certificate of Participation. Other specific awards for outstanding achievements during the year can be given as well. This is a good time to invite parents and administrators, so that you may acknowledge their assistance, and publicly thank them for their interest in the choral program.

As a music educator in the choral area, you should belong to the Music Educators National Conference (MENC), and to the American Choral Directors Association (ACDA). These professional organizations publish informative journals each month, and hold exciting conferences every year. Membership also offers you the opportunity to contribute your ideas, and to voice your opinion of various issues facing choral music educators.

Mini-Projects

1. Listed below are the five high school choirs under your direction. Consider these choirs as well as the times of the day in which you are the most energetic and productive. Plan the optimum schedule for you and your choral department, and fill in the time slots below with your decision.

(Notice the longer time designated at the 11:00 class period, allowing for a thirty-minute lunch during the beginning, middle, or end of the period.)

CHOIRS

Boys' Chorus (beginning level)
Girls' Chorus (beginning level)
Mixed Choir (intermediate level)
Concert Choir (advanced level)
Girls' Ensemble (advanced level)
Planning Period

SCHEDULE

8:00–8:55 _____
9:00–9:55 _____
10:00–10:55 _____
11:00–12:20 _____
12:25–1:20 _____
1:25–2:20 _____

2. On approval, order several music–software programs that can be run on a computer to which you have access. Evaluate the programs for use in a middle school/junior high school or high school choral program.

3. To experience the process of ordering music, order three selections of your choice from a music distributor. Make sure you include the title; composer, arranger, and/or editor; publisher, edition number; voicing; how many copies you need; and how you want the music sent.

4. While observing at several schools, take time to visit their choral library. Notice the system used in storing the music, and discuss with the choral director how well it works. Is the music cataloged on computer?

5. Ask to borrow several catalogs of performing attire from local choir directors. Peruse the catalog, familiarizing yourself with available outfits and their cost. Choose several that would be appropriate for middle school/junior high school students and several for high school students.

References

GRASHEL, JOHN. (1993). Research in music teacher education. *Music Educators Journal, 80*(1), 45–48.

HAMANN, SHARI LYNN. (1993). *An evaluation model for CAI in music.* Unpublished masters project, Southern Methodist University.

HOFFMAN, BETH (compiled by). (1994). Managing technological resources. *Teaching Music, 2*(1), 36–37.

Opportunity-to-learn: Standards for music instruction. (1994). Reston, VA: Music Educators National Conference.

The school music program: A new vision. (1994). Reston, VA: Music Educators National Conference.

WILLMAN, FRED. (1992). New solutions to curricular problems. *Music Educators Journal, 79*(3), 33–35.

Additional Reading

BERZ, WILLIAM L., and JUDITH BOWMAN. (1994). *Applications of research in music technology.* Reston, VA: Music Educators National Conference.

BROODY, CHARLES (compiled by). (1990). *TIPS: Technology for Music Educators.* Reston, VA: Music Educators National Conference.

Computer-assisted instruction in music. *Teaching Music*, *1*(6), 34–35.

Focus on technology in music education (entire issue). (1992). *Music Educators Journal*, *79*(3).

GEERDES, HAROLD P. (1987). *Music facilities: Building, equipping, and renovating*. Reston, VA: Music Educators National Conference.

HAMANN, DONALD L. (1990). Burnout: How to spot it, how to avoid it. *Music Educators Journal*, *77*(2), 30–33.

MUETH, LARRY. (1993). MIDI technology for the scared to death. *Music Educators Journal*, *79*(8), 49–53.

Music booster manual. (1989). Reston, VA: Music Educators National Conference.

WILLIAMS, DAVID B., AND PETER R. WEBSTER (1996). Experiencing Music Technology: Software, Data, and Hardware. New York: Schirmer Books.

Appendix: Selected Choral Repertoire

The list of choral literature that follows is categorized first by voicing (mixed, treble, and tenor-bass), and then by difficulty level (Grades 1–6, with Grade 6 as the most difficult). Most of the repertoire has been selected, with permission, from the University Interscholastic League (UIL) Prescribed Music List for the state of Texas (1991–1994).

CHORAL MUSIC FOR MIXED VOICES

Composer/ Arranger	Title	Publisher
	GRADE I	
Bacak (arr.)	Jubilate! Jubilate! (SAB)	Jenson
Crocker	Sing to the Lord (SAB)	Southern Music Co.
Eilers	Bound for Jubilee	Studio 224
Emerson	Shoshone Love Song (3-part mixed)	Hal Leonard
Emerson (arr.)	Didn't My Lord Deliver Daniel (3-part mixed)	Hal Leonard
Emerson	Time Gone (3-part mixed)	Hal Leonard
Emerson (arr.)	Let Me Ride (Swing Down Chariot)	Hal Leonard
Henderson	Storm (unison and speaking)	Gordon V. Thompson
Jothen	Over the Sea to Skye (2-part mixed)	Beckenhorst Press
Kirk	Sing a Song to the Lord	Cambiata Press
Lyle (arr.)	The Colorado Trail (SACB)	Cambiata Press
Nelhybel	Rest in the Lord	Hope Publishing

Composer/ Arranger	Title	Publisher
Palestrina/ Liebergen	O Bone Jesu	Carl Fischer, Inc.
Pergolesi/Hopson	O, My God, Bestow Thy Tender Mercy (2-part)	Carl Fischer, Inc.

GRADE II

Bright	Never Tell Thy Love	Associated Music
Crocker	I Will Sing of the Goodness of the Lord	Jenson
Cruger/Bach/ Collins	Jesu, Priceless Treasure (SSCB)	Cambiata Press
Diemer	Three Madrigals	Boosey & Hawkes
Greenberg (ed.)	Dadme Albricias, hijos d'Eva	Associated Music
Josquin	El Grillo	Canyon Press
Mendelssohn/ Farrell	Cast Thy Burden upon the Lord (SACB)	Cambiata Press
Pfautsch	Prayer	Lawson-Gould
Praetorius/Greyson	Psallite	Bourne Company
Spevacek (arr.)	The Turtle Dove (SAB)	Jenson

GRADE III

Billings/Shaw/ Parker	Chester	Lawson-Gould
Certon	Je le vous dirai	Bourne Company
Cherubini	Pie Jesu	National Music Publ.
Crocker	Jubilate Deo	Jenson
Distler	Maria Walks Amid the Thorn (SAB)	Concordia
Duson	I Asked the River	Neil A. Kjos
Handel/Hines	Be Merciful Unto Me (Saul) (SAB)	Elkan-Vogel
Kodály	Birthday Greeting	Boosey & Hawkes
Mendelssohn/ Palmer	Neujahrslied	National Music Publ.
Vecchi	Fa una canzona	Lawson-Gould

GRADE IV

Bennett	O Sleep, Fond Fancy	Bourne Company
Berger	A Rose Touched by the Sun's Warm Rays	Augsburg Fortress
Clausen	Set Me as a Seal from a New Creation	Mark Foster

Composer/ Arranger	Title	Publisher
Croce/Bennett	O Sacrum Convivium	Harold Flammer
Duson	What Is a Heart?	Neil A. Kjos
Fauré	Tantum Ergo	Walton
Mendelssohn/ Robinson	Die Nachtigall	Hinshaw Music
Persichetti	Agnus Dei	Elkan-Vogel
Stravinsky	Ave Maria	Boosey & Hawkes
Victoria	O Vos Omnes	GIA Publications

GRADE V

Bartók	Four Slovak Folk Songs	Boosey & Hawkes
Brahms	Im Herbst	Hinshaw Music
Bright	Rainsong	Associate Music Publ.
Costeley/Shaw/ Parker	Allon, Gay Bergeres	G. Schirmer
Debussy	Dieu! qu'il la fait bon regarder! (from *Trois Chansons*)	Durand Company
Dello Joio	Come to Me, My Love	Marks Music Corp.
Handl/Petti	In Nomine Jesu	J. & W. Chester, Ltd.
Haydn	Alles hat seine Zeit	C. F. Peters
Hennagin	Walking on the Green Grass	Boosey & Hawkes
Holst (arr.)	I Love My Love	G. Schirmer
Leisy	Dance to the Music of Time	Lawson-Gould
Mozart	Sancta Maria, Mater Dei (K. 273)	Novello
Pfautsch	Musicks Empire (from *Triptych*)	Lawson-Gould
Stevens	Like as the Culver on the Bared Bough	Associated Music Publ.

EXTENDED WORKS, GRADE VI

Brahms/Klein	Ziegeunerlieder, Op. 103	G. Schirmer
Britten	Festival Te Deum	Boosey & Hawkes
Dello Joio	The Mystic Trumpeter	G. Schirmer
Foss	Behold! I Build An House	Mercury Music
Handel	Coronation Anthem No. 4 (Let Thy Hand Be Strengthened)	G. Schirmer
Hindemith	Six Chansons	Associated Music Publ.
Jannequin	Le Chant Des Oyseaux	Editions Salabert
Mozart	Regina Coeli	G. Schirmer
Pachelbel	Deus In Adjutorium	Marks Music Corp.
Pinkham	Christmas Cantata	Robert King

CHORAL MUSIC FOR TREBLE VOICES

Composer/ Arranger	Title	Publisher
GRADE I		
Artman	All the Pretty Little Horses (2-part)	Studio 224
Bach	Come Together, Let Us Sing (unison)	E. C. Schirmer
Crocker	Children of the Heavenly King (2-part)	Southern Music Co.
Fleming	The Lord Himself (unison)	Gordon V. Thompson
Haydn/Hopson	Sound the Trumpet! (2-part)	Coronet Press
Purcell/Kirk	Shepherds, Tune Your Pipes (SA)	Pro-Art Publications
Rao (arr.)	Good Night (2-part)	Boosey & Hawkes
Rinker	Where Go the Boats? (SA)	Music Corp. of America
Saint-Saëns/ Martens	Ave Verum Corpus (SA)	Walton Music
Sleeth	Hallelujah, Glory Hallelujah (2-part)	Sacred Music Press
GRADE II		
Bacon	Buttermilk Hill (SA)	Boosey & Hawkes
Britten	Jazz Man (unison)	Boosey & Hawkes
Casals	Canco a la Verge	Tetra Music Corp.
Copland/Fine	Simple Gifts (2-part)	Boosey & Hawkes
Henderson	The Yak (SA)	Gordon V. Thompson
Kjelson (arr.)	I Walk the Unfrequented Road (SA)	Belwin-Mills
Mendelssohn	Evening Song (Abendlied)	Gentry Publications
Perry	Alleluia! Sing with Joy (2-part)	Shawnee Press
Rhein (arr.)	Hush-A-By, Bairnie (2-part)	G. Schirmer
Thompson	My Master Hath a Garden (SA)	E. C. Schirmer
GRADE III		
Baksa	Three Precious Gifts	Shawnee Press
Brahms/McEwen	My Beloved (SA)	Zia Music Press
Britten	Fancie	Boosey &Hawkes
Cherubini	Like As a Father	Music 70
Copland	The Little Horses	Boosey & Hawkes
Felciano (arr.)	O Come, O Come, Emmanuel	Marks Music Corp.
Mendelssohn	Ich Wollt', Meine Lieb' (SA)	National Music Publ.
Mendelssohn	Lift Thine Eyes (from *Elijah*)	Carl Fischer
Persichetti	Hist Whist (SA)	Carl Fischer
Purcell/Erb (ed.)	Sound the Trumpet	Lawson-Gould

Composer/ Arranger	Title	Publisher

GRADE IV

Bartók	The Wooing of a Girl	Boosey & Hawkes
Bell	O Sacrum Convivium	Gordon V. Thompson
Clausen	Laudamus te (Orff instruments)	Mark Foster
Duson (arr.)	Danny Boy (SSAA)	Neil K. Kjos
Fauré	Tantum ergo	Broude Brothers
Monteverdi/ Boepple	Angelus ad pastores ait	Mercury Music
Pfautsch	Hello Girls	Lawson-Gould
Rutter (arr.)	Tomorrow Shall Be My Dancing Day	Oxford
Spencer	Nova, Nova, Ave fit ex Eva	National Music Publ.
Thompson	Come In (from *Frostiana*)	E. C. Schirmer

GRADE V

Bach	Suscepit Israel (from *Magnificat*)	E. C. Schirmer
Brahms	Ave Maria, Op. 12 (SSAA)	Carl Fischer
Casals	Nigra Sum	Tetra Music Corp.
Debussy	We Sing to Spring (Salut Printemps)	Hinshaw Music
Duruflé	Tota pulchra es (from *Quatre Motets*)	Durand Company
Fauré	Ave Maria	Broude Brothers
Fine	The Knave's Letter	G. Schirmer
Hanson	How Excellent Thy Name (SSAA)	Carl Fischer
Holst	Ave Maria (double choirs)	H. W. Gray Co.
Kodály (arr.)	Dancing Song (SSAAA)	Oxford
Mendelssohn/ Stone	Surrexit Pastor Bonus	Tetra Music Corp.
Mulholland	Heart We Will Forget Him (SSAA)	National Music Publ.
Nelson	Vocalise	Jenson
Pfautsch	Laughing Song (SSAA)	Lawson-Gould
Poulenc	Ave Verum	E. C. Schirmer
Victoria	Duo Seraphim (SSAA)	Tetra Music Corp.
Watson	Five Japanese Love Poems	G. Schirmer

EXTENDED WORKS, GRADE VI

Britten	Missa Brevis in D	Boosey & Hawkes
Diemer	Fragments from the Mass	Marks Music Corp.
Porpora	Magnificat (SSAA/SSAA)	Colombo

CHORAL MUSIC FOR TENOR-BASS CHOIRS

Composer/ Arranger	Title	Publisher
GRADE I		
Bach/Lefebvre	Alleluia	Galaxy Music Corp.
Crocker (arr.)	The Drunken Sailor (2-part)	Jenson
Green (arr.)	The River (CCB)	Cambiata Press
Larson	We Come with Songs of Gladness (TB)	Pro-Art Publications
Lawrence (arr.)	Drink to Me Only with Thine Eyes (CCB)	Cambiata Press
Rinker	Where Go the Boats (2-part)	Music Corp. of America
Scoggin (arr.)	The Colorado Trail (TBB)	AMC
Swenson (arr.)	Scarborough Fair (CCB)	Cambiata Press
Vulpius/Scoggin	Good Christians All, Rejoice and Sing	AMC
Wheeler (arr.)	The Male Song Bag (TTB)	Dickson/Wheeler
GRADE II		
Arcadelt/ Johnstone	Ave Maria (CCBB)	Cambiata Press
Bach/Siltman	Jesu, Joy of Man's Desiring (CCB)	Cambiata Press
Crocker (arr.)	Drill Ye Tarriers (TTB)	Jenson
Eilers	Bound for Jubilee (TTBB)	Hal Leonard
Giles (arr.)	Poor Lonesome Cowboy (CCBB)	Cambiata Press
Gray	Boatman Stomp (3-part)	G. Schirmer
Nelson	Four Anthems for Young Choirs	Boosey & Hawkes
Shearer	Golden Slumber (TTBB)	Southern Music Co.
Siltman (arr.)	This Train (CBB)	Cambiata Press
Williamson	Jenny Kiss'd Me (TB)	Boosey & Hawkes
GRADE III		
Bartholomew (arr.)	What Shall We Do with the Drunken Sailor?	G. Schirmer
Brahms/Pfautsch	Five German Folk Songs	Lawson-Gould
Fauré/Boyd	Ave Verum (TB)	Roger Dean Publishing
Frackenpohl	Lovers Love the Spring (TBB)	Marks Music Corp.

Composer/ Arranger	Title	Publisher
Heyne (arr.)	Four Hymns for Male Voice (TTBB)	Augsburg Fortress
Ravenscroft/ Owen	We Be Three Poor Mariners (TBB)	Studio 224
Schubert/Ehret	Holy, Holy, Holy	Marks Music Corp.
Sheppard (arr.)	Companions All Sing Loudly	Boston Music Corp.
Siltman (arr.)	Steal Away (TTB-TBB)	Southern Music Co.
Vaughan Williams (arr.)	The Farmer's Boy	Stainer & Bell

GRADE IV

Bartholomew	Old Ark's A-Moverin' (TTBB)	G. Schirmer
Butler	As Beautiful as She	Witmark & Sons
Cherubini	Like as a Father (3-part)	Music 70
Clausen	Pretty Saro (TTBB)	Southern Music Co.
De Cormier (arr.)	Tumbalalaika	Lawson-Gould
Grieg/McKinney	Brothers, Sing On!	J. Fisher & Bro.
Mendelssohn	Herbstlied (TB)	National Music Publ.
Persichetti	Sam Was a Man (TB)	G. Schirmer
Thompson	Stopping by Woods on a Snowy Evening (from *Frostiana*)	E. C. Schirmer
Viadana/ Davidson	O Sacrum Convivium	E. C. Schirmer

GRADE V

Bruckner	Inveni David	C. F. Peters
Copland (arr.)	Ching-A-Ring Chaw	Boosey & Hawkes
Copland/Fine	The Boatman's Dance	Boosey & Hawkes
Cornelius	Grant Them Rest Eternal	Music 70
Duson (arr.)	Loch Lomond	Neil A. Kjos
Goldman (arr.)	Hava Nageela	Lawson-Gould
Kodály	Soldier's Song (TTB)	Boosey & Hawkes
Mathias	O Salutaris Hostia	Oxford
Pfautsch	Go and Tell John	Hope Publishing
Schubert	Die Nacht (TTBB)	Roger Dean Publishing
Shaw/Parker (arr.)	Shenandoah	Lawson-Gould
Thiman	She Is My Slender Small Love	J. Curwen & Sons
Victoria/ Temperley	O Sacrum Convivium (TTBB)	Oxford

Composer/ Arranger	Title	Publisher
	EXTENDED WORKS, GRADE VI	
Bartók	Five Slovak Folksongs	Boosey & Hawkes
Creston	Two Motets	G. Schirmer
Schubert	Ständchen	Lawson-Gould
Thompson	Testament of Freedom	E. C. Schirmer

Index

A

A *cappella* singing, 194
  rehearsing, 202
Accompaniment
  conductor-accompanist commu-
    nication, 144, 146
  considerations in music selection,
    78–79
  organ, 79
  for pop ensemble, 251
  taped, 246, 251
ACDA. *See* American Choral
  Directors Association (ACDA)
Acoustics, 191
Adolescence
  changes during, 157
  definition, 156–157
  energy level, 159
  gender differences, 160
  opposite sex interests, 157, 160
  physical changes during, 211
  sensitivity to criticism, 158, 159
  vocal development, 209–210
Advanced choir
  curriculum, 60–61
  mixed, 41
  ordering music for, 82
  sample concert program, 97–99
  seating arrangements, 45
  sightsinging, 199
Advertisement of choral program, 23
Aesthetic, in rehearsal, 172

Alto–tenor voice, 216–217
American Choral Directors
  Association (ACDA), 218, 295, 296
Amplification, tone quality and, 248
Amplifier, 251
Announcements, 168
Anthologies as repertoire source, 85–86
Aptitude, musical, evaluating, 64–65
Archibeque, Charlene, 168
Areas of silence, 217
Argento, Dominick, 8
Arrangements, selection of, 79–80
Association for Technology in Music
  Instruction (ATMI), 293
ATMI Technology Directory, 293
Attendance
  at rehearsals, 164
  in student evaluations, 62
Attention span, 159, 166
  accommodating, 133, 170
Attitude in student evaluations, 63, 66
Audience considerations in music
  selection, 81
Audition
  collecting personal data, 31–32
  conclusion of, 40
  evaluating musical abilities,
    32–36
  form for, 37
  implementing, 37
  for musical productions, 255
  for pop ensemble, 245–246, 251
  repertoire and, 81–82

Aural map, 107–108, 142
Aural skills, 202
    computer programs, 290
Awards banquet, 21–22, 293–294
    location for, 294

B

Barham, Terry J., 219–221, 236
Baritone, new, 215
Barresi, Anthony, 212–213, 221
Barresi on Adolescent Voice, 222
Bassin, Joseph, 12
Beginning choir
    curriculum, 58–59
    ordering music for, 82
Behavior management. *See also*
  Discipline
    goal of, 162
    need for, 161
    during sectional rehearsals,
        169–170
    understanding age group,
        156–160
Boatmen Stomp (Gray), 225–232
Boyer, Ernest L., 6
*Boy's Changing Voice: New Solutions
  for Today's Choral Teacher* (Barham
  and Nelson), 236
Breathing, 149, 194
    exercises to develop, 183,
        184–186
    marking the score, 118, 124–125
    in popular music, 248
    support for changing voices, 225,
        239
Broadway musical. *See* Musical pro-
  ductions
Budget. *See also* Finances
    alternative income sources,
        271–272
    general operation costs, 271
    justifying requests, 270, 271
    unusual purchases, 271
Buffer voices, 44
*Building Support for School Music: A
  Practical Guide,* 5
Bulletin board, 168, 269
Burnout, teacher, 265

C

Cambiata Vocal Institute of
    America, 216n
Cambiata voice, 215, 216
Card file, 87, 270, 279–280
    composer card, 280
    title card, 280, 281
Carnegie Foundation for the
    Advancement of Teaching study, 9
Cataloging music, 270
    computer database, 274
    sequence of events, 273–274
CD-ROM, 290
Certificate of Participation, 293
Changing voice, 160. *See also* Vocal
  mutation
    alto-tenor plan, 216–217
    cambiata plan, 215
    music for, 212, 215–216, 217,
        222–237
    repertoire lists, 236–237
    seating arrangements for, 45
    theories of, 213–222
    unison singing, 58
    vocal exercises, 216–217
Chanson on Dessus le marche d'Arras,
    136, 139–140
Chaperones, 267
Check–out system for music, 276
Chest voice
    blending with head voice,
        187–189
    during vocal mutation, 213
Choir
    advanced mixed, 41
    beginning, 41
    intermediate–ability, 41
    numbers and types offered, 40–43
    T-shirts and memorabilia, 158
    training, 40–41
Choir day, 24
Choir members
    communication with, 144–147
    getting to know, 170–171
    motivation for participating, 19
    recruiting friends, 25
Choir robes, 284
Choral blend in pop ensemble, 246

Choral director
    burnout, 265
    earning respect, 161
    qualifications, 9–10, 14, 23
    serving as role model, 160
    sharing with colleagues, 84
Choral Journal, 218
    music reviews, 85
Choral library, 82–83, 272–273
    card file system, 279–280
    cataloging, 273–274
    music distribution system, 276
    ordering music, 273
    organizing system, 272–273
    responsibility for, 270
Choral literature, sources of, 83–86
Choral memorabilia, 22
Choral Music in Print, 86
Choral Parent Organization, 22
    committees, 267–268
    constitution, 268
    fund-raising role, 271–272
    helping with musical production, 255
    officers' duties, 266–267
    organizing, 266
    thanking, 294
    transportation services, 250
Choral program
    budget constraints, 1
    building student pride, 21–22
    components of successful, 19–20, 162–163
    developing leadership skills, 22
Choreography
    adjusting to off-campus stages, 250
    for pop ensembles, 247–248
Christmas music, 10, 78
Church choirs, recruiting choral members from, 26
Coaches, support for choral program, 24
College choir, sample concert program, 102–103
Collins, Don L., 57, 216n, 236
Communication
    between conductor and choir, 144
    of directions, 146–147
    nonverbal, 125, 144
    verbal, 145

Compact discs, 290
Computer database
    for cataloging music, 270, 274
    to organize choral library, 87, 88, 272–273, 289
Computer system. *See also* Software
    built-in sound capabilities, 290
    hardware selection, 290–293
    instructional uses, 289–290
    management purposes, 289
    security provisions, 292
Computer-Assisted Instruction (CAI), 293
Concert choir, 1
    choosing number and type of, 74
    establishing reasonable schedule, 171–172
Concerts as repertoire source, 83
Conducting
    communicating with choir and accompanist, 144–147
    error-detection skills, 142, 147, 148
    establishing parameters, 143–144
    facial expressions during, 124, 144
    feedback to singers, 150–151
    introducing new compositions, 144
    in musical analysis, 117
    problem-solving, 147–150
    rehearsals, 141–152
Cooksey, John, 218–219, 236
Cooper, Irvin, 210, 213, 215–216
Cooperation in student evaluation, 63
Curriculum. *See also* Selection of music
    advanced choir, 60–61
    beginning choir, 58–59
    content and sequencing, 57–58
    development of, 55–56
    intermediate-level choir, 59–60

D

Delegating responsibilities
    for musical productions, 265
    to prevent burnout, 265

Dictation, rhythmic and melodic, 200–201
Diction, 114, 196
  books on, 197–198
  with foreign language texts, 195–196
  nonregional, 195
  solo vs. choral singing, 195
Director for musical productions, 255. *See also* Choral director
Discipline. *See also* Rules
  empty threats, 162
  preventive, 162–172
  reactions to, 160–162
  structuring learning environment, 162–163
Distribution of music, 276
Donations, 272
Drill–and–practice rehearsal style, 55–56
Dynamics, 190
  of adolescent voice, 238–239
  for changing voices, 223
  extreme, 77
  marking the score, 124
  musical analysis, 116
  relative, 187
  supporting soft sound, 187
  terminology, 187

E

Ear training, 201–203
Emerson, Roger, 231
End-of-the-year activity, 21
Environment
  for changing voices, 220–221
  creating positive and supportive, 166–167
  physical surroundings, 163
Equal-voice music, 212
Equipment, recommendations, 286–288
Evaluation of students. *See also* Grades
  on aptitude or achievement, 64–65
  on attendance, 62
  on attitude and cooperation, 63

  on knowledge and skills, 64
  negative, 150–151
  purpose of, 62
  on singing accuracy, 63
Extreme notes
  approach, 77
  duration of, 77
  vowels on, 76
Eye contact, 167

F

Feedback
  from conductor to singers, 150–151
  positive, 167
Feeder schools, 23–24
Female choirs. *See* Treble choirs.
File cabinets for music storage, 277–278
Finances. *See also* Budget
  parent organization's role, 271–272
  student treasurer's function, 269–270
Fire, Fire, My Heart, 135–136, 139
Fisher, Robert E., 15
Folder cabinet, 276
Foreign language texts, 78, 224
  diction, 196–197
  introducing, 196
  understanding, 197
Form, musical analysis, 114
Foundations and Principles of Music Education (Leonhard and House), 3
Fund–raising
  parent role in, 22, 267, 271–272
  performance ticket sales, 253, 270, 272
  student responsibilities, 272
  T–shirts and memorabilia, 158, 272

G

Gackle, Lynn, 211–213
Girls' choirs, levels offered, 42–43
Good Timber Grows (Emerson), 232–235

Grades. *See also* Evaluation of students
    computerized, 289
    establishing percentages, 66
Grashel, John, 64
Gray, Michael A., 232
Grouping by ability, 283
Growing Up Complete: The Imperative for Music Education, 5
Guidance counselors, 24, 294

H

Hamann, Shari Lynn, 291
Harmony
    for all voice parts, 232
    exercises, 194
    musical analysis, 115
Head voice, blending with chest voice, 185, 188–189
Higgins, William R., 292
High School: A Report of Secondary Education in America, 6
High school choir
    possible offerings, 41–43
    sample concert program, 101–102
Historian, 268
Hoffer, Charles, 8
House, Robert W., 3
Hymnals, for sightsinging exercises, 199

I

Instructional programs and games, 290
Instruments, purchasing, 286–287
Intermediate–level choir
    curriculum, 59–60
    sightsinging, 199
International Phonetic Alphabet, 195
Intervals, singing accurate, 192
Intonation, 190–195
    factors affecting, 191–192
    vocal production and, 194–195
Issues in Music Education, 9

J

Jazz choir, 43. *See also* Pop ensembles.
Johnson, John Paul, 211

K

Karpinski, Gary S., 293

L

Leadership, 172
    developing skills, 22
    electing officers, 269–270
    student, 268–269
Legato line, 204
Leonhard, Charles, 3
Librarian, student, 270
Lift, 118
Lift point, sopranos and altos, 213
"Lift Thine Eyes" (Mendelssohn), musical analysis, 108–123
Listening skills, 202
    computer programs, 290
    for conductor, 147, 149–150

M

Mabry, Gary, 180
McKenzie, Duncan, 216–217
Madrigals, 136, 140, 245
Male choirs, seating arrangements, 49
Marking the score, 118–125. *See also* Musical analysis.
    breathing, 118
    important entrances, 118, 123
    numbering measures, 146
Massage, 129, 137
Melody, musical analysis, 114–115
MENC. *See* Music Educators National Conference (MENC)
Mendelssohn, Felix, 108
Mental imagery, 182
Microphones, 251
Middle school/junior high school choir
    changing voices, 223
    energy level, 159
    performance attire, 283, 285
    possible offerings, 40–43
    repertoire lists, 236
    sample concert program, 99–101
    scheduling, 282
MIDI. *See* Music Instrument Digital Interface (MIDI)

Mixed chorus, 2, 41
    advanced, 42
    beginning, 40
    intermediate level, 42
    music for, 301–303
Motivation for participating
    extrinsic, 18–19
    intrinsic, 19
Movement. *See also* Choreography.
    in pop ensemble performances,
        246, 247–248
    in rehearsal, 203–204
Music. *See also* Repertoire.
    cataloging, 273–275
    distributing, 276
    ordering, 273
    quality of life issues, 8
    social aspects, 5–6, 8
    storing, 276–279
    where to find, 83–86
Music conventions, 83
Music education
    for all students, 9
    importance in curriculum, 4–8
    nonmusical benefits, 8
Music Educators Journal, 288
Music Educators National
    Conference (MENC), 8, 296
    Action Kit for Music Education,
        4–5
    address, 295
    instrument and equipment rec-
        ommendations, 286
    Music Educators Creed, 12–13
    Religious Music in the Schools,
        10–11
    scheduling recommendations,
        281
Music folder, 276
Music history, 116–117
    on rehearsed pieces, 136–137,
        140, 145
Music Industry Conference,
    287–288
Music Instrument Digital Interface
    (MIDI), 289–290
Music literacy, activities promoting,
    199–200

*Music Teaching in the Junior High and
    Middle School* (Swanson), 217
Music theory, computer programs, 290
Musical analysis. *See also* Score study.
    aural and visual study, 107–117
    before rehearsal, 128, 165
    conducting considerations, 117
    during rehearsal, 124
    historical, 116–117
    relationship of parts, 116
Musical productions
    auditions, 255
    benefits, of, 252
    delegating responsibilities, 255
    problems with, 253–254
    publicity, 256
    repertory agents, 254
    scheduling, 254–255
    school involvement, 25, 252–253
    selecting the show, 254
    ticket sales, 253, 270, 272
    time commitment, 253
Musicianship sheets, 66–70
    first level musician, 67
    second level musician, 68
    super musician, 70
    third level musician, 69
Musicianship skills, 197–204
    ear training, 202
    movement, 202–205
    for pop ensemble, 246
    sightreading, 198–201

N

National Coalition for Music
    Education, 4
National Standards for Arts
    Education, 56–57, 134, 138, 140,
    141
Nelson, Darolyne L., 219–221, 236
Notation system, computerized, 290

O

Octave, tuning, 194
Off-campus performances, 23
    stage considerations, 250

Officers
    election of, 22
    of parent organization, 266–267
    student, 269–270
*Opportunity–to–Learn: Standards for
    Music Instruction* (MENC), 286
Ordering music
    information needed for, 273
    timing of, 81–83
Organ accompaniment, 79
Over–sized music storage, 279

P

Parent organization. *See* Choral
    Parent Organization
Peer pressure, 24, 157–158, 172
Performance attire
    age considerations, 285
    appearance from stage, 285–286
    care of, 285
    casual, 283
    choir robes, 284
    expenses, 250, 285
    formal, 284
    involving students in selection,
        158, 283
    longevity, 286
    parents' committee for, 268
    for pop ensemble, 249–250
Performance schedule, 12
    time factor, 61
Performances. *See also* Musical pro-
    ductions
    attendance, 62
    off campus, 23
    on campus, 23
    educational aspects, 11–12
    preparation for, 55–56
    outside the school, 23
"Personal Skills: Passport to Effective
    Teaching" (Fisher), 15
Philosophy of music education
    formulating, 5–13
    importance of, 2–4
Philosophy of Music Education, A
    (Reimer), 11–12
Phrasing

    activity for, 204
    for changing voices, 232
Physical activities
    in rehearsal, 202–205
    stretching, 129, 137
    during warm–up, 131, 179–182,
        202–205
Piano, 286
    dynamic, 187, 190
    electronic, 251
    moving, 287
    overusing during rehearsal, 194,
        202
    performance, 287
    reduction of orchestral parts,
        78–79
    tuning and upkeep, 36, 271
Piano students, recruiting for choir,
    26
Pitch
    singing below, 149
    temperature effects, 191
Planning period, 282
Pop ensemble, 243–245
    accompaniment, 251
    auditions for, 245–246, 251
    benefits of, 244
    choreography, 247–248, 250
    concurrent choir membership,
        245
    in high school, 43
    performing outfits, 249–250
    problems with, 244–245
    programming, 247
    repertoire, 245, 258–262
    sound equipment, 251–252
    time and money commitment,
        246
    tone quality, 248
    transportation, 250
    variety and size of, 244
Posture, 194
    seated, 179, 180
    standing, 179, 181
Powell, Steven, 192, 194
Praetorius, Michael, 196–197
Private vocal instruction, 177–178
    during vocal mutation, 219

Problem areas
  correcting, 149
  diagnosis, 148–149
  evaluation, 150
  identifying, 148
  isolating, 147–148
  placing in context, 149–150
Professional journals, as repertoire
  source, 85
Professional organizations, 294–295
Programming
  achieving variety in, 93
  chronological order, 96
  considerations in music selection,
    92–93
  dinner order, 96
  first selection, 94
  order of choirs performing, 95
  placing unusual compositions, 94
  pop ensemble performances, 247
  sample programs, 97–104
  theme order, 97
  varying difficulty level, 93
Psallite (Praetorius), 196–197
Puberty
  defined, 157
  physical changes during, 157
  voice change, 210–211
Publicity
  for musical productions, 256
  parents' committee, 267
Publishers and publishing, 11
  as repertoire source, 83–84

R

Range
  of changing female voice, 212
  of changing male voice, 215, 217,
    221
  considerations in music selection,
    76–77, 222–223
  determining, 33, 37–38
  extension, 184–185
Recordings
  compact disc, 290
  as repertoire source, 84–85
Recruitment, 19, 252–253
  sources of, 23–26

Register consistency, 184–185
Rehearsal
  aesthetic in, 172
  attendance, 62, 164
  beginning, 128
  conducting, 141–152
  ending, 133, 137
  enhancing understanding,
    145–146
  first piece, 132
  flexibility of, 170
  flowchart, 143
  middle portion, 132–133
  music handling system, 165
  planning, 127–141, 142–143,
    145, 159, 165
  punctuality, 164
  sample plan, 133–137
  sectional, 169–170, 282
  sharing order of, 164–165
  sightsinging, 131–132
  warm-up exercises, 129, 131,
    137–138
  working with entire group,
    168–169
Reimer, Bennett, 11–12
Relaxation exercises, 182
Religious music. *See* Sacred music
Renaissance music, breath-support
  requirements, 224
Repair
  of music, 276–277
  of performance attire, 285
Repertoire. *See also* Selection of
  music
  balanced, 75
  for changing voices, 232,
    236–237
  educational requirement, 74
  level of difficulty, 74
  for mixed voices, 301–303
  for pop ensembles, 245, 258–262
  revisiting previously performed
    literature, 82–83
  selection of, 73–81
  for tenor-bass choirs, 306–308
  for treble voices, 304–305
Resonance, 183, 186–187
Retreats, 21

Revecy venir du Printans, 135,
    138–139
Rhythm
    musical analysis, 116
    sightsinging exercises, 200
Risers, choral, 286, 287
Rules
    consequences for breaking, 163,
        164
    consistency in enforcing, 163
    involving students in, 163
    stating positively, 163

S

Sacred music, 10–11
    placing in performances, 95
Scales, sightsinging, 200
Scheduling, 280–283
    before and after lunch, 282
    of musical productions, 254–255
    during regular school hours, 281
School Music Program: A New Vision,
    9, 289
Score study. *See also* Musical analy-
    sis.
    for conductor, 142
    before rehearsal, 128
Scrapbook, 22, 268
Seating arrangements, 43–49
    for changing voices, 45
    choir sections, 44–49
    for male choir, 49
    for mixed choir, 45
    mixed positions, 45
    placing individual voices, 44
    for treble choir, 49
Section leaders, 269
Selection of music. *See also*
  Repertoire
    accompaniment considerations,
        78–79
    balanced, 93
    for changing voices, 212,
        215–216, 217, 222–237
    intonation considerations, 192
    multicultural aspects, 10
    for on-campus events, 23
    order of, 166

for performances, 74
    potential audience, 81
    programming considerations,
        92–93
    ranges and tessituras, 76
    for sightsinging exercises, 199
    size of choir, 80
    text considerations, 77–78
    texture, 80–81
    vocal maturity, 80
Seltzer, Vivian Center, 157
Show choir, 2. *See also* Pop ensem-
    bles.
Sightsinging
    advanced level, 60–61
    in auditions, 33–35, 39
    beginning, 59
    books for, 201
    choice of music for, 199
    content and achievement stan-
        dards, 138
    contests, 201
    examples, 34–35
    intermediate level, 59–60
    of new compositions, 144
    placement in rehearsal, 198–199
    rehearsal exercises, 131–132, 135
    teaching methods, 197–201
Sing We and Chant It, 137, 140–141
Singing
    posture for, 179–182
    testing accuracy, 63
Single sex choirs, 41, 42, 160,
    237–238
Size of choir, repertoire selection
    and, 80
Snake, 252
Software
    copyright guidelines, 292
    evaluation of, 291
    selecting, 290–293
    sourcebooks, 292–293
Solfège syllables, 198, 199
Solo
    diction for, 195
    instrumental, 251
    prepared vs. unprepared in audi-
        tions, 32–33, 37
Sound board, 252

Sound equipment
    MENC recommendations, 286
    for pop ensemble, 251–252
    setting up, 250
Speakers, main and monitor, 252
Storing music
    in cardboard boxes, 278–279
    document repair, 276–277
    in file cabinets, 277–278
    oversize or major works, 279
Stretching exercises, 129, 137
Students
    grouping by ability, 283
    involvement in outfit selection, 283
Swanson, Frederick, 217
Syncopation, 124
    sightsinging exercises, 132

T

Talking in the classroom, 164
Tardiness
    to rehearsals, 164
    in student evaluations, 62
Teaching Choral Music (Collins), 236
Technology, classroom, 288–289
    instructional uses, 289–290
    management uses, 289
Telephone committee, 267
Tempo
    considerations in programming, 93
    marking changes, 124
Tenor-bass choir, music for, 306–308
Tessitura
    of changing female voice, 212
    of changing male voice, 215, 217, 221
    considerations in music selection, 76–77, 223
    determining, 33, 37–38
Testing
    musical knowledge and skills, 64
    of singing accuracy, 63
Text
    appealing to adolescent singers, 232
    in music selection, 77–78
    musical analysis, 108, 113
    translations, 78

    understanding of, 196
Texture
    considerations in music selection, 80–81
    musical analysis, 115–116
The Boy's Changing Voice: New Solutions for Today's Choral Teacher (Barham and Nelson), 219–221
Theme concert, 97
Tonal memory test, 34, 35–36, 39
Tone quality in pop ensembles, 248
Tongue trill, 185
Tonic, speaking pitch as, 220
Topp, Dale, 166
Training choirs, 40–41. *See also* Beginning choirs.
Training the Boy's Changing Voice (McKenzie), 216
Transcriptions, selection of, 79–80
Transitional piece, 94
Transportation, 250
Treble choir
    music for, 304–305
    seating arrangements, 49
Tuning, vertical vs. horizontal, 192–194

U

Unified vowels, singing with, 192
Unison singing, 58

V

Verbal instruction, minimizing, 167–168
    Rule of seven, 168
Vocal exercises. *See also* Vocal techniques.
    for breathing, 183–184
    for changing voices, 216–217
    for flexibility, 189
    for intonation, 192–193
    for placement and resonance, 185–186
    for register consistency, 186–188
Vocal lines for all voice parts, 232
Vocal maturity, considerations in music selection, 80

Vocal mutation. *See also* Changing
  voice.
    developmental stages, 218–219,
      221–222
    female, 211–213
    male, 213–222
    visual and aural signs of,
      210–211, 212, 221, 237
Vocal production
    components of, 178
    intonation and, 194–195
    for musical performances,
      253–254
Vocal techniques, 177–197. *See also*
  Vocal exercises.
    breathing, 182–184
    dynamics, 189–190
    flexibility, 188–189
    intonation, 190–194
    mental imagery, 182
    placement and resonance,
      184–186
    physical preparation, 179–182
    posture, 179–182
    register consistency and range
      extension, 186–188
Voice, 178–179
    testing during vocal mutation, 219

type, genetic predetermination,
  219
Voice parts, marking, 117–118
Vowels
    modification, 149
    singing with unified, 192, 194

W

Wardrobe manager, 270
Warming up
    for auditions, 37
    content and achievement stan-
      dards, 138
    mental preparation, 129
    physical preparation, 129, 137,
      179–182
    during rehearsal, 129, 131,
      137–138, 166
    to release energy, 159
    sample exercises, 134–135,
      137–138
    using primary vowel sounds, 192
    vocal preparation, 129, 131, 137
Willman, Fred, 291
Word stress, 114
Working with the Adolescent Voice
  (Cooksey), 218, 236